THE LOST WORLD OF BYZANTIUM

THE LOST WORLD OF
BYZANTIUM

JONATHAN HARRIS

YALE UNIVERSITY PRESS
NEW HAVEN AND LONDON

For information about this and other Yale University Press publications, please contact:
U.S. Office: sales.press@yale.edu   www.yalebooks.com
Europe Office: sales@yaleup.co.uk   www.yalebooks.co.uk

Typeset in Minion Pro by IDSUK (DataConnection) Ltd
Printed in the United Kingdom by Gomer Press Ltd, Llandysul

Library of Congress Cataloging-in-Publication Data

Harris, Jonathan.
  The lost world of Byzantium / Jonathan Harris.
    pages cm
  Includes bibliographical references and index.
  ISBN 978-0-300-17857-9 (hardback)
1. Byzantine Empire—Civilization. 2. Byzantine Empire—Relations. I. Title.
  DF521.H275 2015
  949.5'02—dc23

                                                                2015016348

A catalogue record for this book is available from the British Library.

10 9 8 7 6 5 4 3 2 1

*In memory of Mabel (1896–1966), Ethel (1892–1974)
and Grag (1900–1992)*

Contents

Illustrations and Maps

Maps

Preface and Acknowledgements

This book is a personal journey through the long history of Byzantium, built around the questions that have always puzzled me and the personalities and events that have long intrigued me. Above all, I wanted to investigate why Byzantium lasted for so long in spite of all the upheavals and invasions that threatened its existence and why in the end it disappeared so completely. Inevitably, in pursuing that line, I left a great deal out which another author would have put in while aspects that others might consider peripheral or even irrelevant have found their way in. The same applies to the Further Reading section at the end. It is not meant to be comprehensive – rather, just a few ideas for the next step – and it is restricted to works in English that are widely available. A great deal more has, of course, been written. Then there is the matter of Byzantine names. While in general I have tried to transliterate them as closely as possible to the original Greek, I have not stuck rigidly to that. So I have Phokas rather than Phocas, and Kantakouzenos rather than Cantacuzenus, but Heraclius rather than Herakleios and Porphyrogenitos rather than Porphyrogennetos or Porphyrogenitus. Where there is a recognised English equivalent of a Greek first name, I have used it, so Constantine rather than Konstantinos, John rather than Ioannis. The spelling, like the coverage and the reading, is my own choice.

On the other hand, however personal a take on Byzantium *The Lost World* might be, in writing it I have been deeply influenced both directly and indirectly by others. As it now is, the book has benefited enormously from the comments of two supportive anonymous reviewers and from those of Heather McCallum and Rachael Lonsdale of Yale University Press. Liz Hornby meticulously copy-edited the text. Andrew Sargent kindly read a draft as an interested non-specialist and saved me from numerous inconsistencies, solecisms and omissions. Working in the History department at Royal Holloway has also been a significant influence. I could not have written the book at all if I had not had the opportunity to try out my ideas on the undergraduate students who have taken my courses on Byzantium and its Neighbours and the Fall of Constantinople. Their responses, questions and objections forced me to clarify and refine my ideas and in some cases rethink them altogether. I am indebted, as well, to three heads of department – Jonathan Phillips, Sarah Ansari and Justin Champion – for the support that they have given to my research and teaching, and to Penelope Mullens and Marie-Christine Ockenden for making the administrative side of things run so smoothly. At the end of the day, it is a great privilege to write history from inside an academic department, especially one that is so large and diverse.

Royal Holloway, University of London
January 2015

Prologue

In many places there are remarkable remains of ancient monuments, though one cannot help wondering why so few have survived...
Ogier Ghiselin de Busbeq, ambassador of the Holy Roman Emperor in Constantinople, 1555–1562

In the middle of the sixteenth century, the capital city of the Ottoman sultan was one of the largest and wealthiest cities in the world, its streets thronged by a rapidly growing population of over 400,000 people, the centre of an empire that stretched from the Crimea to Algiers. Popularly known as Istanbul, its official name was Kostantiniyye, or Constantinople. Its ruler, Süleyman the Magnificent (1520–1566), was not only one of the greatest military leaders that the empire had ever produced but also the caliph of Islam, so the city boasted some three hundred mosques to reflect his spiritual as well as his worldly power. On a hill in the centre of town, a huge and splendid new mosque was under construction. When finished it would boast four minarets and a complex of schools, bath houses and hospitals. Known as the Süleymaniye, in honour of the reigning sultan who had commissioned it, the mosque formed a fitting centrepiece to the capital city of the leader of the faithful and the most powerful Muslim ruler of the day.

In 1544, a Frenchman called Pierre Gilles arrived in this imperial metropolis. Classically educated and a keen naturalist, Gilles was on a mission for his sovereign, Francis I, to seek out ancient manuscripts to take back to the royal library at Fontainebleau. He ended up staying much longer than he intended, for, when King Francis died in 1547, the scholar and his mission were forgotten and Gilles found himself marooned in Constantinople without the money for his passage home. After three years, to make ends meet, he had to enlist as a mercenary in the sultan's army as it marched east to do battle with the Persians. In the meantime, during his enforced stay in Constantinople, he wandered through its streets and came to know its layout intimately. It was not the contemporary city that intrigued him, though. He felt that all the grand new mosques only had the effect of making the place even more dingy at street level. Rather, as a classically trained man of letters, he looked for remains of the ancient past when the city had been known as Byzantion. Disappointingly, there was almost nothing classical to see, but Gilles soon became fascinated by the survivals from later centuries when Constantinople had been the capital of a Christian rather than a Muslim empire and Greek rather than Turkish had been spoken in its corridors of power. His contemporaries were coming to refer to this defunct body politic as the Byzantine empire, or Byzantium, and since it had finally disappeared only a century before, much more remained to be seen than is visible today. Whenever he could, Gilles eagerly sought out the surviving monuments of this lost world. He prowled around the most obvious Byzantine building, the towering former Christian cathedral of Hagia Sophia ('Holy Wisdom'), which still dominated the centre of the city opposite the sultan's palace of Topkapi. Outside the cathedral, he slipped and fell down a trench, where he discovered seven mysterious standing columns. Some people told him they were part of what had once been the Great Palace of the Byzantine emperors but Gilles himself was quite sure that they were the remains of a portico which once surrounded the city's main square, the Augousteion. He descended beneath the streets and, in a small boat, glided between the mighty columns of an underground cistern, its vaulted roof lit only by his flickering torch. He clambered on to the portico which marked the eastern end of the Hippodrome where the Byzantines had once gathered to watch chariot races, and from his vantage point he could see the dolphins leaping and diving in the Bosporus beyond.

Uncovering the Byzantine past was not, he discovered, an easy task. Too great an interest in antiquities was liable to arouse suspicion from the locals, the Christians living in the city being as hostile as the Turks in this respect. Taking measurements, something for which Gilles was rather obsessive, was to invite denunciation to the authorities as a spy. If one attracted such unwelcome attention, the only way to escape unpleasantness was to offer to buy everyone some wine. The old Land Walls that guarded the western edge of Constantinople were easy enough to visit and Gilles could pace out the distance between the inner and outer fortifications. Hagia Sophia, on the other hand, had to be viewed with rather more circumspection since it was now the mosque of Aya

Sofya and non-Muslims were not welcome inside. Gilles managed to get in by mingling with the crowds and so was able to examine its soaring dome unnoticed. When it came to the measurements though, he had to pay a Turk to do it for him.

Fascinating though these survivals from the past were, Gilles was only too well aware that they represented but a fraction of the Byzantine monuments that had once adorned Constantinople's skyline. So many churches, monasteries and palaces mentioned in the literary texts, in which he was widely read, had simply disappeared. He knew that there had once been a second palace of the Byzantine emperors at Blachernae near the Land Walls, but he was quite unable to locate it. He looked for the church of the Holy Apostles, said to be second in grandeur only to Hagia Sophia, but no trace of it was to be found, not even the foundations. One monument was being dismantled before his very eyes. Outside Hagia Sophia, he came across a gigantic bronze leg protruding from a pile of scrap. He was tempted to measure it but dared not, for fear of attracting attention. Even without measuring, he could see that the leg was longer than he himself was tall. Further studiedly casual glances at the scrap heap revealed a nose that was about twenty centimetres long, and the legs and hooves of a horse. From his reading, Gilles knew exactly what this was. He was one of the last people ever to see the great equestrian statue of the emperor Justinian I, which for a thousand years had stood on a tall column in the central square of Byzantine Constantinople. The emperor had sat astride his prancing steed, his right hand imperiously raised in warning to his foes, his left grasping an orb surmounted by a cross. Now his statue lay in a heap on the ground, awaiting its final destruction, and already workmen were starting to cart the pieces off to a foundry where they were to be recast into cannon. The Turks, Gilles concluded, had always been the enemies of statuary, and indeed of all architectural design and decoration, which was hardly fair given the splendid buildings for which they were responsible. For all his preoccupation with its monuments and their dimensions, Gilles did not warm to contemporary Constantinople or its people, and as he departed he vowed he would never go back.

* * *

Some years later, while he was living in Rome after his return from the east, Gilles wrote up his experiences in his *Antiquities of Constantinople*, which was published posthumously in 1561. The disappearance of so many of the physical remains of the powerful and prosperous society that Byzantium had once been prompted him to ask the obvious question. How had it happened that the once mighty Christian rulers of Byzantine Constantinople had lost everything and come to be enslaved by 'infidels'? It was, he concluded, simply a matter of character formed by the climate of that particular part of the world:

> For this reason, although Constantinople seems, as it were by nature, formed for government, its people have neither the decencies of education nor any strictness of discipline. Their affluence makes them slothful . . . [and] wholly incapable of making any resistance against those barbarous people by whom, for a vast distance, they are encompassed on all sides.

Gilles was by no means the first person to attribute the downfall of Byzantium to indolence and moral laxity and he certainly was not the last. The theme was taken up some two centuries later by Edward Gibbon, who in the later volumes of his magisterial *Decline and Fall of the Roman Empire* emphasised the 'cowardice and discord' of the 'Greeks' as he and many others preferred to call the Byzantines. Even today, a perception remains that there was something wrong with the Byzantines which explains why they are no longer marked on the map. They ignored political and economic reality in favour of ceremony, antiquarianism, dogmatic disputation and church decoration when they should have been equipping legions to defeat their numerous enemies. Consequently, while the achievements of ancient Greece and Rome are seen as having deeply influenced the world as it is today, and feature regularly in television programmes and school curriculums, Byzantium is largely ignored.

There is, however, one very inconvenient fact that suggests that Byzantium should not be dismissed so lightly. If its inhabitants really were so utterly supine and pathetic that they were incapable of defending themselves, then why did their society last so long? History is littered with ephemeral power blocs, like those of Alexander the Great and Attila the Hun, built up through brilliant military conquest only to fall apart after the death of the charismatic founder. Byzantium, by contrast, was one of the longest lasting human institutions. If the inauguration of Constantinople in 330 CE is taken as its beginning and the capture of the city by the Ottoman Turks in 1453 as the moment of its downfall, it endured for over a thousand years. That record of survival is all the more impressive in that it took place in the most adverse of circumstances. One of the perennial trends of human history is that people are constantly on the move, whether fleeing oppression or ecological disaster, seeking a better life or in some cases aiming to conquer and plunder. There are times when the movement slows to some extent. Between 31 BCE and 180 CE, the Roman empire benefited from just such a situation, allowing it to maintain very wide borders that were never challenged at multiple points. Byzantium, which was a continuation of the Roman empire in a very different form, had no such luxury. Throughout its history, it found itself at the end of a kind of ethnic bowling alley where waves of peoples moved westward from the steppes of Asia and from the Arabian peninsula.

It was this one factor, more than anything else, that determined what Byzantium was to become. Its distinctive society and ethos were formed in response to the phenomenal and constant pressure on its borders. In the face of the challenge, military prowess alone was no longer enough. Defeat one group in battle, and three more would arrive to take their place. A completely new way of thinking would have to emerge that sought other ways of defusing the threat, whether by integration and settlement, or by bribery and covert action – or, most extraordinary of all, by creating a visual splendour that would overawe their enemies and draw them into the fold as friends and allies. The empire regularly met with catastrophe and yet was able to survive and recover time after time. If these aspects of Byzantine civilisation have not been as fully appreciated as they might have been, the Byzantines themselves are partly to blame. In their literature, art and ceremonies, they pulled off one of the greatest deceptions in history, presenting their society in terms of absolute continuity with the past: to the very end they insisted on describing themselves as 'Romans' as if nothing had changed since ancient times. In reality, Byzantium was constantly evolving and adapting in the face of endless threats. It is easy to accept the Byzantines at their own estimate and miss the very nature of Byzantine society. Consequently Gilles, Gibbon and all the others who have pondered on why Byzantium disappeared have been asking the wrong question. The real issue is not why it came to an end but why it survived at all, and even at certain times flourished and grew in the face of such overwhelming odds.

CHAPTER ONE

Twilight of the Gods

I have described the triumph of barbarism and religion.
Edward Gibbon, 1776

The crumbling monuments of Constantinople were not the only traces that remained in the 1540s, a century after the downfall of Byzantium. Throughout western Europe, the libraries of kings, dukes and cardinals were filled with manuscripts of religious and classical texts in Greek that had once been carefully copied by Byzantine scribes. With the empire gone, the Turks had little use for its surviving books and happily sold them to envoys like Pierre Gilles who carried them back to their homelands. Others were brought out by refugees. These codices contained everything from the Gospels and the Psalms to the precious writings of the ancient Greek philosophers which for centuries had been unavailable in the west.

One of these manuscripts is Graecus 156, which is still preserved in the Vatican Library in Rome. There are hundreds of Byzantine manuscripts in the Vatican but this one is different. Its new clerical owners did not want it to be read and, until the middle of the nineteenth century, access to it was severely restricted. At some point in the past, several pages were carefully and deliberately cut out and their content is now lost forever. As a voice of subversion and opposition, it is amazing that it survived at all. Dating from the tenth century, Graecus 156 is a later copy of a historical account written in Greek about five hundred years after the birth of Christ. Its author was Zosimus, an obscure official about whom almost nothing is known, but who was a vital witness to the transition of the Roman empire to its successor state, Byzantium.

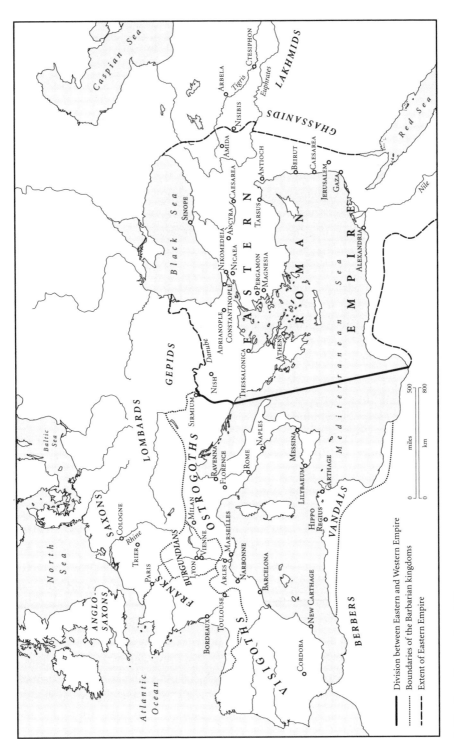

1 The Byzantine empire c. 500

Zosimus was a witness from the losing side. He recounted the history of the empire up to the year 410 but made it clear from the outset that the story he was telling was one of decline and disintegration and that the empire of his day was not what it used to be. By the time he was writing, half of the empire's territory had been lost. The western provinces had ceased to be under the rule of the emperor and had been parcelled out among various Germanic tribes whom Zosimus – in common with his fellow citizens – contemptuously labelled 'barbarians'. North Africa was ruled by the Vandals, Spain by the Visigoths, Gaul by the Franks and Burgundians, Britain by the Angles, Saxons and Jutes. Even Italy and the empire's old capital city of Rome were lost and now belonged to the king of the Ostrogoths. Instead, the eastern city of Constantinople had become the capital of what was left of the empire: the Balkans, Asia Minor, Syria, Palestine and Egypt. How had it come to this? Zosimus had no doubts on that issue. When a state becomes displeasing to the gods, he declared, its affairs will inevitably decline, for the empire had abandoned the Olympian deities who had brought it prosperity and victory in the days of its greatness and turned to the new-fangled religion of Christianity.

Nor did Zosimus hesitate about who was to blame for this impious abandonment of traditional worship and for the consequent decline of the empire: his history points the finger directly at the man who had been emperor between 306 and 337 as 'the origin and beginning of the present destruction of the empire'. His name was Constantine and he was an upstart. True, his father Constantius had been an emperor but, as Zosimus acerbically recorded, Constantine himself was illegitimate, the product of a one-night stand with an innkeeper's daughter. Somehow the boy had been able to get to the palace and worm his way into his father's affections ahead of Constantius' legitimate sons. In those days, the Roman empire still stretched from Syria in the south-east to Britain in the north-west, and when Constantius had marched off to secure the empire's northern frontier, the ambitious Constantine had followed him. Constantius got as far as York but there he died in 306. The soldiers of his army promptly proclaimed young Constantine – the son of a harlot, as Zosimus calls him – as the next emperor. That was all very well but there were plenty of other men in the empire who aspired to supreme power and before long Constantine was at war with one rival after another. In 312 he defeated Maxentius, at the Milvian Bridge on the river Tiber, and became master of Rome and of the western provinces. In 324 he disposed of his former ally, Licinius, and so finally, Zosimus regretfully recorded, the whole empire was in the hands of Constantine alone.

Zosimus goes on to recount how Constantine, now in his fifties and the most powerful man in the world, no longer needed to conceal his 'natural malignity'. That aspect of his character emerged, claims Zosimus, when he developed a suspicion that his young wife Fausta was having an affair with his son by an earlier marriage, Crispus. The young man was immediately executed. But Constantine devised a worse fate for Fausta: he had a bath house heated to excess and then had his wife locked in it until she eventually suffocated. When the deeds were done, Zosimus continued, Constantine suddenly began to feel pangs of guilt. Killing rivals in battle was one thing, terminating his own wife and son quite another. Perhaps he feared the gods might visit some terrible retribution on him, as they had done on the mythical Tantalus who murdered his son Pelops: that unnatural father had been sentenced to spend eternity standing up to his neck in water, suffering from a raging thirst, tormented by the cool water that receded just out of reach whenever he bent to drink. Eager to avoid such a fate, Constantine consulted priests and sages, but they all gave him the same unwelcome verdict, that the stain of so dreadful a crime could never be expunged.

At this point it happened that an Egyptian Christian turned up in Rome. By the early fourth century, Christians represented a substantial minority of the empire's population and the Church had a strong following in some of the larger cities. Emperor Diocletian (284–305) had taken a very dim view of this growing religious cult and in 303 had issued an edict ordering that churches be demolished and copies of the scriptures be destroyed. Christians who held high office in the state were to be demoted and they were ordered to make sacrifices to the gods, on pain of death. The decree was implemented, albeit sporadically, and a considerable number of Christians died for their beliefs, but the Church as a whole was not destroyed and there were even a few Christians at the imperial court. Acquaintance with some of these got the Egyptian visitor admitted to Constantine's presence and he assured the emperor that the God of the Christians would pardon even the most heinous of deeds. According to Zosimus, Constantine took the bait. He reversed the policy of Diocletian, put an end to the persecutions, began openly to favour the Christian Church and neglected the worship of the Olympian gods. Zosimus was horrified by this impiety and by Constantine's abandonment of the religion of his forefathers.

That was not all: Zosimus levelled a second charge against Constantine, that he was responsible for building a new and completely unnecessary city that drained the population and resources of the empire. According to Zosimus, the emperor's religious conversion had not made him popular with the people of Rome, especially when he attempted to prevent the traditional pagan cere-monies taking place on the Capitoline Hill, so he decided to move east and transfer his residence there. At first he opted to build a new city near the site of ancient Troy on the Dardanelles strait in Asia Minor, but after a few years he changed his mind and moved on. Finally he decided to opt for the city of Byzantion. To make it worthy of his presence, he decided that he would completely rebuild it, providing it with replicas of all the grand buildings and monuments that were to be found in Rome: a senate house; a central forum, known as the Augousteion; a stadium for chariot racing, the Hippodrome; and a grand imperial residence, the Great Palace. There were to be many churches and a great cathedral dedicated to the Holy Wisdom of God, or Hagia Sophia, but Constantine hedged his bets and made sure there were a few pagan temples too. The new metropolis was renamed in his own honour as Constantinople or 'city of Constantine'. Zosimus deeply disapproved of the whole project and resented the huge sums, extorted by taxing other parts of the empire, that had funded it. Constantinople acted, he said, like a magnet for settlers from all parts of the empire, eager to cash in on imperial patronage. The population had soared and the streets had become dangerously crowded. Land for building had grown so scarce that suburbs had sprung up beyond the city walls and piles had been driven into the sea to support platforms on which still more houses could be built. The city was, in Zosimus's eyes, a swelling ulcer that would one day burst and pour forth blood, a monument only to Constantine's vanity and wasteful extravagance.

There was a third accusation that Zosimus added to those of impiously abandoning the worship of the traditional gods and of founding a completely unnecessary city. Effective though Constantine was in eliminating his internal rivals, he was less successful in dealing with the barbarians that were massed on the empire's borders. When confronted by some five hundred barbarian horsemen who had invaded Roman territory, Zosimus claims, Constantine simply ran away. Moreover, while the pious, pagan emperor Diocletian had seen to it that the frontier had always been well defended by stationing soldiers in fortifications along its length, Constantine decided to quarter the troops in cities. Not only did this leave the frontiers undefended, it undermined the military ethos of the empire, allowing the troops to become lazy and self-indulgent. The Christian religion furthered the process, in Zosimus's view, undermining the manly virtues that had made Rome great by promoting chastity and renunciation of the world as the new ideals. Monks, particularly, appalled him because they were 'useless for war and other service to the state'. In the palaces of the emperors, eunuchs rather than soldiers came to dominate the corridors of power. Thus, even though it was not until about a hundred years after Constantine that the frontiers finally broke down, Zosimus emphatically blamed him for the decline of the empire and for the loss of the western provinces. 'When our souls are fertile we prosper,' he concluded, 'but when sterility of soul is uppermost we are reduced to our present condition.'

* * *

Zosimus's highly jaundiced views on Constantine and the decline of the empire were not shared by everyone. It was hardly surprising that Christians took a very different line on the man who had saved their Church from persecution and set it on the path to become the empire's official religion. One of the first to voice his gratitude was the bishop of the town of Caesarea in Palestine, a certain Eusebius. A contemporary of Constantine, he had experienced the horrors of Diocletian's persecution at first hand and, once it was over, he hastened to sing the praises of the new regime in a flattering biography of Constantine. The circumstances of the emperor's birth were carefully avoided and the account opens with the young Constantine residing in the imperial palace. Already, Eusebius claimed, a virtuous spirit was drawing him towards a morality superior to that of the pagans around him. Indeed, his virtue and good looks inspired envy in the palace, so that he was forced to flee and head for Britain to join his father. So it was that God arranged it that Constantine should be on hand when his father died, and naturally he was chosen to succeed him. When it came to vindicating his grip on power against his enemies, God took care of that too. While encamped outside Rome in 312 preparing to do battle with his rival Maxentius, Constantine allegedly had a vision of a cross-shaped device superimposed on the sun with the words 'Conquer in this'. That night, Eusebius wrote, Jesus Christ himself appeared to Constantine and commanded that he should make a replica of the device that he had seen in the sky and place it, as his standard, at the forefront of his army in the battle to come. It was this that led Constantine to victory at the battle of the Milvian Bridge and prompted him from then on to favour the Christian Church and to issue an edict putting an end to the persecution. Eusebius makes no mention of the murders of Crispus and Fausta, nor of Constantine's guilt at their murder driving him into the arms of the Church.

For Eusebius, Constantine's achievement of sole rule of the empire in 324 gave him full scope to develop his generous and pious nature. His refounding of Byzantion as Constantinople was not a waste of money and resources but an act of Christian devotion. The new city was designed to be a purely Christian one, unpolluted by pagan worship: the temples that Zosimus mentions have no place in Eusebius's account. Nor, maintained the good bishop, did Constantine neglect the frontiers and give entry to the barbarians. On the contrary, he subjected them to Roman rule and, rather than Romans paying annual tribute money to barbarians, it was now the latter who came humbly to lay their gifts at Constantine's feet. Far from being the ruin of the empire, Constantine was its saviour.

Clearly Constantine was one of those leaders who evoked either fervent devotion or bitter hatred in their subjects. From a more detached viewpoint it is possible to see Constantine's reign as neither an unmitigated disaster nor the inauguration of a golden age, but rather as a process of transformation as the empire adjusted to the new and dangerous world around it. It is in Constantine's time that all the characteristic elements of Byzantine civilisation can first be discerned: a monumental and impregnable capital in Constantinople; dominant Christianity; a political theory that exalted the office of emperor but also placed restraints upon it; an admiration of ascetic spirituality; an emphasis on visual expression of the spiritual; and an approach to the threat on the borders that went beyond the purely military.

* * *

In some ways, Zosimus was right to complain about the new and rapidly growing city of Constantinople. By about 500, the place was desperately overcrowded, and as a result it was dangerous and volatile. It only needed some tiny pretext for a riot to erupt in the streets. In the early years of the fifth century, the city's archbishop or patriarch, John Chrysostom, was immensely popular and his fiery sermons always attracted a large congregation. Unfortunately he was not liked by Empress Eudoxia, the consort of Arcadius (395–408). Chrysostom had criticised her when she had helped herself to some property in Constantinople without taking much notice of the rights of the owners and she was deeply offended by some of his sermons which, while mentioning no names, denounced powerful, scheming women. In June 404 Chrysostom was sent into exile but his supporters took their revenge. Determined that no one was to be consecrated patriarch in Chrysostom's place, a large crowd of his supporters broke into the cathedral of Hagia Sophia and set fire to it. By morning it was a smoking ruin.

It was not only religious issues that raised passions in early Byzantine Constantinople. The chariot races that were held in the Hippodrome attracted huge crowds of supporters for the two main teams, the Greens and the Blues. Successful charioteers enjoyed wide celebrity: poems were composed in their honour and their statues were as prominent in public places as those of the emperor. It was not unusual for fights to break out between rival supporters but what really terrified the imperial authorities was when the Blues and the Greens joined forces. In 498, several Green supporters were arrested for throwing stones. A crowd of their fellows gathered to demand their release from the emperor, the elderly Anastasius (491–518), but they received a blank refusal and a troop of soldiers was sent to disperse them. That was the signal for a general riot in the Hippodrome when the place was full to capacity for the races. The crowd started to throw stones at the imperial box, where the emperor had just taken his seat to preside over the event. One large rock, hurled by a black man in the crowd, narrowly missed Anastasius and the emperor's body-guards made a rush on the perpetrator and cut him to pieces with their swords. By now the exits to the Hippodrome had been sealed, so the crowd resorted to arson, setting fire to the main gate so that considerable damage was done to the stadium and the area round about. Eventually order was restored, after a few prominent malefactors had been singled out and punished, but it was another lesson in how quickly the crowded city could transform itself into a war zone.

While Zosimus might have been right about Constantinople's volatility, in other respects he failed to appreciate the value of the new city. It had not come into being, as he claimed, simply because of Constantine's need to escape from Rome and his own colossal vanity. There were very good reasons for creating a new city at that time and in that place. For some years, the emperors had ceased to base themselves permanently in Rome – the old capital was just too far from the threatened frontiers and some forward base needed to be found. In the western half of the empire, Milan and Trier were often used, while in the east, Antioch and Nikomedeia served the purpose. Constantine was seeking to create his own alternative base but he wanted somewhere worthy of permanent imperial presence, which was why, once he had decided on Byzantion as the site, he worked so hard to adorn the place with fine buildings reminiscent of Rome. Constantine also had strategic considerations in mind, for the site had not been randomly chosen, whatever Zosimus might say about his initially favouring the site of Troy. Constantinople was in a perfect position on the Bosporus, halfway between the Danube and Mesopotamian frontiers, a much more practical site than Rome, given the pressure on the borders. Moreover, as even Zosimus had to admit, it provided a secure refuge, for it was situated on a narrow and easily defended promontory between the sea and one of the finest natural harbours in the world, the Golden Horn. Constantine made the site even stronger by sealing it with a defensive wall on the landward side. In the following century, a new set of fortifications – the Theodosian Walls, or Land Walls – were constructed, enclosing a larger tract of land within the city. Constructed of limestone blocks five and a half metres thick, they effectively made Constantinople impregnable by land. A single span of wall was built along the seaward sides of the promontory too, effectively protecting it from attack by a hostile fleet. If the site did have a weakness, it was the lack of a fresh water supply, but that was remedied by the construction of aqueducts to bring in the water and underground cisterns to store it. What Zosimus was never to know was that, when times became hard and the empire was beset on all sides, Constantinople was to become one of its greatest assets, surviving siege and blockade time after time. Even the pretentious buildings and wide-open squares were to prove their worth, making Constantinople a showcase capital, impressing visitors with the empire's wealth and power and bolstering its claim to be the centre of the Christian world.

* * *

Significant though the foundation of Constantinople was, the pervasiveness of the Christian religion is undoubtedly the element that most sharply distinguishes the Byzantine empire from the Roman world that preceded it. In Roman times a plethora of local deities and cults had existed alongside the official worship of the Olympian gods. In Byzantium there was only one religion, and only by accepting it could you be a loyal subject of the emperor. Whatever Eusebius and other Christian writers tried to suggest, this change did not happen overnight. Constantine's personal conversion did not immediately lead to that of the whole empire but rather inaugurated a gradual Christianisation. After his victory at the Milvian Bridge in 312, Constantine rode into Rome in triumph and erected a monumental arch to celebrate his success, but nowhere on it were there any specific Christian references apart from a vague statement that the victory was won 'at the prompting of the deity'. In 313, he issued an edict of toleration which brought the persecution of Christians to an end. Later in his reign he made Sunday a public holiday, entered into friendly correspondence with Christian bishops and began to subsidise the Christian Church with public funds. On the other hand, the emperor made no serious attempt to outlaw the worship of the old gods, and their temples and sanctuaries continued to operate much as before. Even after Constantine's death in 337, there was no concerted attempt to force Christianity on all the people of the empire. His son, Constantius II (337–361), did order some temples to close but many of his measures were undone by the next emperor, the pagan Julian. In his short reign, Julian (361–363) attempted to restore the worship of the old gods, but after his unexpected death all the emperors were Christians. Even then, they trod carefully and there was a broad tolerance for all beliefs.

Only in the later fourth century did it become safe to introduce active and sustained anti-pagan measures. By then, with the adoption of Christianity by the emperor and court, conversions had inevitably increased apace and in many cities Christians had become the majority. The murky and at times brutal process by which Christianity became the state religion really began with the accession of Theodosius I (379–395). At first, pagan temples were picked off one by one, but in 391 Theodosius felt strong enough to introduce a decree completely outlawing the act of sacrifice, an important part of pagan worship.

How this legislation was interpreted on the ground depended on the local situation. In many places, where Christians were the majority anyway, the pagan cults disappeared with very little fuss. That was certainly the case in Constantinople, but not in the empire's second city at that time, the great Egyptian port of Alexandria. In the fourth century Alexandria had a population of about 300,000 with nearly four hundred places of worship belonging to pagans, Christians and Jews. The Christian community was a flourishing one that could claim the evangelist St Mark as the founder of their Church. Their archbishop was regarded as one of the most important in the Christian hierarchy, ranking third after the pope in Rome and the patriarch of Constantinople and one of only five entitled to style himself 'patriarch'. On the other hand, Alexandria also had a vibrant, vocal and numerous pagan community and was a centre for classical learning, boasting the second most important school of philosophy after that of Athens and a library containing some 490,000 papyrus rolls of ancient Greek literature. There were a number of magnificent temples. The Tychaion was dedicated to the goddess Fortune, the Caesareum to the cult of long-dead emperors. Most splendid of all was the Serapeum, whose great colonnaded hall was dominated by a monumental statue of the god Serapis.

Sooner or later, the two groups were bound to come into conflict and the flash point was usually Christian attempts to replace temples with churches. In 361, the Christian patriarch of Alexandria, George, decided that an abandoned temple of Mithras should be cleared away and the site dedicated to Christian worship. Work began, but when some skeletons were unearthed and paraded around disrespectfully by a group of Christians, a riot broke out. The pagans stormed the cathedral, dragged out the unfortunate George and beat him to death. In the end, of course, it was the Christians who prevailed, for with imperial authority on their side they could hardly lose. In 391 another patriarch, Theophilos, applied to the emperor Theodosius for permission to demolish the pagan temples in the city. That was willingly granted and Theophilos marched with a gang of supporters to begin the work. When they got wind of what was happening, a large band of pagans seized weapons and attacked the Christians. There were running battles in the streets before the pagans rushed to the

Serapeum and barricaded themselves in. The stand-off was only defused when an imperial edict was read out promising an amnesty to those who had participated in the violence, provided that they vacated the Serapeum at once. Most took advantage of this offer and the Christian mob then surged in. By the time they had finished, the famous building had been completely demolished, the columns pulled down and the towering statue of Serapis smashed to bits. Scarcely a trace of the magnificent temple remained.

Much the same happened at Gaza in the province of Palestine. The prosperous city's chief landmark was the enormous circular Marneion, the centre for the cult of Marnas, the local god of agriculture and plenty who was identified with the Greek deity Zeus. The costly marble paving of its sanctuary was considered so sacred that no one was allowed to walk on it. Here, if anywhere, paganism seemed to be secure, for the Christians were a tiny minority among the 20,000 inhabitants. When in 395 the Christians of Gaza elected as their bishop an uncompromising monk called Porphyry, he arrived to a frosty welcome from the local pagans. They piled thorn bushes in the approach road to Gaza to hinder his progress and it was not until late in the night that he finally got through. Christians were regularly attacked and beaten up in the streets. Incensed by these provocations, Porphyry complained to the imperial authorities, obtaining a decree that the temples in Gaza should be closed. The local officials in Gaza, doubtless fearing trouble, neglected to enforce the order and the Marneion stayed open. There was only one thing for it. Porphyry decided to travel to Constantinople and appeal to the emperor himself.

Arriving at the imperial palace, the bishop and his companions found it difficult to get to see the emperor, now Theodosius's son Arcadius. They did, however, secure an audience with the empress Eudoxia, who was sympathetic to their request and promised to persuade her husband to agree to the destruction of the Marneion. That proved easier said than done. Although Arcadius was a pious Christian, when Eudoxia cornered him later he protested that he received a handsome tax revenue from the wealthy pagans of Gaza and that he had no desire to antagonise them. Porphyry was not discouraged. He waited some weeks until the empress had given birth to a son and, on the day of the christening, he stood outside the doors of the cathedral with a petition which he managed, with the empress's connivance, to place in the care of the servant who was carrying the baby. Thus, when the imperial party assembled in the palace, the emperor could hardly avoid receiving the petition. He had been ambushed and he knew it but he weakly gave in. The very next day, Porphyry received a written imperial order and set out for Gaza with an official called Cynegius who was charged with seeing the job done.

Once in Gaza, Cynegius gathered a troop of soldiers and marched on the Marneion in May 402. The pagans were not going to give in without a fight and they barricaded the heavy doors of the temple, so the soldiers and local Christians headed off to attack other undefended temples, which they looted and burned down. Ten days later they reconvened to debate the best way to net the biggest prize, the Marneion itself. With their plan finalised, they marched on the temple and smeared the doors in pitch, sulphur and pork fat. When this incendiary mixture was ignited the doors went up in flames and the conflagration soon spread to the rest of the building. By the end of the day, the Marneion was a smoking ruin. Once the ashes and passions had cooled, Porphyry announced his plan to build a new church on the site using money that he had been given for the purpose by Eudoxia. It was to be of a different shape and design to the temple that had preceded it so the site had to be completely cleared. Five years later the new church was complete. The marble pavement which had survived the fire was, on Porphyry's orders, relaid in the market-place where it could be walked on by all and sundry, including the dogs and pigs. Even a generation later, many pagans still avoided the marketplace so that they would not have to defile it.

These dramatic episodes marked the end of public expressions of pagan worship in Byzantium. By 423 the emperor Theodosius II (408–450) considered the likelihood of a pagan revival to be so remote that he could afford to be generous and issue a law guaranteeing pagans security of property provided that they did not attempt to make public sacrifices. This gesture of reconciliation aside, the last stages of the process of Christianisation have the atmosphere of a witch hunt. By the early fifth century, the pagans were an embattled minority and often the victims of brutal persecution. The most shocking incident occurred in Alexandria in 415. One of the teachers at the school of philosophy there was a woman, Hypatia, who numbered among her pupils some of the foremost intellectuals of the day, both Christian and pagan. Hypatia herself remained unconverted to Christianity and that, along with her refusal to play the backstage role considered appropriate for women, attracted the animosity of some elements within the church of Alexandria. One day as she rode through the streets of Alexandria in her carriage, Hypatia was set upon and dragged out by a gang of Christians. She was carried off to a church, stripped naked and beaten to death on the altar. It was an isolated incident and most Christians were as horrified by it as the pagans were, but it casts a very ugly light on the process of Christianisation and goes some way to explain the bitter tone of Zosimus's history and his complaint that learned and virtuous philosophers were persecuted for their beliefs.

It was not only pagans who suffered in this religious revolution. Christians who subscribed to a version of the faith that differed from the officially recognised one were in the line of fire as well. For what Constantine had probably not realised when he adopted Christianity was that the Church was divided by a number of issues. The most serious of these was the question of exactly who Jesus Christ was and what relation he bore to God. It was in the ever-fractious city of Alexandria that the controversy developed. A priest called Arius had been teaching that Jesus had been created and was therefore a secondary God. Other Christians held that Christ was equally divine with God the Father. Hoping to bring the debate to an end, Constantine convened a council of the whole Church at Nicaea in 325, a meeting which was later to be known as the First Ecumenical Council. The three hundred or so bishops who attended the meeting drew up a creed, or list of beliefs, that broadly took the line of Arius's opponents, describing Jesus as being of the same essence as God.

That was not the end of the matter. Arius and his supporters continued to preach their version of theology and towards the end of his reign Constantine began to be more sympathetic towards them. After his death, his successor Constantius II favoured the Arians (as did several later emperors). That meant that those who supported the decisions of the Council of Nicaea were branded as heretics and were subject to persecution. Their leader was the outspoken patriarch of Alexandria, Athanasius, who was three times shipped off to exile in cold and remote parts of the empire. In the later fourth century, the pendulum swung the other way. Theodosius I, who was so militantly anti-pagan, was also a convinced adherent of the decisions of the Council of Nicaea. In February 380, he issued a law announcing that henceforth all Christians should follow the faith as defined by that council and that only they could claim to be members of the universal Church. A few months later, he put his edict into practice by deposing all bishops who were deemed Arians and replacing them with supporters of Nicaea. The following year, a second ecumenical council was summoned to Constantinople to reinforce the theological decisions made at Nicaea. The 'poison of Arian sacrilege' was outlawed and the faith as defined at Nicaea and Constantinople, and reinforced by the decisions of the Council of Chalcedon of 451, remained the official doctrine of the Byzantine empire throughout its existence. Woe betide anyone who thought differently: from now on, it was heretical to believe, as the Arians did, that Christ was less divine than God.

Along with pagans and heretics, Jews were another group who could not be easily fitted into the new, all-embracing orthodoxy. Their position under the Roman empire had always been a difficult one. Since the crushing of the Jewish revolts in Palestine in 70 and 135, there had been ongoing large-scale Jewish emigration from Jerusalem and Palestine, so that by Zosimus's day there were large and often prosperous communities all over the empire, especially in Egypt and Syria. Generally these Jewish communities existed peacefully alongside their neighbours, but as Christianity became the majority religion, matters started to change. Local clergy became concerned that many new Christians were not adequately aware of the difference between their faith and Judaism and that they were happy to attend both church and synagogue. Sermons started to be preached, pointing out how Christianity's acceptance of the divinity of Jesus marked it out from Judaism. The most celebrated of these preachers was John Chrysostom, the future patriarch of Constantinople, whose series of eight homilies on this theme, delivered in Antioch in 386–387, had been met with thunderous applause. Playing to the gallery, Chrysostom could not resist lobbing the accusation that it was the Jews who were responsible for the death of Christ and that they therefore had 'no chance for atonement, excuse or defence'.

The dissemination of such views sometimes led to tension on the ground and there were clashes between Jews and Christians, just as there were between Christians and pagans. In around 490, a Christian mob in Antioch burned down a synagogue and dug up some of the corpses in the cemetery next to it. In Alexandria matters developed into a major confrontation in 413 when, incensed by Christian attacks, the Jews of the city decided to mount a concerted response. Word was passed that all Jews should wear a rough ring of palm bark on their fingers so that they would know each other in the dark. Then one night they ran through the streets shouting that a church was on fire. As Christians rushed from all directions to extinguish the blaze, the Jews were waiting for them and many Christians were murdered. When the extent of the carnage became apparent the next morning, the patriarch of Alexandria led crowds of his flock through the streets to attack Jewish houses and synagogues. Within days the entire Jewish community of Alexandria had been forced to leave and most of their property was taken over by the Christians.

The attitude of the Christian imperial authorities towards the Jews was ambivalent. The governor of Alexandria was outraged by their expulsion, no doubt because the absence of such a large and wealthy part of the city's population would seriously diminish his tax revenue. From 425 specific laws were in place to protect the Jews and prevent attacks on their houses and synagogues. Yet, even in the corridors of power, dogmatism had managed to creep in. Jews were forbidden from holding posts in the imperial administration and in 388 Theodosius I passed a law forbidding them to marry Christians. In 531 it was announced that Jews could no longer act as witnesses against Christians in the law courts. Jewish communities survived in Byzantine cities but anyone not subscribing to the official religion was more or less disadvantaged.

Having a different faith was not the only way to find oneself marginalised in early Byzantine society. The Christian religion promoted celibacy as an ideal and restricted sexual activity to monogamous relationships between men and women. Those whose inclinations lay outside those limits were in danger. Under the classical Roman empire, sexual relations between members of the same sex were not illegal, and even emperors openly had male lovers, although there seems to have been a widespread prejudice that the passive role in any such relationship was unbecoming of Roman citizens. As Christianity slowly became the official religion of the empire, the authorities began to legislate on what had previously been a matter of private choice. As in the case of paganism, the emperors proceeded very slowly. In 342 a vaguely worded statute was introduced that forbade men to marry other men but prescribed no precise punishment, and nearly fifty years later another law banned homosexual prostitution. In 533, however, legislation expressly forbade sexual relations between men, and a number of high-profile individuals were prosecuted and punished with torture and exile. Curiously, they were all bishops. From then on, wrote a contemporary chronicler, 'those who experienced sexual desire for other males lived in terror'.

* * *

So far, the picture of the transition from Rome to Byzantium appears to be a depressing one, where intolerance became enshrined in government and legislation. For Edward Gibbon, writing in the eighteenth century, these developments seemed distasteful enough. But for anyone living in the post-1945 world, the persecution of dissidents, Jews and homosexuals has a horribly familiar ring. The parallel, however, is inappropriate. The regime that came to power in Germany in the 1930s billed itself as likely to last for a thousand years yet barely managed twelve. Byzantium, by contrast, achieved the feat. That was because, alongside the undeniable narrow-mindedness of emerging Byzantine religion and culture, there were other aspects that held the imagination and engendered the loyalty of its populations, and drew awe and admiration from outsiders – aspects that were to prove very useful in the difficult times to follow. Four examples are enough to illustrate how this came about. First, Christianity brought to Byzantium a conception of rulership that combined political and religious leadership under one head of state, and this encouraged political stability. Second, it was a rulership that invited its subjects to give their assent to each new ruler and offered them a surprisingly direct relationship with him. Third, it provided public services that catered for the most basic needs of its citizens and promoted a spiritual ethos that captured their hearts and minds. Lastly, it developed a new form of art and architecture that sought to express the immaterial and spiritual in visual form.

Turning first to rulership, Byzantine political theory was deeply influenced by the crisis faced by the Roman empire between 235 and 284, when a series of military disasters had led to political instability. Since the emperor seemed unable to defend the frontiers, there were endless revolts and usurpations in the provinces. Changes of ruler took place with bewildering regularity and most imperial incumbents reigned for only a few months. In response, some emperors had sought to enhance the prestige of their office by associating it with the divine. Whereas in the past, deceased emperors had been honoured as gods, Aurelian, who ruled in the 270s, claimed that he was 'lord and god' in his own lifetime. Diocletian was more modest, claiming to be a kind of representative on earth of Jupiter, the king of the gods, but the intention was the same: to discourage the idea that the throne could simply be grabbed by anyone who had the military force to do so.

This tendency to merge government and religion continued after the emperors became Christian, although the door was now closed on any notion that they were somehow divine. Bishop Eusebius of Caesarea, the author of the laudatory biography of Constantine that contrasts so starkly with Zosimus's version of events, was largely responsible for developing a Christian version of divinely sanctioned rulership. In 336, as part of the celebrations of Constantine's thirty years on the throne, Eusebius incorporated his ideas on the matter into a flattering speech that was delivered in the emperor's presence. Perhaps surprisingly, he was perfectly ready to admit that the office of Roman emperor had always been special in the eyes of God, even in the days when those who occupied it had been pagans. After all, in the Gospel of Matthew, Jesus Christ had advised his listeners to 'Render to Caesar the things that are Caesar's and render to God the things that are God's', a clear injunction that Christians had a duty to the Roman emperor just as they had to God. Nor could it have been mere coincidence, Eusebius argued, that the birth of Christ had taken place during the reign of the first Roman emperor, Augustus (31 BCE–14 CE). Clearly it had been God's plan from the beginning that the Roman empire would become Christian and would be the state in which all Christians would live. Now, with the conversion of Constantine, the emperor was a Christian and so his office was even more important than it had been in the time of Christ. The *basileus*, as the Byzantines tended to call their emperor, was a deputy, placed on earth to rule over the Christian people, an earthly reflection of the real ruler, almighty God.

This new conception of the imperial office was to have far-reaching implications for the scope of the emperor's role. In pagan times, although the emperor had been chief priest, it had not been his responsibility to police the plethora of temples and cults. The Christian deputy of God, on the other hand, would certainly be responsible for ensuring that the Church was protected and able to flourish. That meant subsidising the Church from state funds and discouraging and ultimately suppressing paganism, but it went much further. When there were disputes over doctrine, the emperor became involved, with Constantine presiding over the Council of Nicaea in 325 and his successors over subsequent ecumenical councils. Effectively the emperor was playing a part in the formulation of doctrine, a task that might have been thought to belong more properly to priests and theologians. Consequently, as the fourth century progressed, the imperial office came to be seen as somehow holy. Chronicles of the time referred to 'the sacred emperor', and in his portraits he was depicted with a halo. It was a prime example of the blurring of any distinction between secular and religious that came to characterise Byzantium.

In a modern world where representative democracy is widely seen as the ideal form of government and religion is considered a matter of personal conscience unconnected with loyalty to the state, this kind of theocracy may seem simply a cloak for dictatorship and megalomania. How better to control the masses than by swathing yourself in a religious aura and denouncing any political opposition as tantamount to heresy? On the other hand, it should be remembered that this was a form of government that developed in, and was appropriate to, a dangerous and uncertain world: Byzantium's frontiers were under constant pressure. It promoted a certain stability as, although there were periods in Byzantine history when individual emperors came and went in coups and counter-coups, the prestige of the office itself remained undimmed. No usurper could hope to be accepted as emperor unless he could look the part by installing himself in the Great Palace in Constantinople and playing his role in the appropriate round of religious ceremonies. Taking the capital was easier said than done, and many revolts petered out when their leader failed to do so.

A second important feature of the Byzantine empire was that the imperial office, with its religious mystique, genuinely engaged the loyalty of the mass of the population, who played an important role in the accession of a new emperor. The new incumbent would appear in the imperial box in the Hippodrome of Constantinople, which could seat 100,000 people, and there be acclaimed by the crowd, who thus gave their assent to his accession. The emperor was also remarkably accessible to ordinary subjects. His gardens in the Great Palace were open to the public from soon after daybreak until nine o'clock and again after three in the afternoon. During processions on festival days, onlookers could pass him petitions. In 369, a widow called Berenice did so, complaining of a powerful court official called Rhodanos who had used a trumped-up charge as a pretext to seize her property. After investigating the matter, Emperor Valentinian I (364–375) had the man executed in the Hippodrome in front of the gathered crowd and gave all his property to Berenice. Perhaps most important of all, the Byzantine emperor was not an untrammelled despot who could do whatever he wanted. The same religious ideology that gave him his power placed strict limits on it and the Church could place sanctions on him when he overstepped the mark. In the year 390, Emperor Theodosius I arrived in Thessalonica with his army only to be met by riots as the local inhabitants protested about having to provide billets for the soldiers. The emperor was incensed but he bided his time, waited until the citizens were gathered in the local hippodrome to watch a chariot race, and then ordered his troops to shoot arrows into the crowd. Several thousand people were killed. Satisfied with a job well done, Theodosius continued his march west but when he reached Milan retribution caught up with him. The city's bishop, Ambrose, had heard about the events in Thessalonica and refused to let the emperor into the church to receive communion. The stand-off lasted for several days until the emperor showed his remorse by introducing a law that those who had been sentenced to death or confiscation of property should be granted thirty days' grace before the penalty was carried out in case evidence should emerge of their innocence. Only then was Theodosius allowed in. Byzantine theocracy might not be to our contemporary taste but it was a system that worked for Byzantium and survived remarkably unchanged for the whole of the empire's long history.

∗ ∗ ∗

There was a third area in which the transition from Rome to Byzantium brought benefit to the empire's people. At the same time that the Christian Church was defining Byzantine political theory, so it was also coming to be the main source of public welfare for the vast majority of the urban population. In the days when the Roman empire had been peaceful and stable, municipal government had been the responsibility of the wealthy citizens of each town who constituted its *curia*, or senate. These *curiales* were responsible for collecting the taxes but they vied with each other to spend lavishly, from their own fortunes, on public buildings and services, from bath houses to aqueducts. When times grew hard from the third century on, however, there were fewer wealthy men and those who remained were less inclined to part with their wealth for the common good. Some sought to escape the burden by moving to villas in the countryside, others by becoming senators of Rome or Constantinople, who were exempt from serving on the municipal *curia*. At the same time, the populations of many cities were increasing as people drifted in from the countryside in search of work, often becoming a homeless population living on the streets. The imperial authorities did almost nothing about the problem but the Christian Church did, and its efforts went far beyond mere remedial charitable donations. In major cities, it organised large-scale distributions of food so that at one point no less than 75,000 people were reckoned to be receiving these hand-outs in Alexandria alone. Urban churches were not buildings standing alone but usually had a complex of buildings around them offering various services free of charge. These included hostels for the poor where they could be clothed, housed and fed, and hospitals where treatment was given free of charge to those who could not pay. John Chrysostom, the same man who had preached inflammatory sermons against the Jews in Antioch in the 380s, established several hospitals in Constantinople after he became the city's patriarch in 398.

The town of Caesarea in Asia Minor, which was about 611 kilometres east of Constantinople, was particularly well served in this regard. Prosperous and staunchly Christian, its citizens had destroyed all the pagan temples in the city by the 360s and in 370 elected as their bishop a member of a prominent local family called Basil. The new incumbent was an adherent of the Nicaean definition of the Christian faith and so had a rather tense relationship with the emperor in Constantinople, Valens (364–378), who subscribed to the Arian view. The emperor allegedly decided to have the troublesome bishop sent into exile but when he came to sign the order the pen broke three times. So Valens gave up and Basil was allowed to remain in post and to carry out a project to improve the lives of his flock. Just outside Caesarea, he established a complex of buildings for various charitable purposes. They included a hostel for the poor, another for travellers, a refuge for lepers and a hospital. The latter was staffed by both physicians and nursing attendants and treated both illness and physical injuries. There is no indication that these services were restricted only to Christians and it is recorded that when Basil died in 379 he was mourned by pagans and Jews, as well as by his co-religionists.

Providing poorhouses and hospitals was, of course, simply an extension of Christian charity, but the activities of Christian bishops came to extend far beyond that. As the wealth of private citizens waned and the imperial authorities became increasingly distracted elsewhere, bishops found themselves taking over responsibility for all kinds of things. Theodoret, who became bishop of the Syrian town of Cyrus, near Antioch, in 423, took over the maintenance of bath houses, bridges and aqueducts throughout his diocese because nobody else was going to. In Alexandria, the diocese owned its own fleet of ships to bring food and supplies into the city. It was all part of the process whereby the Church came to pervade the whole of life.

These developments might give the impression that the Christian Church simply purchased the adherence of a large section of the population by hand-outs. That was not in fact the case. The new faith inspired a devotion and enthusiasm that it is difficult at this remove to comprehend. It has to be said, though, that it was not always the established Church and its bishops that gave rise to this enthusiasm but sometimes individual ascetics and holy men. Even before Constantine's conversion, many Christians had felt that belief in Christ alone was not enough and that one should follow his example literally and give everything to the poor. The pioneer was an Egyptian called Anthony who, round about the year 300, divested himself of all his worldly goods and headed off into the desert. For twenty years he hid away in a deserted fort at Pispir on the east bank of the Nile, living a life of abstinence and contemplation. What Anthony had not bargained for, however, was the admiration that his example would excite. As his presence at the fort became known, a few hardy individuals made their way there to follow his example. Then more came and still more, so that the desert came to resemble a small city and Anthony's fame spread throughout the empire. Even the emperor Constantine wrote to him to ask his advice. Desperate to pursue his life of solitude, Anthony retreated further into the desert but he could never quite escape his celebrity. On a rare visit to Alexandria, he found the streets thronged with his admirers, pagans as well as Christians.

Anthony's followers became known as *monarchoi*, 'those who live alone', from which the English word 'monk' is derived. As time went by, many of them took to living in communities or monasteries, but in the Byzantine world the highest religious calling was always seen as that of the solitary hermit. Some of these hermits became famous for their self-denying lifestyles and commanded the kind of celebrity which would now be reserved for film stars. Most celebrated of all the ascetics was Symeon Stylites. He grew up a Christian, tending his family's flocks in Syria, and being of a religious inclination he became a monk and entered a monastery. He remained there for about ten years but it was not a happy experience. He was not popular in the monastery because he was just too rigorous in observing the rules. While his fellow monks would fast for two days, Symeon would go without food for a whole week. Finally, it was all too much and the abbot asked him to leave. He wandered for a time around the countryside of Syria, much as Anthony had done in the deserts of Egypt, before he settled on a suitably desolate place where he chained himself to a rock. However, he soon encountered the same problem that Anthony had. His very reputation for holiness attracted large crowds of people seeking him out, thus disrupting the solitude he craved. They tended to cluster around him and tried to touch him. Moreover, while in Egypt Anthony had been able to withdraw ever further into the desert, that option was not really possible in Syria, where there were no great tracts of desert on the same scale.

Since he was unable to go away, Symeon went up. In about 412 he found a nine-metre-high antique column standing alone not far from Antioch. Perhaps it was left over from some demolished pagan temple. Symeon managed to get himself to the top and there he stayed, completely unprotected either from the heat of the sun or from the winter frost. He had a number of disciples who took up residence at the base of the column and they passed food and water up to him on ropes. Not surprisingly, this bizarre lifestyle took its toll. No doubt because he spent most of his time standing, Symeon's left foot developed a malignant ulcer which oozed pus, and in the end virtually the whole foot rotted away. The leg above was infested with worms and these sometimes fell off and dropped to the bottom of the column. There Symeon's disciples would reverently pick them up and, at his request, put them back on him so that they could cause him even more pain. As with Anthony, Symeon's reputation for holiness soon drew in the crowds. The area around his column became a permanent encampment and hundreds of visitors would turn up every day. On one occasion 1,244 of them were counted. A walled enclosure had to be built to prevent the throng from pressing too closely around the base of the column. Symeon remained up there for over forty years and when he finally died, in 459, he remained standing, stiff with rigor mortis. A splendid church was then built on the site of the column to accommodate those who continued to travel there to pray to the saint.

As with the quasi-religious status of the Byzantine emperors, this obsession with monks looks strange from the perspective of a far-removed time, place and culture. Yet holy men were perceived to provide a range of both spiritual and material benefits. There was a genuine belief that as a result of their ascetic struggles, holy men like Symeon were nearer to God than were weaker human beings, including the ordinary clergy. Consequently they were able to act as channels of divine grace, dispensing good counsel, intercession through prayer, and, ultimately, salvation, that could never be obtained simply by going to church on Sundays. There were also huge benefits to be gained from them in the here and now. Many of the visitors to Symeon's column brought sick people for him to heal which, according to his biographers, he regularly did. Others, particularly farmers, came to implore his prayers for a change in the weather to enable them to harvest their crops successfully. Symeon was also consulted on what might be considered purely secular matters. Delegations from local villages used to troop over to see him and seek his mediation in law suits or solicit his advice about the right time to plant crops. Perhaps the most important role of all played by Symeon Stylites and other holy men is that they often acted as protectors of the poor and vulnerable against the heavy hand of government authority. In a world where communication was slow and uncertain, imperial administrators had absolute power in their own districts and ample scope to abuse it. Appeals for justice to the distant emperor in Constantinople, or even to the governor in Antioch or Alexandria, were likely to go unheard. A far better bet was to call on the local holy man for help. When a delegation approached Symeon to complain about the activities of a local official who was extorting money from the poor and vulnerable, the holy man dispatched a messenger with the words 'Do not take by force what does not belong to you.' The official, of course, took little heed but when he dropped dead of a heart attack the very next day no one put it down to coincidence. Such dramatic outcomes were doubtless extremely rare but the holy man did have one great advantage in confronting powerful men: he was completely invulnerable. Threats of confiscation or violence were useless when levelled against someone who had no possessions and who voluntarily subjected his body to excruciating pain. While urban sophisticates like Zosimus may have loathed monks, to the poor and the oppressed they were champions and protectors. They were another way in which the mass of the people could make their voices heard and identify with the empire's claim to exist for their protection and benefit.

* * *

Some of the events of the period might suggest that the early Christian Church was anti-intellectual, anti-artistic, and altogether philistine. Incidents like the murder of Hypatia, and the destruction of architectural monuments including the Serapeum and the Marneion, leave a disturbing impression of fanaticism and cultural vandalism. Zosimus recorded with horror the riot in Constantinople in the summer of 404 when some militant Christians burned down not only the cathedral of Hagia Sophia but also the senate house along with its gallery of statues of the muses that were carved in a rare kind of marble that was no longer quarried. Their loss, he lamented, reflected the universal contempt for art and beauty. The same attitude can be detected towards the rich inheritance of classical literature. Spiritual celebrities like Anthony and Symeon Stylites were scarcely educated and spoke only their local Coptic and Syriac languages: they knew nothing of Latin or Greek. Many Christians felt that it was inappropriate to read the works of Homer, Aristophanes and Lucian with their tales of gods, nymphs and heroes, and felt that believers should restrict themselves to the Bible and other edifying matter. During the process of Christianisation it looked for a time as if these works of literature might share the fate of the temples.

That did not happen, for while one cultural tradition was being eroded, another was developing which was to incorporate many aspects of the old. Classical literature is a case in point. Influential Christians, such as Basil of Caesarea, argued that these works were worthy of study for the beauty of their language and style, and their view prevailed. The Greek classics were not thrown on the bonfire when the empire became Christian but were carefully preserved and studied throughout the Byzantine period. The same applied to religious art, a fourth defining characteristic of Byzantine civilisation. While the Serapeum and Marneion had been wrecked, the marble statues of pagan gods and goddesses that lined the streets of Constantinople were left untouched. Christians were perfectly happy for them to be preserved for their beauty and artistry alone, provided that they were not objects of veneration. Pagan art was also sometimes subtly adapted for the needs of the moment. When Constantine wanted a likeness of himself to adorn one of the main squares of Constantinople, he made an interesting choice. Rather than commission a new one, he simply reused a statue of the sun god Apollo that he had purloined from a temple in Asia Minor, leaving in place the seven rays that emanated from its head.

The synthesis between the old classical culture and the new Christian one can also be seen in architecture. When Christianity had been a small and persecuted sect, its adherents had met secretly in houses. What came to be the word for 'church', *ekklesia* in Greek, originally just meant 'assembly', the gathering together of Christians. Now, with ever-increasing numbers of Christians, large, dedicated buildings would need to be found to accommodate them all on Sundays. That raised the problem of what these buildings should look like, because at this stage there was no Christian tradition of architecture on which to draw. There were pagan temples but Christians wanted to mark their churches out as different. Porphyry of Gaza stoutly resisted the suggestion that the Marneion should simply be converted to Christian use: the place had to be destroyed, erased and purified before the new church could replace it on the site. Instead Christians turned to another classical model, the basilicas, large public buildings that existed in all the towns of the empire and provided the setting for legal proceedings or audiences with the governor. They were fairly simple buildings, rectangular in shape, with a flat ceiling and a pitched roof, sometimes with side aisles as well. They had the great advantage of providing a large covered space where everyone could see and everyone could hear. One of the earliest of these Christian basilicas was that built in the 320s over the site of the burial place of St Peter in Rome and dedicated to that saint. Another was constructed by Constantine in Jerusalem over what was believed to be the tomb where Christ was laid after his crucifixion, known as the church of the Holy Sepulchre. Many others followed, including the original cathedral building of Hagia Sophia in Constantinople which was dedicated in 360.

Now that the size and shape of a church had been decided upon, how should it be decorated on the inside, if at all? The walls could hardly be left stark and bare, for the building needed to be striking and beautiful to reflect the high purpose for which it had been constructed. So early basilicas were adorned with pastoral scenes, trees and plants. Before long, however, some people began to argue that the decoration should not be neutral but should have some kind of spiritual or instructive purpose. Pictures could show the example of martyrs who had given their lives for the faith during the persecutions, or stories from the Gospels, showing Christ's miracles, teaching, crucifixion and resurrection. This idea, however, evoked strong opposition in some quarters: it smacked of idolatry and of the statues of the gods that had adorned pagan temples. While on pilgrimage in Palestine in 394, Epiphanius, bishop of Salamis on Cyprus, was horrified to see a painted image of Christ on a curtain hanging in a church. He angrily tore it down and went his way. That was not the end of the matter. Epiphanius then had to face the complaints of the congregation and the demand that if he really did not like their curtain he might at least have had the goodness to replace it with another one at his own expense.

In any case, Epiphanius lost the argument. By the early fifth century, it was generally accepted that churches should be decorated with appropriate scenes from scripture to inspire and instruct the congregation. The new philosophy was put into effect in the basilica of Santa Maria Maggiore in Rome, which was reconstructed and redecorated between 432 and 444. The interior decoration is a series of mosaics in which the images are made up of thousands of tiny coloured cubes of marble. A series of panels in the nave depicts a cycle of stories from the Old and New Testaments with the prophets and angels sporting togas as if they were Roman senators, a clear demonstration of how the old was incorporated into the new. So while the Christianisation of the Roman empire was undoubtedly accompanied by violence, persecution and destruction, it did not represent the end of art and culture, whatever Zosimus might have claimed.

* * *

Perhaps critics such as Zosimus could have forgiven Constantine's vanity project of Constantinople and his odd choice of religion had it not been for the fact that by the year 500 half of the empire had been lost. Pagans placed the blame on the shoulders of Constantine and his Christian successors, but again they were not being entirely fair. The problems faced by the Christian emperors of the fourth and fifth centuries were by no means new, and their pagan predecessors had not been particularly successful in dealing with them either.

The root of the trouble was that by 200 CE, the frontiers of the Roman empire were impossibly long. In the first two centuries after Christ, that had not mattered as the Romans had only to deal with isolated attacks on their borders, allowing them to boast that they had established a *Pax Romana* ('Roman Peace'). During the third century, the situation changed dramatically. In Persia, Rome's neighbour to the east, the ailing Arsacid dynasty, was replaced by the ambitious Sassanians who hoped to expand their empire into the Roman eastern provinces. A series of Roman defeats culminated in 260 when Emperor Valerian, a noted persecutor of Christians, was captured by the Persian King Shapur I and dragged off into captivity, never to be seen again. Around the same time, the Persians captured and sacked the major city of Antioch. The defeats in the east were catastrophic enough, but to make matters worse the northern frontiers came under attack at exactly the same time from another enemy. In 251, the Germanic tribe known as the Goths swept across the Danube, wiped out a Roman army and the emperor who led it, and raided as far south as Asia Minor, where they torched one of the Seven Wonders of the Ancient World, the temple of Artemis at Ephesus. The empire's very existence was now in danger. But from the 260s a series of energetic emperors succeeded in pulling the situation back from the brink, winning a series of military victories that neutralised the immediate Persian and Gothic threats. Zosimus's hero Diocletian negotiated a treaty with the Persians which stabilised the frontier in the east for the time being. With order restored, Diocletian pushed through a series of internal reforms to render the empire better suited to survive in the new dangerous and uncertain environment. The empire was, he decided, too large for one man to rule and he inaugurated a system of two emperors ruling jointly, one in the east and one in the west.

One of the thorniest problems was how to find a long-term solution to the threat to the northern frontier. The enemy there was not a unitary state like the Sassanid empire but a series of independent 'barbarian' tribes. Their attacks on the Roman frontiers had no expansionist aim like those of the Persians. The barbarians were either in search of plunder or, more often, seeking security from some other tribe that was pushing them southwards or westwards. The emperors had therefore long ago realised that it was not a question of winning battles and making treaties. Fighting and slaughtering large numbers of barbarians could only ever be a last resort and could not resolve the threat in the long run: sooner or later another group would take their place. Instead, they sought where possible to integrate newly arrived groups into the empire. In 280, Emperor Probus had settled the Bastarnae tribe, from beyond the Danube, in the Balkans and such arrangements were of great benefit to the empire. In a world where manpower was always in short supply, the settlers were required to provide troops when needed, making them *foederati*, or allies, who thus bolstered the defences. They could be settled on deserted land which they could then bring into cultivation, generating surplus produce and taxes. Whatever Zosimus's slurs on his military competence, Constantine seems to have dealt with the barbarian threat in much the same way as his predecessors had. There is no substantiation of Zosimus's story that he ran away when confronted by barbarians. On the contrary, he successfully pacified the Danube frontier in the 320s, building a bridge across the river so that his troops could carry the war into Gothic territory. In 332, a tribe known as the Tervingi Goths were compelled to surrender and make a treaty with the empire, promising to send 40,000 men to help the emperor whenever he needed them.

It was not only Constantine's supposed cowardice that Zosimus deplored. He believed that by substituting the pacific Christian religion for the manly, martial one of the ancients, and by placing eunuchs rather than virile men of action in charge of the administration, Constantine had undermined the military ethos on which the greatness of Rome had been founded. Again, on examination, neither charge sticks. While some Christians, such as Basil of Caesarea, considered any killing, even in defence of your country, to be sinful, that other prominent Christian of the day, Athanasius of Alexandria, wrote that it was praiseworthy to kill in war and those who did so rightly had monuments erected in their honour. There is certainly no sign of reluctance on the part of Christians to serve in the imperial armies. As early as the 160s, a contingent of Christians had fought on the Danube frontier against the Marcomanni tribe and in 314 the Council of Arles declared that it was quite permissible for Christians to join the army. By the late fourth century a considerable proportion of soldiers must have been Christian. Moreover, a new kind of military ethos started to emerge that was in many ways stronger than the old. Given that the empire was increasingly Christian and its Persian and barbarian enemies were not, defending the Roman borders was defending the Church. That idea was made manifest in the army's insignia and banners. Eusebius claims that Constantine carried into battle against the Tervingi Goths the same

cross device that he had allegedly seen in a vision in 312. Banners were embla-
zoned with the Chi-Rho symbol, consisting of the first two letters of the name
of Christ in Greek, a device which also appeared on coins. So praiseworthy
indeed was the mission of defending the Christian empire that almost any
action to secure victory was justified. In 358, the Christian emperor Constantius
II, Constantine's son, attacked the Sarmatians and the Quadi – tribes that,
although they had been allies in the past, had taken to raiding in the Balkans.
When the fighting men had been crushed in battle, the imperial troops charged
into their villages to round up the non-combatants, killing some, leading others
off to be sold as slaves.

As for the perennially despised eunuchs, they had been a feature of the
imperial court long before the advent of Christianity, for they had the great
virtue of being ineligible for the imperial throne. There is absolutely no
evidence that their role in government was somehow detrimental to the
empire's military fortune. In fact, several successful military commanders were
eunuchs, including Narses who was to bring the Gothic war to a successful
conclusion in the 560s. For this reason too, Zosimus was quite wrong to suggest
that Christianity had robbed the empire of its military ethos.

The loss of the western half of the empire did not come about because of the
incompetence of the Christian emperors or a decline in military prowess. It
was the result of events taking place thousands of miles away on the steppes of
Central Asia, where a nomad people known as the Huns were starting to move
westwards. Fierce mounted warriors, adept at loosing off arrows as they
galloped at high speed, the Huns' approach spread terror among the Germanic
tribes who stood in their way. In 376, a large group of Goths arrived on the
empire's Danube frontier. They made contact with Emperor Valens in
Constantinople, offering military service in exchange for the opportunity to
settle on deserted lands located within the Roman frontier, safely out of reach
of the Huns. Valens was delighted at this opportunity to bring in some valuable
manpower and accepted the offer, on the condition that the Goths turn over
their weapons. He promised that they would be provided with food until they
could harvest their own crops. The Goths duly crossed into Roman territory
but then the problems began. The Roman officials in charge of the transfer
syphoned off much of the money that was supposed to be given to the Goths to
buy food and they accepted bribes from the newcomers to allow them to keep
their weapons. Soon afterwards, bands of starving, armed Goths began
rampaging about the Balkans. Valens was compelled to assemble the eastern
Roman army in an attempt to bring the marauders to heel. On 9 August 378,
rashly refusing to wait for the arrival of the western Roman army, he attacked

the Goths at Adrianople, north-west of Constantinople. His impetuosity proved fatal. The Roman army was virtually annihilated and some 20,000 men were killed. Among the casualties was Valens himself, although nobody knew how or where he died, such was the confusion.

The disaster at Adrianople marked the moment when the Romans lost control of the ever-increasing number of invaders who were coming up against their northern borders. True, the Goths were finally brought to heel after four years of fighting, but they had to be allowed to remain inside the empire with quasi-independent status. In 395, they revolted under their leader Alaric and moved to Italy, where they sacked Rome in 410. In the meantime, the pressure from the Huns sent further waves of migrants up against the Roman border. In December 406, the Rhine frontier collapsed completely and several tribes such as the Vandals and Suevi crossed into imperial territory and began to settle wherever they wanted with the western Roman emperors powerless to prevent them. By the time the last man claiming to be the western emperor, Julius Nepos, was assassinated in 480, all the provinces he had once ruled were under new masters, even if some of them paid lip service to the authority of the eastern emperor, Zeno, in Constantinople.

* * *

Given Zosimus's background, it is hardly surprising that he saw the events of his day, and those of preceding generations, in the light that he did. His philosophy and religion had been sidelined and the state that he equated with the civilised world had been seriously diminished. Inevitably he would blame someone and Constantine represented everything that he disliked and despised. Time and distance give a different perspective. Wrong choice of religion, corrupt character and moral decadence seem to have had very little to do with what happened in the fourth and fifth centuries. Rather, the rulers of the empire found themselves in a new and dangerous situation and fought courageously to respond and adapt. In the process, the empire changed completely, with traditional religion replaced by Christianity and Rome supplanted by Constantinople as the most important city. The new religion pervaded all aspects of life, from warfare and political thought to public services and the visual arts. In short, by around 500 CE, the Roman empire had become Byzantium.

CHAPTER TWO

Outpost of Empire

*He is by nature a meddler and a lover of those things which in no way belong to him
... he has conceived the desire of seizing upon the whole Earth ...*
Procopius of Caesarea

In the great days of the Roman empire, prominent people seldom went to Ravenna. While its harbour of Classis was an important naval base for the northern Adriatic, the town itself was an insignificant settlement of houses built on piles and surrounded by bleak marshland. Then, in the year 402, this provincial backwater was suddenly transformed into the capital of the western Roman empire. Emperor Honorius (395–423), annoyed and alarmed by rioting in Rome, abandoned the city and took his entire court with him to Ravenna. Some of his more fastidious retainers must have been dismayed at the primitive conditions in their new home, but Honorius's choice had not been without good reason. The marshes made it inapproachable by land while the river which linked it to the sea at Classis six kilometres away was too shallow to allow passage to seagoing ships. The city could be supplied by small boats but these had to wait until the tide was in so that they could float up to the defensive wall. Here Honorius was safe from both the rioting rabble and the invading Goths.

The political upheavals that followed served only to confirm Ravenna's new status. When there were no more Roman emperors in the west, the new ruler of Italy, Odovacar, took up residence in the marshy city and avoided Rome as assiduously as Honorius had. The emperor in Constantinople, Zeno (474–491), was not very happy with this state of affairs but for the time being there was very little that he could do about it for he had no troops to spare for an

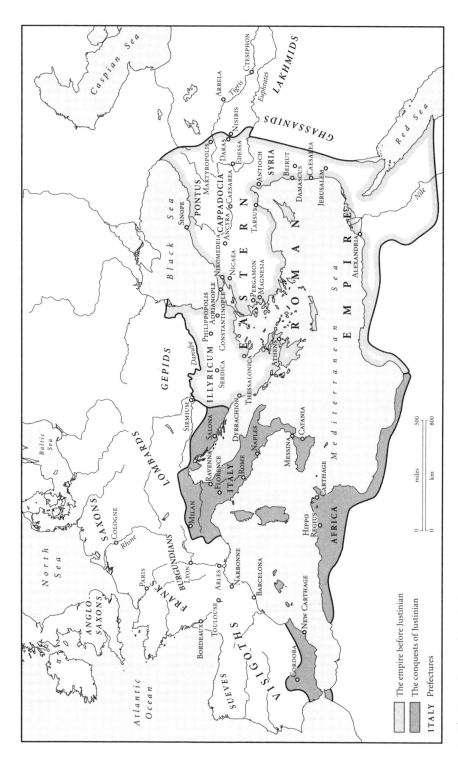

2 The Byzantine empire c. 565

Caspian Sea

LAKHMIDS

Red Sea

GHASSANIDS

ARBELA
Tigris
Euphrates
CTESIPHON
NISIBIS
DARAS
EDESSA
MARTYROPOLIS
SYRIA
ANTIOCH
BEIRUT
DAMASCUS
CAESAREA
JERUSALEM

PONTUS
SINOPE
CAPPADOCIA
NIKOMEDEIA
ANCYRA
CAESAREA
NICAEA
TARSUS

E A S T E R N

Black Sea

PERGAMON
MAGNESIA

R O M A N

Nile

ALEXANDRIA

PHILIPPOPOLIS
ADRIANOPLE
CONSTANTINOPLE
ILLYRICUM
SERDICA
ATHENS

E M P I R E

THESSALONICA

Danube

GEPIDS

SIRMIUM
SALONA
DYRRACHION

Mediterranean Sea

Baltic Sea

LOMBARDS

RAVENNA
FLORENCE
ITALY
ROME
MILAN
NAPLES
MESSINA
CATANIA

SAXONS

COLOGNE
Rhine

CARTHAGE

North Sea

AFRICA

HIPPO
REGIUS

ANGLO-
SAXONS

FRANKS
PARIS
BURGUNDIANS
LYON
ARLES
NARBONNE
BARCELONA

Atlantic Ocean

TOULOUSE
BORDEAUX

NEW CARTHAGE

SUEVES

VISIGOTHS

CORDOBA

0   500 miles
0   800 km

The empire before Justinian
The conquests of Justinian
ITALY Prefectures

expedition to recover Italy. In the end he resorted to what was to become the Byzantines' standard tactic for dealing with enemies who were too strong to be tackled head-on: he paid someone else to do it. Zeno made contact with Theodoric, ruler of the Ostrogothic tribe. For some years the Ostrogoths had been an unwelcome presence in the Balkans. Technically they were allies, *foederati*, but they frequently grew discontented with their terms of employment and attacked Byzantine cities in the area. In 488, Zeno made an agreement with Theodoric that he hoped would both rid him of the Ostrogoths and bring Italy back under his sovereignty. The Ostrogoths would march west, dispose of Odovacar, and then rule the country in Zeno's name. Arriving in Italy the following year, Theodoric had little difficulty in sweeping aside Odovacar's armies in the field, but then his adversary retired to the safety of Ravenna and a long stalemate ensued. Theodoric controlled most of Italy but he was quite unable to breach the defences of Odovacar's stronghold. After three years of frustration, Theodoric finally accepted a negotiated settlement, mediated by the archbishop of Ravenna. Theodoric and Odovacar solemnly agreed to rule Italy jointly and, in March 493, Theodoric's army was finally permitted to march into Ravenna. Not surprisingly, the agreement was unworkable and it lasted precisely ten days. Theodoric then invited Odovacar to a banquet to celebrate their friendship and in the midst of the festivities stabbed him to death.

So it was that Theodoric came to reside in Ravenna and it has to be said that in spite of his violent path to power, both the city and Italy as a whole prospered under his rule. Styling himself king of the Ostrogoths, he carefully maintained the fiction that he ruled merely by permission of the emperor in Constantinople. Although he himself was an Arian Christian, he made no attempt to interfere with the beliefs of the majority of his subjects, Chalcedonians, who accepted the definitions of the faith prescribed by the councils of Nicaea and Chalcedon, that Jesus Christ was equally human and divine. Determined that all Christians should live together peacefully in Ravenna, he built a new cathedral and churches just for his co-religionists, making sure that these Arian churches were no less splendid than the Chalcedonian ones. When he ordered the construction of an impressive new church dedicated to Christ the Redeemer (later known as Sant'Apollinare Nuovo), no expense was spared on the mosaic decoration. There were also separate baptisteries in Ravenna where the two groups could christen their children according to their own rites.

Not all parts of the former Roman empire in the west enjoyed such relaxed and tolerant rule. In North Africa, now under the rule of the Vandals, there were sporadic attempts to force the Chalcedonians to adopt the Arian line.

In Italy, however, life remained much as it had been when a Roman emperor, rather than a Gothic king, had ruled in Ravenna. In Rome, the senate still met and the city's bishop, known as the pope, presided unhindered over its Church even though – adhering to the official doctrine from Constantinople – he was a staunch supporter of Chalcedon. When things did change it was not because of the Ostrogoths but because of the new emperor who had taken power in Constantinople. The tumultuous events that followed were to transform Ravenna from the capital of Ostrogothic Italy to a vital outpost of the Byzantine empire.

* * *

When Emperor Zeno had died childless in 491, he had been succeeded by a civil servant called Anastasius who married Zeno's widow, Ariadne. The couple were by no means young at the time of Anastasius's accession and they produced no children. So when Anastasius died in 518, allegedly at the age of ninety, there was again no heir. For want of anyone better, the officials of the palace accepted the commander of the palace guard, Justin, as the new incumbent. As a soldier and man of action, Justin was in some ways well suited to the position of emperor, but he too was by now rather elderly and he had never had any formal education. He was therefore quite unable either to read or to signal his assent to the documents brought to him for approval. The latter difficulty was overcome by the use of a stencil which enabled the emperor to sign his name, but he also needed someone reliable to read and explain the content. That was why he came to rely very heavily on his clever nephew, Justinian, who now replaced him as commander of the palace guard. Not only did Justinian read his uncle's documents, he even took to writing some of them and sending them out under his own name. In due course, this indispensable right-hand man was appointed co-emperor and on his uncle's death it seemed only natural that he should succeed him.

Justinian I (527–565) is one of the few Byzantine emperors whose physical appearance can be reconstructed both from written descriptions and from a realistic portrait. Contemporaries noted that he was of medium height, with a round face and florid complexion. His mosaic portrait in the church of San Vitale in Ravenna confirms that description, showing a dour middle-aged visage under a richly jewelled crown. In short, the new emperor was nothing remarkable to look at. His reign, on the other hand, was to be momentous.

It was in Justinian's time that the trends that had been transforming the empire since the reign of Constantine reached their culmination, particularly the process of Christianisation. In the decades before Justinian's accession, it had still been possible for pagans like Zosimus to live quietly in the empire. No sooner was the new emperor in power than he attempted to wipe out the last vestiges of the old religion. He aimed the blow at the one area where the last pagans were still influential. They had been excluded from the court and naturally had no place in the Church, but they were still a major voice in higher education, where the curriculum was based on the ancient Greek classics. In 529, an edict was issued forbidding the teaching of philosophy at Athens, thus putting an end to a tradition that stretched back to the days of Socrates and Plato, and robbing many pagan intellectuals of their livelihood.

Despairing of the future, many of them gazed longingly at the non-Christian world beyond the imperial borders. They had heard great things about the new king of Sassanid Persia, Chosroes I, who was, it was rumoured, the very type of philosopher king presented as the ideal ruler in Plato's *Republic*. Under Chosroes's benevolent oversight, the reports claimed, there was no crime in Persia: valuables could be left unguarded in the street and no one would think of touching them. So, in about 531, a group of seven learned pagans crossed the border and made for Chosroes's court at Ctesiphon. On arrival, they were cruelly disappointed. Chosroes, though friendly and welcoming, was not the earnest student of philosophy they had expected, and, needless to say, there was plenty of crime in Persia. The ruling classes, far from being detached philosophers, were rapacious, overbearing and oppressive. What really shocked these fastidious intellectuals was that, even though polygamy was permitted, men still felt the need to commit adultery. After two years in Persia, the philosophers decided to return home and accept whatever fate awaited them there. By that time, Justinian had mellowed somewhat and, although they were not welcomed back with open arms, they were generally left to live out their lives unmolested. True, every now and then the authorities bestirred themselves. One summer's day in 559, a number of prominent pagans were arrested and their books, statues and pictures were piled up in one of Constantinople's main squares to be burned. Yet such incidents were now very rare. One of the emigrants who had returned from Persia, Simplicius of Cilicia, was able to continue his studies and went on to write a series of influential commentaries on the works of Aristotle before his death in 560. But this was to be the last generation of pagan intellectuals in the Byzantine empire, for many of them now adopted Christianity, even if only in name, as it was becoming impossible to live in the empire without conforming to the majority creed.

Among these nominal Christians may well have been a certain Procopius of Caesarea. Outwardly, Procopius was an educated Christian attached to court circles. As Eusebius had done in Constantine's time, he produced a laudatory speech in praise of the reigning emperor, extolling Justinian's building programme and assuring his listeners that 'when the emperor is pious, divinity walks not afar from human affairs'. He also wrote a long account of the wars fought in Justinian's reign, although curiously its references to the emperor are few and far between. All the while, Procopius was preparing another work, his so-called *Secret History*, which was never to be published in his lifetime. Here the author poured out his real feelings, heaping on Justinian and his wife Theodora all the bile that Zosimus had dealt to Constantine. Not only was the man a wastrel who was indifferent to the well-being of his subjects but his persecutions of those who failed to conform to the established religion were turning the world upside down. It was a strident protest but this was a dying voice. When Procopius's generation of pagans passed away, there were no more to replace them.

The last pagans were not the only ones to feel the weight of Justinian's Christianising zeal. It was under his militantly Christian regime that harsher legislation against homosexuals was introduced, and there was that same ambivalent attitude to the supposed enemies of Christ, the Jews. Imperial legislation that protected their lives and property remained in force but Justinian could not resist interfering. He introduced a law that if in any year Passover fell before Easter, it could not be celebrated until after the Christian festival. The measure probably soon fell into abeyance or may never have been enforced at all, but it typifies Justinian's dislike of diversity. The group on which Justinian's wrath fell most heavily, however, were those Christians who refused to accept the official definition of Christian belief as defined by the councils of Nicaea and Chalcedon. In 528, the emperor introduced a law banning 'heretics' from acting as witnesses in cases where the litigants were Chalcedonian Christians. It is unlikely that he had the Arians in mind here – by now they had ceased to be a significant force inside the empire even though many of the barbarian rulers of western Europe professed this version of the faith. Much more worrying to Justinian were the views of the so-called Monophysites.

In the eastern provinces of the empire, especially in Alexandria, many clergy and theologians were unhappy with the definitions of the Council of Nicaea in its statements about Christ's divinity. They felt that the council had not gone far enough in stressing Christ's divine – as opposed to his human – nature. By the mid fifth century, Dioscurus, patriarch of Alexandria, was arguing that the two natures in Christ, the divine and the human, were so intimately united that they became physically one. The Council of Chalcedon in 451 had attempted to resolve the issue by declaring that Jesus was both perfect man and perfect God, but the formulation did not please the followers of

Dioscurus who – believing that Christ was predominantly divine, with a minimal human aspect – became known as Monophysites. Had this been just a squabble between theologians, the imperial authorities might have been tempted to leave them to it, but unfortunately it was much more than that. By the late fifth century most of the inhabitants of the eastern provinces of Syria, Palestine and Egypt supported the Monophysite point of view, fuelling discontent and alienating them from the Chalcedonian emperor in Constantinople.

Under the emperors Zeno and Anastasius, various attempts had been made to find some sort of compromise between the Chalcedonian and Monophysite positions. Justinian was having none of that. No sooner had his uncle Justin attained the throne in 518 than he contacted the pope, who had strongly disapproved of the compromise policy, and promised to uphold the true faith as defined at Chalcedon. Life started to be made very difficult for those who did not accept the council's definitions. In the Monophysite heartlands of Egypt and Syria, sporadic persecution began with 'heretical' bishops being ousted from their sees and replaced with Chalcedonians. Monophysite monks and nuns were forcibly thrown out of their monasteries. Justinian was soon to discover, however, that there were limits on how far uniformity could be imposed. Small minorities such as homosexuals, Jews and the few remaining pagans could be pushed around, but there were far too many Monophysites for the strong-arm tactics to work in their case. The ousted bishops went underground and continued to minister to their congregations. There was even opposition within staunchly Chalcedonian Constantinople, for Justinian's wife Theodora was herself a Monophysite. She succeeded in having some exiled bishops recalled and in 535 she even managed to get a Monophysite, Anthemios of Trebizond, appointed as patriarch of Constantinople. As soon as his real beliefs became known, Anthemios was removed from office but he spent the next twelve years living secretly in Theodora's palace. Even the zealous Justinian had to accept defeat and return to a search for compromise.

Although Justinian was unable to impose a uniform doctrine, there could be no doubt that the empire was now overwhelmingly Christian and the dominant faith was influencing ever more aspects of everyday life. Eusebius and other theorists had established the idea that the Roman emperor was the representative of God and that the boundaries of the empire were the same as those of the Christian faith. Indeed, for most of their history, the empire's inhabitants referred to themselves as Romans, the name 'Byzantines' being a modern invention. Given the theological importance of the office of emperor, it was only to be expected that public ceremonies would have religious overtones. For centuries, the return of an emperor to his capital city had been a significant public occasion, so when Justinian made a ceremonial entry into Constantinople in August 559, after some weeks away supervising the building of fortifications in Thrace, he was met at the city gate by the prefect and other civic dignitaries, and escorted along the main street, the Mese, by a colourful procession. But when the cavalcade reached the church of the Holy Apostles, it came to an abrupt halt. The emperor got down from his horse and went into the church to pray, and only when he emerged could the ceremony continue. Church services and imperial ceremonial came increasingly to resemble each other, with the same hymns being sung at both.

It is also during Justinian's reign that those aspects of Byzantine Christianity that were later to mark it out from the Christianity of western Europe can be clearly discerned. One was that intense admiration for the individual holy man, a sentiment that Justinian shared with the vast majority of his subjects. In the spring of 530 news reached the emperor that Savas, the leader of a community of monks that lived in the desert near Jerusalem, was on his way to Constantinople. The hermit had visited the capital once before but had had some difficulty obtaining an interview with Emperor Anastasius because the officials on the door took one look at his dirty and much-patched robe and had sent him on his way. Justinian made no such mistake. He sent imperial galleys to escort Savas's ship on the last leg of its journey and, when it had docked, the hermit and his party were lodged in the Great Palace. When they were shown into the audience chamber, Justinian leaped from his throne and ran to embrace Savas, kissing him, with tears streaming down his cheeks. After agreeing to build a hospital and a church of the Mother of God in Jerusalem, Justinian received the holy man's blessing, although this was pointedly not extended to Theodora on account of her Monophysite sympathies. Only a holy man would both enjoy such a reception and be able to risk the emperor's displeasure with impunity.

Justinian's treatment of Savas was by that time very typical, but in another respect his reign shows evidence of a development in Byzantine religion. Christianity had consciously differentiated itself from Judaism by allowing its places of worship to be decorated and by including images of Jesus and his disciples for instructive purposes, in spite of the objections of Epiphanius and others. There were, however, certain implications in depicting Christ. He was, after all, God incarnate, so in portraying him an artist was portraying God. So, if an image of the haloed emperor was to be treated with respect and veneration, then one of Christ certainly should be too. Images of Jesus began to be produced not in mosaic for display on the walls of churches but painted on wood, making them easy to move and carry around. They did not depict Christ in the context of a Gospel story but alone and facing outwards, making direct eye contact with the viewer. These icons can only have been made for private, emotional veneration. If there were those who feared that such veneration of an image of wood and paint amounted to idolatry, during Justinian's reign stories began to circulate that suggested otherwise. The people of Edessa in Syria claimed that they had in their possession the so-called Mandylion, a portrait of Christ that had come into being not through the work of an artist but by a miracle. Hundreds of years before, the ruler of their city, Abgar, had written a letter to Jesus Christ, begging him to come to Edessa and cure him of his painful gout. Jesus was unable to leave Palestine so instead he pressed a cloth against his face, leaving an imprint of his features on it. This he sent to Abgar, who was at once healed. The inhabitants of Camuliana in Asia Minor claimed that they had a similar cloth with Jesus's picture on it. Justinian ordered that the image by carried through the cities of the region so everyone could see it and, in 574, it finally arrived in Constantinople. The existence of these miraculous images seemed to confirm that the veneration of icons of Christ was not only permissible but had divine authority.

* * *

Just as Justinian's reign marked the continuation of earlier religious trends, so he had to deal with those same threats on the frontiers that had existed since the crisis of the third century. Procopius was keen to present Justinian as utterly incompetent in his dealing with the empire's enemies, but that was by no means fair, especially in the earlier part of his reign. The Sassanid Persians were still poised on the eastern border, waiting for the opportunity to invade and occupy as much territory as they could. In 530, at Daras on the frontier, the Byzantines heavily defeated a Persian army for the first time in a century. Although the following year the Persians invaded the Byzantine eastern provinces and routed the defending army at Callinicum, their losses were so huge that they had no choice but to negotiate. In 532 the two sides agreed to maintain an 'Eternal peace' from then on.

Of course, this kind of military and diplomatic response could not resolve the other constant threat, the tribes living along the empire's Danube border. Wave after wave of migrating peoples were still arriving. The Hunnic empire had ceased to be the main power in the region after the death of its leader Attila in 453, but it was soon replaced by other ethnic groups such as the Slavs and the Turkic speaking Kutrigurs and Avars. In search of land and plunder, they raided into Byzantine territory just as the Goths had before them. In 548, the Slavs reached as far as Thrace, where they captured and completely destroyed the town of Topiros. In 558 the Kutrigurs invaded across the Danube and almost reached as far as Constantinople before they were driven back. Justinian attempted to contain the raids by throwing defensive walls around the cities of the region and by constructing a chain of fortresses along the southern bank of the Danube. Like his predecessors, however, he knew that such military solutions could not remove the basic problem.

There was an alternative. For centuries, as already recounted, the emperors had been defusing the barbarian threat by allowing limited numbers of them to settle in the empire and to serve as allies when needed. After the disaster at Adrianople in 378, it became much more difficult to exercise control over these settlers. Those Goths who had been given land in the Balkans ended up revolting and going to war with the empire. So the empire's rulers resorted to subtler tactics to convince the leaders of the tribes that peace and alliance with the empire was the most sensible course. In early 381 Theodosius I had invited the leader of the Goths, Athanaric, to Constantinople. Fearsome warrior though he was, Athanaric had no experience of urban life, having passed his days on the march and in small settlements of huts. The sight of the great public squares, the Hippodrome and the Great Palace, left him amazed. He had, he said, heard about these marvels but he had never believed them to be true. He is said to have exclaimed that the emperor must be a god on earth and that if anyone lifted a hand against him, he would be asking for death. This kind of psychological impact succeeded in persuading barbarians to throw in their lot with the empire.

Much the same can be said about the euphemistically termed 'annual subsidies' that the emperors took to paying to some recalcitrant tribes. During the 460s, some three hundred pounds of gold were paid every year to a group of Goths led by Valamer. Justinian made similar payments to the Avars. On one level such payments were simply a bribe to buy off potential attacks, but they also acted in the same way as Athanaric's visit to Constantinople. Payments were made in the Byzantine gold coin, the nomisma, which weighed more than any other coin in circulation at the time. Stamped with the emperor's image, the nomisma was a beautiful object, as impressive as the monuments of the capital. It was even said that the ruler of Sri Lanka had judged the Byzantine emperor to be greater than the king of Persia, simply by comparing their coins. Those who received them were well aware of their beauty and prestige: they often accompanied a powerful chief to his last resting place, as grave goods.

While Justinian was not the first to resort to such tactics, he does seem to have extended them slightly. Back in 512, the emperor Anastasius had settled the Heruli tribe on land around the town of Singidunum (modern Belgrade) in return for military service in the Byzantine army. They did provide the required service but they remained an unruly presence in the Byzantine Balkans, often plundering the areas around their settlement. In 528 their leader, Grepes, was invited to Constantinople with twelve of his relatives and some of his more prominent followers. No doubt he would have been as awe-struck at the sight of the imperial city as Athanaric had been. He received generous gifts and renewed his promise to serve the Byzantine emperor whenever he was called upon to do so. There was one noticeable difference from Athanaric's 381 visit. In a public ceremony, Grepes and his fellow visitors were all baptised as Christians, with Justinian himself standing as godfather. The Heruli were being drawn more closely into the Byzantine orbit by accepting the officially defined, Chalcedonian faith rather than Arianism. The move was not entirely successful. Whatever Grepes had done, many other Heruli went on as before and continued to rob their Byzantine neighbours. In his *Secret History*, Procopius poured scorn on Justinian for his generous gifts to barbarians like the Heruli which he said drained the treasury without bringing any tangible benefit. Nevertheless, the visit of 528 was the beginning of a process whereby the Heruli were slowly absorbed into the empire and disappeared as a distinct people and as a threat. Linking 'orthodox' Christianity with the integration of threatening peoples was to be used again and again in the future.

* * *

There was a strong link between Justinian's desire to impress the barbarians and draw them into the empire's service and his extraordinarily ambitious building programme. Successive emperors had left their mark on Constantine's new city by erecting some new monument or building. Theodosius I had shipped an eight-hundred-tonne marble obelisk from Egypt and set it up on the central spine of the Hippodrome on a plinth carved with figures of himself and family watching the races. Justinian planned to leave a much greater mark on the visual appearance of the city and he was extremely fortunate in being provided with both the means and the opportunity to do so.

The means had been bequeathed to him by the thrifty emperor Anastasius, who had left 320,000 pounds of gold in the treasury on his death. Justinian had no intention of leaving it there. The opportunity came in January 532, when the Blue and Green circus factions joined forces for another demonstration in the Hippodrome, demanding the release of some of their members who had been imprisoned for affray. Before long it became clear that the disorder was even worse than that faced by Anastasius in 498. The crowd spilled out into the

Augousteion and, as the looting and fighting intensified, fires broke out which, with no one to extinguish them, joined together into one huge raging conflagration. The flames spread to a hospital where many of the patients perished in their beds. Watching events unfold from the windows of the Great Palace, Justinian made preparations to flee the city by ship until he was allegedly persuaded to stay and fight by the redoubtable Theodora. Order was only restored when troops were sent to pen the rioters in the Hippodrome. In the ensuing massacre, some 30,000 people were killed, and for the next few days an awed hush descended on the city as the population contemplated the enormity of what had just happened. Many of the city's most prominent monuments were now smouldering heaps of rubble. The main entrance to the Great Palace, the Brazen Gate, was gone and so was the Senate House. The cathedral of Hagia Sophia, which had been rebuilt after being torched by the supporters of John Chrysostom in 404, had once more been burned to the ground.

Justinian cannot have been that aghast, because within a month of the riot, workmen were starting to clear the site: the emperor must have begun hatching his plans almost before the ashes had cooled. Given the now complete identification between Church and empire, the priority had to be a new cathedral. But Justinian did not just want a replica. The first two cathedrals on the site had both been rather unimaginative rectangular basilicas, although the second building had been surrounded by an impressive colonnade. The new cathedral had to be something striking that would instil visitors such as Athanaric and Grepes with astonishment at the supernatural powers of the Byzantine emperor. So Justinian chose the revolutionary design of Anthemios of Tralles for a square rather than rectangular structure, surmounted by a gigantic dome. Work went ahead with astonishing speed as Justinian threw money at the project. Two teams of 5,000 workers were employed to work on it night and day, and vast sums were expended on it. Some 40,000 pounds of silver were used to embellish the sanctuary alone. The new Hagia Sophia was thus probably one of the most expensive buildings ever constructed, but it was worth every penny. When it was dedicated on 27 December 537, it was indeed an object of wonder. Its dome, fifty-five metres high, towered above the streets and would have been visible for miles around, even from ships well out to sea. The building was even more impressive on the inside, where the sense of size and space was overwhelming. The effect was enhanced by the mosaic decoration which covered the entire space of the dome, and the columns of different coloured marble – red, purple and green – which supported the galleries. From the forty small windows around the base of the dome, sunlight suffused the building from different angles at different hours of the day, shining in from the upper windows and illuminating the gold mosaics and marble columns with dazzling light. No wonder Justinian was tremendously pleased with his new cathedral. He was even said to have boasted that he had outdone Solomon, the Old Testament king who had built the Temple in Jerusalem.

The new cathedral was only part of Justinian's ambitious building programme, which reached into parts of the city that had been untouched by the 532 riot. The second largest church in Constantinople was the Holy Apostles, where Constantine himself lay buried. By 527, however, the building was in poor repair and Justinian decided to remodel it completely. The new design was a low-slung rectangle surmounted by four small domes, grouped around a larger central one. Throughout the city another thirty-three churches were built or rebuilt, all in the new domed style, thus giving Byzantine Constantinople its characteristic cityscape of domes interspersed with columns. Everything that Justinian commissioned was designed to enhance the prestige of the empire in general and himself in particular. The entrance to the Great Palace was reconstructed and decorated with imposing mosaic portraits of Justinian and Theodora. A short distance away in the Augousteion, a column was erected and topped with a statue of Justinian on horseback, the very one of which Pierre Gilles was later to get a final glimpse. As usual, Procopius was ready with a dry comment, sneering that Justinian disregarded no detail of his building programme, except the cost. Yet in beautifying Constantinople and adding to its almost mystical aura, Justinian was enhancing one of the qualities that was to help the empire to survive in the years to come.

* * *

While in many respects Justinian's reign prefigured the future of the Byzantine empire, in others it was the last hurrah of the Roman past. Some old Roman institutions, such as the consulate, disappeared during his reign, but other aspects were consciously retained. Justinian himself spoke Latin rather than Greek and when the corpus of the empire's laws was codified and rationalised, it was issued in Latin. Nowhere was Justinian more Roman than in his decision to launch a series of wars of reconquest against the Germanic rulers who had taken over the western half of the empire. Perhaps he was uneasily aware of the criticism of pagans like Zosimus that Rome had declined from the moment it adopted Christianity, or maybe it was simply that he had the opportunity, given the wealth at his disposal. He certainly dreamt of an empire that once again stretched from Britain to Syria. Whatever his precise motives, it was a campaign unlike any the Byzantines were ever to fight again and in the end its outcome was disastrous.

Justinian's attention fell first on North Africa. For years, the emperors in Constantinople had looked on helplessly as the Vandals had first conquered Carthage and the area round about and had then subjected the Chalcedonian population there to sporadic persecution. In 468 a fleet had been sent to reconquer the lost province and it captured the town of Tripoli without much difficulty. The Vandals, however, had played for time by entering into peace negotiations and then waiting for a favourable wind. When the weather was right they had launched burning ships which were carried into the midst of the Byzantine fleet in the harbour at Mercurium. Many of the invading vessels were set alight, while others were attacked by the Vandals who sailed into the harbour to take advantage of the chaos. The battered survivors beat a hasty retreat to Sicily. It was said that the disaster cost the Byzantine treasury almost as much as Justinian was later to lavish on the cathedral of Hagia Sophia.

So humiliating was the defeat that for two generations no one in Constantinople dared to suggest that another attempt should be made to wrest North Africa from the Vandals. No one, that is, until Justinian. In 530, the king of the Vandals was overthrown and replaced by his cousin, Gelimer. Justinian professed himself to be horrified and wrote to Gelimer demanding that he restore the rightful king. When he received a defiant response, he gathered his advisers and proposed going to war. Their reaction was not very positive. The 468 disaster was immediately raised and it was also objected that the troops were tired after a recent war with the Persians. Then there was the expense, and success was uncertain. Justinian was momentarily swayed by these arguments but at this opportune moment a bishop arrived at court and begged an audience with the emperor. He announced that God had instructed him in a dream to plead with the emperor for the suffering Chalcedonians compelled to live under Arian rule in North Africa. That clinched it. Justinian decided to go to war.

There were some good reasons why Justinian could be confident and ignore his advisers. The Byzantine army had changed radically from the lumbering columns that had been massacred by the Goths at Adrianople in 378. Cavalry was now a much more significant element, in response to the fast-moving tactics of their enemies. As it was expensive to equip and mount a horseman, some units were actually the personal retainers of wealthy commanders who paid them out of their own pockets. These well-heeled commanders were all the more important to Justinian because, unlike Constantine, Valens and Theodosius I, he never personally led his troops into battle and needed to find a reliable general to lead the reconquest of the west. His choice fell on Belisarius, who had a household cavalry of over a thousand men. It was a slightly controversial appointment. It had been Belisarius who had inflicted the notable defeat on the Persians at Daras in 530 but the following year he had come off worse when he engaged a retreating Persian force at Callinicum, and some said that he had fled from the engagement across the river Euphrates in a boat. It is likely, though, that Belisarius's wealth was an inducement for the choice, for Justinian was reluctant to commit too great a proportion of his resources to the project: he only provided Belisarius with 15,000 men, a fraction of the force that had come to grief in 468. The general's own personal resources would be vital if the campaign were to succeed.

In the event, the choice turned out to be a good one and the prophets of doom were proved wrong. Belisarius's campaign was a stunning success. Landing at Caput Vada in what is now Tunisia in the summer of 533, the Byzantine force took the Vandals completely by surprise and marched on Carthage without encountering any opposition. Only when it was a mere fifteen kilometres from the town did Gelimer arrive with his army to bar the way. In the sharp encounter that followed, the outnumbered Byzantines routed the Vandals, and a few days later they marched triumphantly into Carthage. Early the following year, King Gelimer and the Vandals surrendered, restoring the province of North Africa to imperial rule. By the late summer, Belisarius was back in Constantinople to take part in a triumphal parade, after which the captive Gelimer had to kneel before the feet of the victorious Justinian in the Hippodrome. The extraordinary victory in Africa was commemorated in the mosaics that decorated the interior of Justinian's new Brazen Gate.

So swift and complete had the victory over the Vandals apparently been that Justinian immediately turned his thoughts to new conquests, and a suitable pretext soon presented itself. In Ravenna, the great Theodoric, the Ostrogoth conqueror of Odovacar, had died in 526 and had been buried in the splendid mausoleum that he had prepared for himself. He had been replaced by his eight-year-old grandson, Athalaric, with the boy's mother, Amalasuntha, as regent and guardian. Sadly, Athalaric proved to be something of a handful for his long-suffering mother, falling into bad company as he grew older and indulging in prodigious drinking bouts. Amalasuntha began to fear for her political future, which looked bleak regardless of whether her wayward son lived to achieve his majority or whether he drank himself to death. She therefore entered into secret negotiations with Justinian, hoping to secure Byzantine military help against her enemies. Events, however, moved too fast for her plans. In October 534, young Athalaric died and his nearest surviving relative was his elderly and scholarly cousin, Theodahad. Left to himself, Theodahad would probably have been perfectly happy to continue the previous arrangement, reigning as titular king while Amalasuntha took care of the real business of governing. But he was not to be left to himself. Suspicions grew about Amalasuntha's contacts with Constantinople and some of Theodahad's advisers, whose relatives had been executed under Amalasuntha, urged him to strike before she invited imperial forces into Italy. In the spring of 535, the former regent was arrested and sent away from Ravenna to close confinement on the shores of Lake Bolsena. Shortly afterwards she was murdered in mysterious circumstances.

Justinian now had a pretext for war and he made preparations for a three-pronged attack on the Ostrogoths. One force, under Mundus, was to advance up the Dalmatian coast, while a fleet under Belisarius was to set sail, ostensibly for Carthage but in reality to strike at the island of Sicily. Meanwhile an alliance was made with the Chalcedonian Franks that they were to cross the Alps and attack the Arian Ostrogoths from the north. Not all the prongs were successful. The Franks proved reluctant to move against the Ostrogoths until they could be sure of winning, and Mundus's force suffered a reverse near the town of Salona. Belisarius's fleet, however, landed unopposed on Sicily, at Catania. By the end of 535 Syracuse had been captured and Sicily restored to imperial rule. Theodahad now put out peace feelers to Justinian, sending the pope to Constantinople as his envoy, but was constantly thwarted by the hawks at his own court who opposed any concessions whatever. When peace negotiations were clearly stalled, Justinian ordered Belisarius to cross the Straits of Messina in the summer of 536 and to march north on Naples. There was little resistance. The Byzantine troops were cheered by the local Chalcedonian population as they marched through Calabria, and the towns along the route opened their gates to the liberating army. There were even deserters from the Ostrogoths who joined the ranks of Belisarius's army. Only when the Byzantines reached Naples itself did they encounter serious resistance. The Ostrogothic garrison closed the gates and held out for several weeks in the hope of being relieved. But the incompetent Theodahad sent no aid and Naples fell when Belisarius's men found a way in through the fortifications via a disused aqueduct. After pausing in Naples to resupply and reinforce, Belisarius marched north again. In December 536, he walked unopposed into the old imperial capital of Rome.

Thus far the invasion of Italy had followed much the same pattern as that of North Africa, and when news of the capture of Rome reached Justinian early in 537 he must have thought that another easy victory was within his grasp. This time, however, resistance was to be stiffer. The Ostrogoths became exasperated with Theodahad's ineffectual leadership and the army gathered at Regatta to air its grievances. Vittigis, a successful general, was elected as king and Theodahad fled for the safety of Ravenna, only to be overtaken and killed before he could get there. The new leader at once prepared to counter-attack, and in February laid siege to the Byzantine forces in Rome. By now Belisarius had only some 5,000 men under his command and with these he had to man the defensive walls that stretched for some eighteen kilometres. Nevertheless, by a heroic effort he held out for a year and nine days until reinforcements finally arrived from the east. In March 538, Vittigis abandoned the siege and withdrew northwards, pursued by the Byzantine army. A force sent into Lombardy seized Milan while Vittigis fell back on his last stronghold, the impregnable city of Ravenna.

Here at least, Vittigis could hold out and force Justinian to come to terms. After all, it had taken Theodoric three years to induce Odovacar to surrender back in the 490s. Proposals were sent from Constantinople offering peace if Vittigis would cede the whole of Italy south of the river Po, and the Ostrogoths were ready to accept these terms. Belisarius, however, refused to ratify the agreement since he saw no point in compromise when total victory was within his grasp. The stalemate was only broken when the Byzantines resorted to a trick. A message arrived from some Ostrogoths who were exasperated by Vittigis's failure, promising to open the gates of Ravenna if Belisarius would declare himself emperor of the west and resume the imperial title that had lapsed in the previous century. The Byzantine general pretended to accept, then once his troops were inside the walls, he loyally took possession of the city in the name of the emperor. Thus it was that in May 540, Ravenna was absorbed into Justinian's expanding empire.

* * *

Even in this moment of triumph, some sensed that all was not well. As he watched the Byzantine troops marching into Ravenna, Procopius, who served as Belisarius's secretary on the campaign, recalled that:

> An idea came to me, to the effect that it is not at all by the wisdom of men or by any other sort of excellence on their part that events are brought to fulfilment, but that there is some divine power which is ever warping their purposes . . .

In their desire for total victory and refusal to accept any compromise, Justinian and Belisarius had over-reached themselves. To provide troops and supplies for the Italian campaign, other frontiers had been left virtually undefended and, as he retreated towards Ravenna, Vittigis had made a last desperate attempt to take advantage of this Achilles heel. He found two Italian priests who, in return for a large sum of money, agreed to carry his letters east to the Persian king. It was a long and hazardous journey which inevitably involved crossing Byzantine territory, and the priests would have found it difficult to communicate once they entered the Persian empire. But they were lucky. No one thought to question Italian clerics as they would have had they been Goths, and when they reached Thrace they fell in with a multilingual interpreter who accompanied them for the rest of the journey. In the autumn of 539, they arrived at the court of Chosroes at Ctesiphon and presented him with Vittigis's letter. They warned the Sassanid ruler that Justinian's ambitions knew no bounds and that once the kingdom of the Ostrogoths was overthrown he would inevitably turn on Persia. Chosroes was, in theory, bound by the so-called 'Eternal Peace' that he had agreed with the Byzantines seven years before, and he could hardly have believed that his empire was seriously threatened. On the other hand, the opportunity to raid into Byzantine territory unmolested was too tempting to miss.

In the spring of 540, Chosroes invaded Byzantine Syria with a large army and, encountering no opposition, laid siege to the city of Sura. A delegation headed by the bishop was sent out by the inhabitants to negotiate. Chosroes rejected their terms but insisted on providing a military escort for them back to the city gate. The townspeople on the walls felt rather flattered to see their bishop being so honourably treated and flung wide the gate to welcome him home, but the Persian soldiers who were with him then threw a large stone, which they had brought with them, under the gate to prevent it from closing. On their signal, the entire Persian army charged forward and poured in through the open gateway. As Sura burned and its inhabitants were being rounded up to be slaves, some Byzantine ambassadors arrived to remind Chosroes of the Eternal Peace. As they rode together through the carnage, the victorious Persian king pointed out to the envoys a woman being dragged away by one of his soldiers: she was still clasping the hand of her toddler who, unable to keep up, had fallen to the ground and was being pulled along through the dust. Tears welled up in Chosroes's eyes and he angrily cried out that God should punish the man responsible: he meant, of course, Justinian. He then dismissed the ambassadors with the words: 'Tell the Emperor Justinian where in the world you left Chosroes, son of Kavad.'

From Sura, Chosroes made a leisurely progress westwards and it became obvious that the great city of Antioch itself was now his target. Justinian dispatched his nephew Germanos with a small force of three hundred men to shore up the defences. Like Rome, Antioch had very long defensive walls, but they were generally in good repair. Unfortunately, there was a weak spot where a tall rock was higher than the adjacent wall, giving the opportunity to attackers to bridge the gap and gain a foothold. Various solutions had been discussed, such as building a tower on the outcrop and connecting it to the wall, but none had been carried out because, it was argued, the work would not be completed before Chosroes arrived. The half-completed works would then be a liability as they would signal to the Persians exactly where the weakness was.

By now Chosroes was at Hieropolis, some four days' journey away. There he was met by a delegation from Antioch and its leader, the bishop of Beroea, pleaded with him to spare their city. Grudgingly Chosroes said that he would accept 100,000 gold pieces to hold off. These terms were rejected by Germanos, for envoys had just arrived from Constantinople bringing Justinian's strict injunction that no money whatsoever was to be handed over to the enemy. Chosroes continued his remorseless advance, capturing and sacking the town of Beroea, and in June 540, less than a month after Belisarius had seized Ravenna, the Persian army pitched its tents by the river Orontes, in sight of the walls of Antioch. The garrison had by now been reinforced by 6,000 men so the inhabitants were confident that they could hold out. They gathered on the walls to shout insults at Chosroes and, when a Persian envoy was sent forward to invite them to buy their safety with a sum of money, he was very nearly killed by a hail of arrows. Chosroes duly ordered the attack to commence.

He led his forces in person and concentrated them on the vulnerable spot which he had easily identified without any help from the Byzantines. The garrison concentrated its best troops there, and they were assisted by young men of the city who had plenty of fighting experience from the brawls between the Blue and Green factions. So at first the Persian attacks met with little success and there was no opportunity to take advantage of the overhanging rock until an unlucky event undermined the defence. In order to concentrate as many men as possible on this threatened stretch of wall, the defenders had rigged up some wooden platforms suspended on ropes slung between the towers that interspersed the walls. These made the space behind the battlements much broader but it encouraged large numbers of defenders to crowd on to them to get a shot at the Persians. So many, in fact, that the entire structure gave way with a mighty crash. Those who heard the noise, but could not see what caused it, supposed that a section of the wall itself had collapsed and fled from their posts. Some of them found horses and started to ride across the city to escape from one of the gates on the other side, but by now the streets had become crowded with women and children who had rushed out of their homes in terror when they heard all the noise. Many of them were trampled down by the fleeing soldiers. The Persians, meanwhile, had taken advantage of the gaps left in the defence to mount ladders against the wall and clamber up to the battlements. They did not advance into the city at once because they simply did not believe that it could have been that easy to get into the third city of the Byzantine empire. Surely some trap must have been set. So the Persians actually started signalling to the remaining Byzantine soldiers that they should escape now and that they would not pursue them. Many accepted the invitation so that while the Persians entered Antioch on one side, a stream of soldiers and civilians was leaving on the other. Only when they were sure that the garrison was gone, did the Persians start to descend into the centre of Antioch. As they advanced they found themselves under attack not from soldiers but from the young supporters of the chariot factions, mostly armed just with stones. So ferocious was the assault that the Persians fell back, but heavily armed, professional soldiers were bound to prevail in the end and the battle turned into a massacre. After the stone-throwing youths had been cut down, the Persians turned on anyone else who was left in the city, slaughtering young and old alike. Then the looting started. As Zoroastrians, the Persians had no compunction about helping themselves to the contents of churches. Chosroes contented himself with the loot from just one church, since there was enough gold, silver and polished marble there even for his needs, and he left the rest to his men. When all the moveable goods had been collected, he ordered the entire city to be burned down.

The rest of Chosroes's time in Byzantine Syria was like a royal progress. He met with some envoys sent by Justinian, who handed over a generous payment in gold to secure his agreement to withdraw. Since there was no Byzantine army in the area to threaten him, Chosroes lingered in the area for a few weeks, almost as if he were on holiday. He marched west as far as the port of Seleucia, where he took a bathe in the sea. He visited Antioch's suburb of Daphne, which boasted a pleasure garden and fountains, and stopped off at Apamea, where he was allowed to enter the city with an escort of two hundred men to attend the chariot races at the hippodrome. Since he knew that Justinian favoured the Blue faction, Chosroes cheered for the Greens, and when it looked as though the Blue chariot might win, he ordered his men to block its path, allowing its Green rival to overtake and pass the winning post first.

Only then did the king begin to lead his army home, the whole column proceeding very slowly on account of the large amount of booty loaded on to carts, and the long train of prisoners. In spite of his agreement with Justinian's ambassadors, Chosroes could not resist extorting money from the cities he passed on his way, since there was nothing to prevent him from doing so.

The fall of Antioch was only the beginning of the disasters that were to befall Byzantium in the second part of Justinian's reign. After their capture of Ravenna in 540, the Byzantines' position in Italy deteriorated rapidly. Belisarius was recalled, partly so that he could be sent east to secure the frontier against Chosroes but partly because his ruse to take Ravenna had raised suspicions about his loyalty. Once he was gone, there was no longer an undisputed overall commander of the Byzantine forces in Italy. There had already been problems before Belisarius's departure, with some of his subordinates opposing his orders. Now there was no one to co-ordinate the leaders of the various garrisons and contingents. Bessas and John led the field army but Constantianus was in charge of the city of Ravenna. The disadvantages of this arrangement became clear in 542 when the Byzantines decided to clear the Ostrogoths out of Verona. The city had been stormed and was all but taken when the commanders got into a dispute about the division of the spoils. While they were preoccupied by their bickering, the Ostrogoths rallied and drove the Byzantines out. In a bid to impose some kind of unity, Justinian did dispatch a supreme commander, Maximinus. But for some reason, Maximinus only sailed as far as the Adriatic coast of Dalmatia and then tarried there for weeks while the situation in Italy slowly worsened.

Not only was the Byzantine command divided, but it was also rapidly losing the support of the Chalcedonian population of Italy. Belisarius had been assiduous in maintaining good relations with the locals, paying them well for their produce when it was needed to feed the army. He was, after all, extremely wealthy, maintaining part of the Byzantine force at his own expense. His successors were neither as wealthy nor as ethical, and saw the campaign as an opportunity to enrich themselves. It was not only the army that started shamelessly plundering the local population. Now that Ravenna was his, Justinian decided that, as a province of his empire, Italy would have to pay its way. He dispatched one of his most efficient tax gatherers, Alexander the Logothete, whose nickname was 'the Scissors', supposedly from his ability to clip the edges of a gold coin without spoiling its circular shape. He imposed a swingeing new tax assessment on the country but at the same time cut back on expenses, particularly payments to the soldiers. He thus succeeded in alienating the locals and destroying the morale of the troops at the same time.

The consequences would not have been so serious had the Ostrogoths remained leaderless and divided. Vittigis had been taken prisoner in Ravenna in 540 and was taken by Belisarius to Constantinople. When it was clear that Belisarius had no intention of declaring himself emperor of the west, the Ostrogoths elected the governor of Verona, Ildibad, as their king. Ildibad was an able leader but he incurred the anger of some of his subordinates for an ill-judged execution. One evening at a banquet, while Ildibad was reclining on a couch and leaning forward to take some food, one of his guards stepped up behind him and cut off his head, leaving the decapitated corpse sitting with the morsel still in its hand. A certain Eraric was then proclaimed king but within a few months he shared Ildibad's fate. Eraric's replacement was Ildibad's nephew Totila.

Unlike his ephemeral predecessors, the new king of the Ostrogoths soon proved himself to be a brilliant commander. Shortly after the Byzantines failed to take Verona in the summer of 542, Totila confronted them in open battle at Faenza. Cunningly he dispatched three hundred horsemen to attack the enemy from behind at the height of the battle, causing the Byzantines to panic and flee in the belief that they were being assailed by a much larger force. Thereafter the Byzantine commanders locked themselves behind the safety of the walls of Ravenna while Totila marched through Italy taking town after town. Naples fell in 543, Rome in 546, and by then little remained to the Byzantines in Italy apart from Ravenna. Part of Totila's strategy was to court the favour of the local population. The Byzantines might share their Chalcedonian faith but they were effectively foreigners, or 'Greeklings' as Totila called them. The Heruli, Persians and Moors who made up a large part of the Byzantine army had even less in common with the Italians, and Totila made full use of the propaganda value of the ruthless exactions of Alexander the Scissors. For those Italians who remained under Byzantine rule, life was almost intolerable. Rome had to endure several years of siege before it surrendered to Totila, during which time the inhabitants were reduced to virtual starvation. Some committed suicide by jumping into the Tiber. If the disasters in Italy were not enough, even the conquest of North Africa, which had seemed so swift and easy at the time, proved not to be as complete as had at first appeared. Although the Vandals had been comprehensively defeated, the Berber tribesmen of the interior remained defiant. In 544, they revolted and killed the Byzantine governor, Solomon, overrunning most of the province and penning the Byzantines into their fortified strongholds.

* * *

It was not only military defeat that marred the second half of Justinian's reign. It was also a time of unprecedented natural disasters. The most catastrophic of these was an outbreak of what was probably bubonic plague, which was first reported on the Nile Delta in Egypt in the summer of 541. Sporadic bouts of plague were not unusual but it soon became apparent that this visitation was on quite a different scale. The infection reached Alexandria in September before spreading to Syria, where it appears to have been particularly virulent, with entire villages wiped out and the corn left unharvested in the fields. By the spring of the following year it had reached Constantinople, where it ravaged the tightly packed urban population. Even Justinian developed symptoms but recovered. The epidemic subsided the following year, but further outbreaks followed in 558 and 573.

The sixth century was also marked by a series of earthquakes. Antioch, which suffered so badly at the hands of Chosroes in 540, was struck in 526, 528 and 551, the 528 tremors killing some 5,000 people. In December 557 Constantinople itself was hit, at around midnight when most people were in bed. The first tremors brought them rushing out into the streets, but casualties were high in the poorer areas of the city where houses and tenement blocks collapsed easily. In some places, pillars from larger buildings were shot up into the air by the force of the tremors and came crashing down on houses nearby. Aftershocks continued to be felt for days afterwards.

From a modern, scientific viewpoint, seismic activity was only to be expected, with Constantinople lying on the North Anatolian fault and Antioch on the East Anatolian. It occurred with such frequency and virulence during the reign of Justinian, however, that contemporaries could only ascribe it to the wrath of God. The Monophysites certainly read that into the horrible death of Euphrasius, the Chalcedonian patriarch of Antioch, in the 526 earthquake. He had been upstairs in his palace when it struck, and when the floor gave way he fell into a cauldron of pitch used by some wineskin makers who had their workshop in the basement. The unfortunate man landed feet first in the boiling pitch and was found with his head lolling over the rim of the cauldron: the rest of him had been burned away to just the bones. Critics of Justinian's stringent tax regime also drew appropriate conclusions, and doubtless some satisfaction, when one of his senior tax officials perished in the 557 earthquake in Constantinople. Anatolius by name, he had been in bed when the first tremors loosened a marble plaque on the wall, which then fell and crushed his skull. Symbolic too was the fate of Justinian's most visible achievement, the new cathedral of Hagia Sophia. It survived the earthquake of 557 but ominous cracks were observed at the base of the dome. Repairs were begun but five months later part of the dome collapsed, sending masonry hurtling down to crush the high altar. The dome had to be rebuilt on a narrower and slightly less ambitious scale and the cathedral did not reopen until 563.

* * *

There was little that Justinian could do about the plague and the earthquakes, apart from remitting the taxes owed by the affected areas. As far as the military situation was concerned, however, he hurled money and troops at the problem. General after general was sent out to deal with the Berbers of North Africa until finally they were crushed by John Troglyta in 547. To deal with Totila, Justinian sent Belisarius back to Italy, but the ageing general had lost his touch. He was unable to save Rome from falling back into the hands of the Ostrogoths and spent most of his time, according to his secretary Procopius, sailing from one fortified coastal town to another and scarcely setting foot on land. He did succeed in wresting Rome back from Totila, but, when he was recalled to Constantinople early in 549, the Eternal City was soon lost again. Matters only improved when a new commander, the eunuch Narses, arrived in Ravenna, the only really secure base that the Byzantines possessed in Italy, bringing with him a sizeable army and supplies of ready money. It was the latter that probably made the difference, enabling Narses to feed and pay his soldiers without squeezing the local Italian population. So, when it came to the final showdown with Totila at Busta Gallorum in the summer of 552, Narses could field about 25,000 men, along with contingents from various Germanic tribes such as the Lombards and the Heruli. Totila's tactic on the day was to feign a withdrawal and then launch a massed cavalry attack on the Byzantine army once it lowered its guard. Unfortunately for him, Narses had guessed what he was up to and when the Ostrogoths charged his own cavalry had been placed on the wings to encircle them. Caught in the trap, some 6,000 Ostrogoths died along with Totila himself.

Even this overwhelming victory did not bring the war to an end. Rome was recovered again shortly after the battle, changing hands for the fifth time since 536, but the Ostrogoths still did not surrender. They found a new king, Teias, and a new army. Narses had to fight at Mons Lactarius in Campania the following year and once more comprehensively crush his opponents. Some cities still held out. It was not until 561 that Verona finally capitulated and Italy could be said at last to have been conquered and restored to the empire.

* * *

After the interminable wars and disasters, Justinian's last years were a far cry from the exuberant optimism of his accession. While North Africa, Sicily, Italy and even a part of southern Spain had been recovered, it had been at an enormous cost in lives and money. No one had any idea exactly how much had been spent on the wars and the building programme. According to Procopius, speculation was rife in Constantinople as to whether the treasury was empty or whether there were substantial amounts squirrelled away behind the walls of the Great Palace. Justinian, of course, was not required to publish his accounts. There were rumblings of discontent and talk that the ageing emperor had lost his grip. Plots to dethrone him, real or imagined, came to feed Justinian's paranoia, and he struck out at those around him blindly. Towards the end of 562 there was a wave of arrests when a plan to assassinate the emperor was uncovered and the suspects implicated several prominent individuals. Even Belisarius fell under suspicion and was disgraced, though he was restored to favour the following year.

As the years went by, a sense of impending doom gripped the inhabitants of Constantinople. Justinian and Theodora had produced no children and there was no obvious successor. One September day in 560, some years after the empress had died, news travelled through the streets that the emperor was not receiving visitors and that he had not been seen for several days. Before long, it was being said that he had died, and crowds descended on the bakeries to stock up with food for the uncertain times ahead. By the end of the day, no bread was to be had anywhere and shops throughout the city were closed. Only then did it emerge that the emperor had cancelled his audiences merely because of a headache.

The panic proved completely unnecessary. When Justinian passed away in his bed on the night of 14 November 565, the transfer of power was orderly and seamless. A message was carried to the residence of the emperor's nephew, Justin, who walked across the Augousteion to the Great Palace just as the dawn chorus was greeting the rising sun. There he was acclaimed emperor by the palace guard, and crowned Justin II by the patriarch. When the day was more advanced he walked through the long corridor that connected the palace with the imperial box in the Hippodrome to receive the cheers of the huge crowd of Blues and Greens that had gathered on the news of the old emperor's demise. Then a solemn funeral procession left the Great Palace, bearing Justinian's body beneath a heavy pall embroidered with scenes of victories over the Vandals and Ostrogoths. He was laid to rest in the church of the Holy Apostles in a great marble sarcophagus. One of the new emperor's first acts was to undo one of Justinian's minor reforms: he revived the consulate and assumed the office himself.

So after all the upheavals of the second half of Justinian's reign, many people must have thought that things would continue much as they had always done. Out at the western edge of Justin II's empire, in Ravenna, it must have seemed that the old order had been re-established. Ostrogothic rule had been toppled and Theodoric's Arian churches had been converted to Chalcedonian worship.

The church of San Vitale, the building of which had commenced under the rule of Theodoric, had been completed and dedicated under Justinian. Mosaic portraits of the emperor and Theodora had been placed on either side of the high altar to stare down imperiously at the congregation. Unlike the equestrian statue in Constantinople, these mosaics have survived: a fitting monument to a man who had seemed to have done so much to strengthen Byzantium but whose legacy was to bring it to the brink of ruin. For the appearance of calm continuity was deceptive. Byzantium was soon to be overwhelmed by a deluge.

CHAPTER THREE

The Deluge

The danger is not without recompense; nay it leads to the eternal life. Let us stand
bravely, and the Lord our God will assist us and destroy our enemy.
Heraclius

Noon in Alexandria around the year 607. The city was entirely deserted, as
most people had withdrawn to their homes to avoid the fierce heat. Only two
monks, John Moschos and Sophronios, were on the streets, heading for the
house of Stephen the Sophist on a business matter that could not wait. When
they knocked on the door of his house, a maid put her head out of an upstairs
window and informed them that her employer was still resting. Perhaps they
could come back later? The monks decided to make for the nearby Tetrapylon,
a crossroads where an arch on four columns provided welcome shade. In the
drowsy heat there was no one else there, apart from three blind men.

The monks sat quietly by a column and opened the books they had brought
with them, but they were soon distracted into listening to the conversation
going on across the way where the trio were telling each other how they came
to lose their sight. One had developed ophthalmitis while he was a sailor, while
another had injured his eyes when working as a glassblower. The third had to
be pressed to tell his tale, but eventually he admitted that when he was young
he took to petty theft to avoid having to work for his living. One day he noticed
a funeral procession passing by, with a richly dressed corpse being taken for
burial in a tomb behind the church of St John. That night, he returned and
broke into the tomb and carefully removed all the clothes from the body,
leaving it in just a shroud. He was about to leave with his haul when it occurred
to him that he might get something for the shroud too, so he turned back to

pull it off. As he did so the corpse suddenly opened its eyes and sat up. It stretched out its gnarled hands towards the horrified intruder and clawed out his eyes. Moschos and Sophronios were so impressed with what they had heard that they decided to creep away and leave the urgent business to another occasion.

The two monks were not natives of Alexandria but were from Damascus in Syria and had taken monastic vows at the monastery of St Theodosius near Bethlehem. From there, in a way that was perfectly acceptable for Byzantine monks, they had wandered from monastery to monastery, visiting Mount Sinai in Egypt and reaching Jerusalem in 594. As they went, Moschos kept a record of the edifying stories that they heard along the way, such as the tale of the blind man of Alexandria, and incorporated them into his book, *The Spiritual Meadow*, which he hoped would provide improving reading for monks, ascetics and those who admired their lifestyle. As the first two decades of the seventh century went on, however, Moschos and Sophronios no longer travelled for moral edification. They were fleeing for their lives as the empire crumbled.

* * *

The crisis had been building up for years, ever since the death of Justinian in 565. Only three years after he was interred in his grand mausoleum, the first crack appeared in the empire's expanded borders. As pressure from the Avars increased on the Germanic tribes in the lands north of the Danube, the Lombard tribe decided to follow the usual route to safety and crossed the border into Byzantine Italy. This was hardly an unprecedented occurrence but the Byzantine governor in Ravenna struggled to deal with the newcomers, allowing them to take over town after town in northern Italy, first Milan in 569 and then Pavia in 571. Lacking the military force to drive the Lombards out, the Byzantines tried all the other methods. Chestfuls of gold coins were sent to the neighbouring Franks to induce them to attack the Lombards, but, although they took the money, they never fulfilled their side of the bargain. Slowly, the Arian Lombards pushed the Byzantines southwards, confining them to Ravenna and other cities of the Italian coast and taking possession of much of the land that had been wrested from the Ostrogoths at such a cost.

Everywhere there were signs that the frontiers were buckling. In the small enclave in southern Spain that had been recovered in the 550s, pressure from the Visigoths was building and they took the city of Cordoba in 572. On the eastern frontier, Chosroes I showed his usual amnesia in the matter of treaties and captured the fortified city of Daras in 573, a disaster that drove Justinian's successor, Justin II, to madness. Most worrying of all was the

situation on the Danube frontier. At the outset of his reign, Justin II had felt
safe enough to cancel the annual tribute payments to the Avars, who were then
involved in a series of wars to defend their hegemony north of the Danube. He
had miscalculated badly. Fast-moving horse archers who sported chains slung
across their bodies and long and unkempt hair, the Avars were as feared by
other tribes along the Danube as they were by the Byzantines. In 567, they had
crushed the Gepids with the help of the Lombards and had then rounded on
their erstwhile allies and driven them across the Alps and over the border into
Byzantine Italy. By 580 they had emerged as the dominant power in the Danube
basin, with the Slavs, Kutrigurs and other tribes paying them tribute and
acknowledging their supremacy. With their powerbase secure, they took to
attacking imperial territory alongside their tributary allies. In around 570 they
put a Byzantine army to flight and in 581 captured the town of Sirmium. They
only gave it back when the emperor agreed to make them an annual payment
of 80,000 gold coins. The ease with which the Avars had seized Sirmium,
however, ensured that the peace would not last long. It was clear to their khan
that he could get anything he wanted. He demanded that a gold couch be sent
from Constantinople along with an elephant, a creature that he had never seen.
The emperor cravenly did as he was told but when couch and elephant arrived,
the khan announced that they were both a grievous disappointment and sent
them back. The raids went on, with the Avars marching to the port of Anchialos
during the summer of 583 and the following year orchestrating an invasion of
the Byzantine Balkans by their Slav allies. These attacks were developing into
something much more serious than raids, as groups of Slavs in particular were
beginning to settle on imperial territory. Well accustomed as the rulers of the
empire were to dealing with threats to their borders by unruly tribes, the sheer
scale and mounting ferocity of the attacks in the late sixth century clearly took
them by surprise.

By now the empire was ruled by Maurice (582–602). He had come to the
throne through the kind of sensible constitutional agreement for which the
Byzantines have never been given adequate credit. The previous emperor,
Tiberius II (578–582), had no son to succeed him and in August 582 his physi-
cians advised him that he had not long to live. Maurice had just returned to
Constantinople from the eastern frontier, where he had inflicted a significant
defeat on the Persians, so Tiberius decided to marry the general to his daughter
Constantia and crown him as co-emperor. On the day of the dual ceremony,
Tiberius gave a memorable speech, assuring his audience that in these troubled
times they needed an exceptional man to lead them and that man was Maurice.
The very next day, Tiberius ate some mulberries that had gone off, and died. So

it fell to Maurice's lot to find some solution not only to the Avars in the Balkans but also the Lombards in Italy and the Persians as well. Against all the odds, he very nearly succeeded.

It was obvious that the empire did not have the resources to counter all the threats simultaneously, so some kind of decision would have to be made on priorities. North Africa was largely at peace anyway while in Italy there was a stalemate, with the imperial forces well dug in behind the walls of Ravenna and in Apulia and Calabria to the south. Maurice accordingly decided that for the moment these western provinces would have to be left to themselves and he made an inspired administrative reform to make the best of the situation. The governors of Carthage and Ravenna were designated exarchs, who would now have complete control of both the military and civil administration. They both commanded the army and also collected the taxes that funded it, directly from the local population. These wide powers gave them the wherewithal to respond efficiently to threats in their area, but it must have been made clear that from now on the exarchs were on their own: appeals for further resources from Constantinople would not be heard. Circumstances also presented Maurice with an opportunity to defuse the threat in the east from Sassanid Persia. The formidable Chosroes I had died in 579 and, in February 590, the Persian king Hormisdas IV was overthrown and replaced by his most successful general, Baram. Hormisdas's son and heir Chosroes II, however, fled to Byzantine territory and wrote to Maurice to ask for his help in retrieving his rightful throne. Maurice provided a force to bolster Chosroes's followers and together they invaded the Persian empire and overthrew Baram. Chosroes then made a treaty with the Byzantines, restoring to them the cities of Daras and Martyropolis and promising undying peace with his benefactor Maurice.

Thus from 591 Maurice was free to turn his entire attention to the Avars, and since diplomatic means had failed he sought an uncompromising military solution. In the spring of 593 he dispatched his general, Priscus, to the Danube frontier with a powerful force. The aim was to drive the Slavs who had settled in the area back over the Danube, and the Byzantine army, which included many veterans returned from the Persian campaign, was successful in every encounter. The Avars protested at this attack on their allies but the Byzantines now felt strong enough to ignore them. During 599 Priscus won a series of impressive victories against both Slavs and Avars in which tens of thousands of them were killed or taken prisoner.

The success, however, was illusory. The Byzantines had failed to deliver a decisive blow since the Slavs operated in small groups which could be elusive and difficult to track down. Summer after summer the army had to return, always with the same result. The cost of these campaigns began to put a serious burden on the empire's finances. Since Roman times, each province was required to pay a wealth tax of about one per cent and a flat poll tax on each adult. The main city of the province was responsible for administration and collection and for passing the proceeds on to the central government. The succession of wars and natural disasters during the sixth century, however, had ensured that the cities and provinces were increasingly impoverished and were less and less in a position either to pay or administer the tax. The resulting shortfalls hampered Maurice's efforts to equip and field an effective army. Maurice's solution to the problems of elusive victory and dwindling finance was a radical but risky one which ultimately was to cost him both his throne and his life. In the autumn of 602, he ordered the Balkan army, now under the command of his brother Peter, not to retire as usual to Thrace at the end of the campaigning season. Instead they were to cross into Slav territory north of the Danube and spend the winter harassing the enemy there, where they would least anticipate it. They would be expected to live off the land and so save the treasury the cost of supplying them.

When news of these orders circulated in the Byzantine camp, there was outrage. Many of the soldiers had captured valuable booty in the previous summer's campaign and they wanted to take it safely home. They protested against the orders and mutinied, choosing as their leader an officer called Phokas. Peter, who had completely lost control of the situation, fled to Constantinople. The army followed him, determined to overthrow the now hated Maurice. When the emperor heard news of the revolt, he at first attempted to cover it up and ordered a series of chariot races to distract the populace. It soon became clear, however, that the people of Constantinople were losing confidence in his rule. Crowds of Blues and Greens roamed the streets shouting insulting slogans and urging Maurice's relative by marriage, Germanos, to seize the throne. Probably fearing that Phokas's army would be allowed into Constantinople by supporters on the inside, Maurice fled the city by night on a ship that carried him with his family across the Sea of Marmara in the hope of making contact with his friend, Chosroes II of Persia. As far as the people of the capital were concerned, his flight meant abdication. The next day the patriarch went out to meet Phokas, who was now camped at Hebdomon not far from Constantinople's western walls, and proceeded to crown him emperor. Phokas then rode triumphantly into Constantinople in a chariot drawn by four white horses, through streets lined with cheering crowds.

So far the transfer of power had been all but bloodless and might have remained so had it not been for the ever-turbulent factions. The Blues and the

Greens had been united in their opposition to Maurice but once he was gone a dispute broke out between them over which group should be stationed where to acclaim the new emperor. When Phokas sent troops to restore order, the Blues started a taunting chant of 'Maurice is not dead!' Fearing that there might be an uprising to restore his predecessor, Phokas gave orders for Maurice to be killed. His soldiers dragged out the former emperor and eight members of his family from the church where they had taken refuge and took them to the harbour of the town of Chalcedon, opposite Constantinople. Maurice and four of his sons, the youngest of whom was only an infant, were decapitated. Their heads were taken to Constantinople for public display on an army parade ground. Their bodies were thrown into the Bosporus, from where some of them were washed up on the beaches to be gazed at by passers-by and gnawed by dogs.

If Phokas had believed that this purge would leave him safe on the throne, he was badly mistaken. The brutality of Maurice's end transformed him from failed statesman to saint and martyr. Rumours spread quickly of the heroism with which he had faced death. The nurse of his youngest child had, it was said, substituted her own child in the hope of saving at least one of the family, but Maurice had noticed the switch and insisted that his own son be presented to the executioner. Moreover, in seizing the throne and ordering the killings, Phokas had brought to an end a period since the reign of Constantine where power had generally been handed peacefully from emperor to emperor. Having set a new precedent, he was increasingly fearful that a counter-coup might be organised against him, and ordered further killings, liquidating first Maurice's relatives and prominent associates, then his wife the former empress Constantia and their daughters. Among the victims were some of the empire's most successful generals who had led the campaigns against the Avars and Persians. That was particularly unfortunate because Phokas was soon to have need of every good soldier he could find.

In the spring of 603, the new emperor sent an embassy to Persia to announce his accession to Chosroes II. It was not well received. Chosroes demanded to know what had happened to his friend and benefactor Maurice, and declared that he had at his court one of Maurice's sons who had survived the massacre. Both the outrage and the claimant were feigned. Chosroes had in fact seen the chance that he had long hoped for of renewing the war with Byzantium. Now he had a pretext, and with the emperor's attention occupied with securing his position in Constantinople, the Persians could be sure of limited opposition. So, in the summer of 604, Chosroes's army crossed the frontier and seized the city of Daras that he had handed back to Maurice in 591. Resistance was sporadic at best and the Persians were able to lay siege to other towns such as Edessa and capture them one by one.

While the Persians probed the eastern defences, the Avars and Slavs also took full advantage of the withdrawal of the Byzantine army to Constantinople. They crossed the Danube in force and pushed south as far as Greece and the Peloponnese. With no Byzantine army to check them, they ceased to withdraw when the summer was at an end and began to settle on Byzantine land. Clearly Phokas was leading the empire to disaster, but in Constantinople all likely focuses of protest and revolt had been ruthless crushed. It had to be from out on the periphery that a successful coup would come. In North Africa, which was one of the few parts of the empire still untouched by war and invasion, the exarch of Carthage, Heraclius, was contacted by disaffected elements in Constantinople. Heraclius had been one of Maurice's commanders in the war against the Persians in the 580s and probably felt little loyalty to the usurper. He dispatched his nephew Niketas with an army to Egypt and his son, also named Heraclius, with a fleet to Constantinople. The idea was that whoever arrived first should depose Phokas and take his place as emperor. It was the younger Heraclius who arrived first with the fleet off the sea walls of Constantinople on 3 October 610. Had there been determined and loyal resistance, Heraclius and his ships would have had little chance. Phokas had in any case taken the precaution of rounding up Heraclius's mother and fiancée, who happened to be in the capital, to keep as hostages.

Nevertheless, the very presence of Heraclius's fleet had the effect of galvanising the opposition within the city. The Green faction had become increasingly opposed to Phokas over recent months and its supporters now took direct action, storming the house where Heraclius's mother and fiancée were held and setting them free. Further mob violence was forestalled when, in the early hours of 5 October, two prominent courtiers walked into Phokas's apartment in the imperial palace and dragged him out of bed. They hustled the completely naked emperor down a flight of steps to the waterside where they put him into a small skiff and rowed him out to Heraclius's flagship. Brought before his nemesis, Phokas showed as much courage as Maurice had in the same situation. When Heraclius demanded to know how he justified his handling of the empire over the past eight years, Phokas spat back: 'No doubt you will rule it better!' At that, Phokas's right arm was sliced off, followed swiftly by his head. His body was later publicly burned in one of Constantinople's main squares. Within a few hours of this brutal murder, Heraclius was in Justinian's cathedral of Hagia Sophia where he was solemnly crowned emperor by the patriarch. Outside on the street, jubilant gangs of Greens burned pictures of Phokas and flags of the Blue faction. In this violent way, political equilibrium had been restored.

* * *

While the coup of 610 may have ended the violence in the capital, on the frontiers the change of rulers only saw the situation deteriorate still further, so that Phokas's last words must have seemed to be prophetic. The Avar and Slav raids intensified as they completely destroyed the town of Justiniana Prima and laid siege to Thessalonica. Although the city's strong defences held them at bay, the countryside was quickly passing out of Byzantine control. In Italy the Lombards seized the remaining Byzantine towns on the coast of Tuscany and the last holdings in Spain were lost soon after. The worst news of all came from the east. Chosroes II had no intention of halting his campaign now that Maurice's murder had been avenged, so that the incursions into Syria continued. In the spring of 614, his army headed south, towards Caesarea on the coast of Palestine, before swinging back inland and making for Jerusalem. There was no imperial army in the vicinity to provide defence so the patriarch of the city, Zacharias, was inclined to open negotiations with the Persians with a view to buying them off. When Jerusalem's Blue and Green factions heard of his plan, they demonstrated in the streets and demanded that their city be defended at all costs. Zacharias reluctantly gave way and took it upon himself to arrange the defence by bringing in a detachment of troops from nearby Jericho. Unfortunately, by the time these reinforcements arrived the Persians were already encamped around Jerusalem and, seeing the size of the opposition, the soldiers fled back whence they had come. On 15 April, the Persians began their assault on the walls, bringing up catapults to hurl rocks at the fortifications. After several weeks, they were able to break down a section of wall and their troops poured through the breach. For reasons that are not entirely clear, the Persians indiscriminately killed the civilian population so that tens of thousands died. They were joined in this by the local Jews, who probably had plenty of scores to settle after years of Christian domination. Churches and monasteries were sacked and burned and anything of value in them was looted. The survivors, including the patriarch, were rounded up and marched into captivity in Persia. The Persians also carried off the so-called True Cross, believed to be the very one on which Christ had been crucified, a trophy that seemed to presage the imminent collapse of both of the empire and the Christian religion.

This catastrophe was very different from the fall of Antioch in 540. Then the Persians had gathered their loot and gone home. This time the army would not be going home because the king planned to conquer the Byzantine empire and incorporate it into his own. Jerusalem was handed over to the Jews and the countryside was occupied. The following year the Persian army began to advance into Egypt while a detachment under general Sahin marched unopposed through Asia Minor and reached the Bosporus at Chalcedon, where Maurice had been murdered thirteen years before. From there the Persian soldiers could gaze over the water at the domes and columns of Constantinople's skyline. Sahin withdrew after a short time, but in Egypt the Persians meant to stay. The factious city of Alexandria fell to them in June 619, robbing the Byzantines of their second city and one of their richest provinces. With the Balkans now almost completely lost to the Slavs and Avars, it appeared only to be a matter of time before the empire was destroyed. That it was not was partly because of the personal genius of Heraclius, but also because of some of the developments that had taken place since the reign of Constantine, the very ones that had so outraged Zosimus. The Christian religion, the visual spirituality expressed through religious icons and Constantine's city of Constantinople, were all to play their part in this moment of supreme crisis.

* * *

Given that Heraclius was to play the leading role in turning defeat into victory, one might ask what he was doing during the first ten years of his reign and why he did not do more to prevent the loss of so much territory. Part of the problem was knowing which enemy to fight first. While Carthage and Ravenna could be left to their own devices under their exarchs, the situation in the eastern provinces and the Balkans could only be retrieved by the intervention of a large army, and Heraclius lacked the resources to launch a major offensive against the Persians and Avars simultaneously. In the early years of his reign he made several attempts to split his enemies by making peace with one so that he could concentrate on the other. His first efforts were directed towards the Persians so that he would have a free hand against the Avars, but Chosroes, scenting complete victory, haughtily turned him down. Eventually a truce was hammered out with the Avars in 618 which involved handing over to them very large amounts of tribute money and leaving them in possession of all the land that they had conquered. It was a brave decision and there must have been those who accused the emperor of abandoning his subjects to the barbarians. Even so, the truce with the Avars did mean that Heraclius could transfer troops from Europe to Asia and bring the whole weight of his army to bear against the Persians.

Wisely, the emperor did not launch his attack immediately. The early 620s found him not marching against the Persians in Syria but encamped with his army in western Asia Minor, one of the few areas still under his control. There he introduced an intensive regime of training, dividing the army in two and staging mock battles in preparation for the struggle ahead. To keep them paid and supplied during this period, he took what was coyly described as a 'loan' from the Church, having the gold and silver communion vessels and candelabra gathered up and melted down into coin. Yet this was not the act of an irreligious man. It had the full approval of the ecclesiastical authorities and Heraclius was to go to unprecedented lengths to clothe the forthcoming campaign with the aura of a righteous war for the defence of the faith. In the past, the Christian religion had not undermined the fighting zeal of the empire's soldiers, as Zosimus had feared, but war had remained, especially in the eyes of many of the Church leaders, a distasteful necessity. Now, in his rallying speeches to the troops, Heraclius made much of the fact that the Byzantines were fighting for the True God against infidels, for the Persians were Zoroastrians. It was a religious duty, he declared, to punish the atrocities committed against Christians in Jerusalem and he promised that those who undertook this pious duty would receive the reward of eternal life in heaven.

These stirring words have often led to Heraclius being labelled as the first crusader, but there was a considerable gulf between the way that the Byzantines waged war against non-Christians and the crusade ideology that was later to develop in western Europe. The obvious difference was the silence of the Byzantine clergy. Whereas in the west the pope launched crusades and the clergy urged the faithful to participate, in Byzantium this rarely happened. While it had been a bishop who had urged Justinian to make war on the Arian Vandals of North Africa in 533, claiming that God had spoken to him in a dream, at no point was any spiritual reward offered by the Church to those who took part. Instead, in Byzantium it was the emperor who took the lead in promising his men that God would reward their efforts. Moreover, alongside this triumphalist ideology there co-existed a curious pragmatism. The Byzantines were never convinced of the glory of dying in battle for its own sake, even when fighting against non-Christians. A handbook of military tactics composed around this time advised that it was better to overcome the enemy with planning and ruses rather than sheer force, and that it was best to avoid pitched battle altogether. Many of the tactics that the handbook proposes distinctly lack the glamour of a glorious crusade. Spread false reports and rumours in the enemy camp, urged the anonymous author, and thus undermine their morale. Encourage your men by faking news of victories that have just happened elsewhere, and, if any of your men desert, allow letters to fall into enemy hands suggesting that they are spies. In Byzantine eyes there was no contradiction

here. After all, the cause of defending the Christian empire was so righteous
that any means of achieving that end was justified.

Another element in the idea of holy war that was peculiar to Byzantium was
the role played by religious images. Icons had been coming to play an ever
more prominent role in Byzantine life, and now Heraclius introduced them
into warfare. Already in 610, when he had set sail from Carthage to topple
Phokas, he had attached an icon of the Virgin Mary to the prow of his ship.
Now, as he prepared to confront the Persians, he took with him into battle an
icon of Christ which was allegedly a miraculous image, not made by human
hands. It may have been the image of Camuliana which had been brought to
Constantinople in 574. In this, Heraclius and the Church were working
together. As the time of crisis approached, Patriarch Sergios ordered that an
image of the Virgin Mary holding the Christ child on her arm should be painted
on to all the gates in the Land Walls of Constantinople. The prototype for these
images was probably the Hodegetria icon ('She Who Shows the Way'), so
named because the Virgin was pointing out the way of salvation, namely the
baby she was holding. It was popularly believed to have been painted as a real-
life portrait of Mary and Jesus by St Luke the Evangelist, and it had supposedly
been brought from Palestine to Constantinople in the fifth century. Now it
took its place on the walls alongside the human defenders.

With his preparations complete, Heraclius headed east in the spring of 624.
It is likely that the Persians were expecting that the emperor's first move would
be to march into Syria and attempt to recover some of the lost territory. If so,
their armies had a long and fruitless wait, for Heraclius never came. Instead,
the Byzantine army marched east through Asia Minor and then north into
Armenia, an area that had long been disputed and divided between the two
empires. From there he turned south and descended on the unprotected
northern borders of Persia itself. News of his arrival came as a devastating
surprise and Chosroes II desperately recalled his armies to defend their home-
land. Before they could arrive, Heraclius was free to capture and destroy one
Persian city after another. As his army approached the Zoroastrian holy city of
Shiz, Chosroes was close to the city with a large force but, when he heard of
Heraclius's approach, he decided to withdraw without a fight. The Byzantine
troops were thus able to enter the town unopposed and they seem to have
taken particular delight in revenging the destruction of churches in Jerusalem
by destroying the temple where a holy fire was kept burning. So successful had
the foray been that at the end of the campaigning season, Heraclius did not
withdraw to Byzantine territory in Asia Minor but decided to spend the winter
with his army in Armenia. The following spring, the Byzantines resumed their

attack. By this time, the Persians were ready and two large armies had been dispatched to intercept him. After leading them on a lengthy chase through the rugged terrain, Heraclius fought on ground of his choosing and routed them one after the other, capturing the golden shield and armour of one of the commanders, who had thrown them away in his rush to escape. The Byzantine army was then free to resume its campaign of destruction.

In desperation, Chosroes and his commanders hit on a plan to force Heraclius to withdraw: they would imitate his tactics by striking directly against Constantinople and thereby force the emperor to hurry back to defend it. Emissaries were sent to the Avars urging them to break the truce and join in a united assault on the Byzantine capital. The khan did not need much persuading as he had already broken the agreement several times, the empire in its weakened state offering too tempting a target. So, when in the spring of 626 Chosroes dispatched his general Shahrbaraz with a large force into Asia Minor, the Avars and their Slav allies were also on the move. The Persians had reached the Bosporus by early June and shortly afterwards, on the other side of the strait, the Avar vanguard arrived at the Land Walls. The allies were able to see each other and communicate with fire signals across the water. As the trap closed, the situation inside the city was ominous. During May there had been riots and demonstrations in the streets and in Hagia Sophia against the high price of food, and urgent messengers were dispatched to acquaint Heraclius with the danger facing the capital.

Whatever Chosroes might have hoped, the news did not induce Heraclius to break off his attacks on Persia or to withdraw westwards. Instead, the emperor sent a third of his force back to reinforce Constantinople while the rest remained in the east. An alliance was made with a local Turkic tribe, the Khazars, and a two-pronged invasion of Persia went ahead in spite of the threat in the rear. Constantinople was left to fend for itself. Heraclius could never have made this daring move had he not known in advance how difficult it would be for the Avars and Persians to take Constantinople: that they would have to find some way to link up across the Bosporus and, once they did, to break through the Land Walls. Perhaps the Avar khan had not been well informed about Constantinople's defences for he seems to have been fairly confident that his army's expertise with siege engines would secure a swift breakthrough. At the end of July, twelve towers and numerous catapults were brought up against the Land Walls to begin the assault, and two days of fierce fighting followed. The Avars achieved little, for the stones hurled by their catapults made almost no impression on the massive limestone blocks of the Land Walls. Even though they heavily outnumbered the defenders, the layout of the walls made it very difficult indeed for an infantry assault using siege towers to succeed. The designers of the fortifications had cunningly created a three-tier structure which was impossible to get close to or penetrate. The main inner wall stood about twelve metres high, punctuated at intervals by ninety-six towers, from which the Byzantines used ballistas and catapults to fire back at the Avars. In front of that stood another outer wall, slightly lower and punctuated by a further ninety-two towers from which fire could also be directed at the Avars. Beyond that was a wide, brick-lined ditch, between fifteen and twenty metres across and between five and seven metres deep, with a stockade made of brick and wood on the city side. Any assailant would have first to cross the ditch and stockade while exposed to withering fire from the outer and inner walls. Even if they did get across and managed to capture the outer wall, they would find themselves trapped in the five-metre-wide corridor between it and the inner wall.

The Avars did manage to manoeuvre some of their siege towers close to the lower walls by filling in some sections of the moat, but that was as far as they got. Some sailors, who had left their ships in the harbour to join the defence, secured a mast to the battlements and lashed to it a small skiff packed with combustible material. This was ignited and the mast was then swung round to bring the skiff crashing against an Avar siege tower, causing it to burst into flames. Foiled, the khan resorted to bluster, sending emissaries to demand the surrender of the city if the inhabitants wished their lives and property to be spared. Otherwise, he threatened, he would unleash the Persians, who were still waiting at Chalcedon, against the city. The Byzantines would probably have been happy to renew the truce and to pay more tribute to the Avars but the demand for complete surrender could never be met. The talks broke down and the siege went on.

The Avar khan now had to carry out his threat to bring the Persians into the battle, but that was easier said than done. The two armies were separated by the Bosporus and neither had a fleet of ships to bring the Persians across to the Land Walls. The Avars had, however, brought with them a plentiful supply of what can only be described as canoes. They were probably fairly crude ones, made by hollowing out a tree trunk, but each one would have been sufficient for bringing two or three men across from the Asian side. Early one August morning, these canoes were launched into the choppy waters to cross over to Chalcedon. As soon as they were afloat, a Byzantine flotilla of seventy ships sallied forth from the Golden Horn and proceeded to sink the canoes with ease, their Slav crews either being shot with arrows or drowning as they fell overboard. Some of those who did manage to swim ashore were killed on the orders of the khan, who was furious at this signal failure. Having borne the brunt of the canoes disaster, it was the Slavs who now decided that they had had enough of the enterprise. They started to withdraw, rebelling sullenly against the leadership of their Avar masters. With his manpower dwindling, the khan had little option but to follow suit, though his cavalry looted and burned several churches in the vicinity as they went. There was now no point in the Persians remaining and they too began to retreat eastwards. By the middle of August, the siege was over.

All Heraclius's inspired tactics and generalship would have counted for nothing had Constantinople fallen in 626. Its geographical position meant that, if it had, Asia Minor would have been cut off from the rest of the empire's scattered territories and there would have been nothing to hold the empire together. There was no other defensible city left under Byzantine control in the east that could have replaced it as a centre of administration. The only alternatives were in the west, Ravenna, Carthage or perhaps Syracuse. Thus the empire would have ceased to exist east of the Bosporus and the Byzantines would also have lost the one fixed focal point that was coming increasingly to define their culture and their view of the world. By surviving against all the odds in 626, Constantinople seemed to have confirmed the Byzantine belief that their empire was the state most favoured by God and the city acquired an almost mythical aura of being under the special protection of the Virgin Mary.

Now that Heraclius's great gamble had paid off, his attacks on his enemy's heartland continued. In September 627, he led his forces into Persia once more, again taking Chosroes completely by surprise. The Persian king had thought he was safe because the summer and the campaigning season were drawing to a close, so it was not until Heraclius's army had reached the site of ancient Nineveh that it encountered a sizeable Persian army barring the way to Ctesiphon. On the morning of 12 December 627, the two armies commenced battle on the wide-open plain and the fighting continued all day long. Heraclius himself was in the thick of it and was at one point hit on the lip by a spear. It was a confused and bloody encounter, but at the end of the day the Persian commander was dead and the Byzantines held the field with twenty-eight captured standards. The remains of the Persian army withdrew while Heraclius marched on to nearby Dastagerd where he allowed his troops to loot and burn one of Chosroes's palaces. The king himself, who had been in the palace until only nine days before Heraclius's arrival, fled by night and took refuge in a remote farmhouse. A few days later, the pursuing Byzantines reached the place. Chosroes was gone by then, but Heraclius is said to have been amazed when he saw the narrow door of the farmhouse. Knowing that Chosroes was a man of considerable girth, he was surprised that the king had ever managed to enter.

The victory at Nineveh did not have to be decisive. The Persian army that had been driven off was still intact, and Chosroes had reinforced it with 3,000 men. But the king's precipitate flight and general mishandling of the war had crystallised opposition in his own court. Led by his eldest son, Siroy, a group of conspirators arrested him on 23 February 628 and murdered him shortly afterwards. Almost as soon as he was crowned, Siroy contacted Heraclius to sue for peace, promising to hand back all territory seized since 602 and to release all prisoners taken in the course of the long war, including the patriarch Zacharias and the other unfortunate souls captured in Jerusalem in 614. His envoys also handed back the True Cross and other relics seized during the sack. Heraclius accepted the terms and withdrew: he had achieved what he set out to do. He was also well aware that Shahrbaraz, the Persian general who had attacked Constantinople in 626, was at odds with the court in Ctesiphon and that civil war was likely to break out before too long. The following year, the Persians duly withdrew from Syria, Palestine and Egypt and the Byzantine eastern borders were restored to where they had been in 602.

When Heraclius returned to Constantinople, his reception was tumultuous. He was met at Hieria on the Asian side of the Bosporus by a huge crowd of citizens, headed by his son Constantine and the patriarch, all holding olive branches and candles. Crossing to the city, Heraclius staged a victory pageant in the Hippodrome, headed by four captured elephants. The most poignant celebration of victory, however, took place in Jerusalem in the spring of 630 when Heraclius arrived with the True Cross to restore it to the Holy City. But he also had accounts to settle. The Jews, some of whom had aided the Persians, were expelled from the city and denied the right to live within three miles of it. The Nestorian Christians, a sect that had been favoured under the Persian occupation, was ejected from the city's churches, which were then given to Chalcedonians. These measures were vindictive but hardly as punitive as they might have been. After all, Heraclius could afford to be magnanimous. He had achieved what wars so seldom achieve, a clear and absolute victory, following years when defeat had seemed a certainty. Few leaders have ever enjoyed that kind of triumph. Of the few who have, none has ever then lost the fruits of their victory so swiftly and so utterly as did Heraclius very soon afterwards.

* * *

Scarcely had the celebrations died down than reports started coming in of Arab raids on the Syrian frontier. They were not taken too seriously in Constantinople. The Arabs frequently used to cross the border in search of loot and it was for the local governor to gather a force and see them off. There had been just such a raid in the spring of 529 when an Arab raiding party had reached the suburbs of Antioch, but they had withdrawn quickly when a Byzantine army had borne down on them, and in general the Arabs, though a nuisance, were not a major threat. They were divided into small tribes and so could not field the kind of armies that the Persians or Avars did. They were, moreover, given to feuds and vendettas so that most of their energy was expended on fighting each other. The easiest way to deal with them was to recruit some of these tribes as allies both against the Persians and other Arabs. One tribe, the Ghassanids, had long been allied to the Byzantines and their territory along the Syrian border served as a buffer against incursions by other Arab tribes. Justinian had welcomed their king, the Monophysite Christian al-Harith ibn Jabalah, to Constantinople in 563 and Heraclius had had a large contingent of Ghassanids with him when he invaded Persia in 624. So in fact the Byzantines had traditionally dealt with the Arabs in exactly the same way as they had with other troublesome peoples on their borders. In any case, Heraclius had far more important matters to deal with than attending to minor border incursions.

The spectacular victory over the Persians and the recovery of Syria and Egypt meant that the Byzantine emperor had once more to confront the problem that had preoccupied Justinian and his predecessors: that of establishing some kind of unity between the Monophysite and Chalcedonian Christians. The ease with which the Persians had occupied the eastern provinces between 613 and 619 must have been at least partly due to the indifference of the local population, who saw no reason to resist the invaders and defend a regime that considered their faith heretical. The Persians had wisely exploited the situation. While the largely Chalcedonian population of Jerusalem had been massacred, the Monophysites were left in peace. Now, with the Persians marching home and Byzantine governors re-established in Alexandria and Antioch, something had to be done to ensure that the eastern provinces were reconciled to rule from Constantinople. It was a problem that was to dog Byzantium throughout its existence. Although Constantinople was an enormous asset that had helped to save the day in the moment of crisis, the increasing concentration there of wealth, power and administration helped to alienate peripheral areas to whose inhabitants the capital looked distant and foreign. Successful as the emperors had been in drawing in foreign invaders and integrating them into the empire's defence, their own Syriac- and Coptic-speaking Monophysite subjects proved to be more of a challenge.

Like others before him, Heraclius decided to try a compromise. In 630, he met with the Monophysite patriarch of Antioch and twelve other bishops to agree some kind of formula that both sides could agree on. They came up with

Monoenergism: the idea that the divine and human natures of Christ had a single active force. In June 633 a synod was organised in Alexandria which proclaimed Monoenergism to be orthodox doctrine. The Monophysites seemed ready to accept it and it looked for a moment as if the schism might be at an end. Inevitably, however, the new doctrine failed to please the Chalcedonians and so strident was the outcry in Constantinople and Rome that Heraclius was compelled to abandon it. In 638, a new compromise doctrine was introduced, Monotheletism, the idea that, while Christ had both divine and human natures, he had a single will. This initiative had even fewer supporters than the previous one, for it was unacceptable to the Monophysites and very few Chalcedonians liked it either. Determined to push it through, Heraclius resorted to force, and the Monophysite clergy were again driven underground. By that time the issue had been overtaken by another wave of invaders.

What Heraclius and his advisers did not know was that, while they had been confronting the Persians and wrestling with theological formulas, in an obscure corner of the Arabian peninsula events had been moving very fast. In the spring of 627, while Heraclius was planning his final invasion of Persia, another round of the interminable Arab tribal wars was drawing to a close. The Quraysh tribe of Mecca was laying siege to the town of Medina. The leader of the heavily outnumbered defenders, Muhammad, was himself a member of the Quraysh, who had fled from Mecca five years before in the face of opposition to his monotheistic religious ideas. The siege ended in failure. The defenders were able to frustrate the attack by digging a network of trenches around the walls, forcing the Meccans to withdraw. The victory marked the beginning of Muhammad's rise to prominence among the Arab tribes. One by one they made peace with him and accepted his religious teaching, which was to become Islam. By the time of his death in 632, Muhammad had imposed an unprecedented political and religious unity on the whole of the Arabian peninsula. It was this unity, rather than the religion of Islam, that posed such a threat to the Arabs' neighbours. Becoming Muslim did not make the Arabs any more warlike. They had always lived by war and Islam did not change that. What it did do was put an end to the centuries of tribal conflict and create a unitary state. That unity survived Muhammad's death, for a successor or representative was elected in the person of Abu Bakr, the first caliph. Consequently, the incursion of 633 that went largely unnoticed in Constantinople was not the usual tribal raid but the precursor of a full-scale invasion.

Only slowly did the gravity of the threat emerge. When the Arabs crossed the frontier in late 633, there was no reaction until early the following year when a local commander called Sergios came to repel them with a small force.

The Arabs did not flee with their booty as they normally did but stood and fought. Sergios died with many of his men and the survivors were carried back to Arabia as prisoners. It was a defeat but not one serious enough to sound alarm bells in Constantinople. From his base at Edessa in northern Syria, Heraclius decided to send his brother Theodore to the area to deal with the problem. When Theodore suffered a bruising encounter with the Arabs at Gabitha, the emperor replaced him with a commander called Vahan. The change of leadership brought a change of fortune and an Arab force was driven back with heavy losses. Heraclius may have thought that the threat had been neutralised for he started to head back to Constantinople.

His withdrawal was premature for, early in 636, a huge Arab army, on a scale never seen before, crossed the frontier. Vahan knew at once that this was an invasion and not just a raid, and sent an urgent request for reinforcements. An imperial army was sent down to join him and when the two forces combined they represented a formidable response to the Muslim attack, even if they were not led by the victor of Nineveh in person. The two armies met in the vicinity of Yarmuk and for several weeks over July and August skirmished and manoeuvred. The advantage was undoubtedly with the Byzantines, who had the larger army and who were fighting on their own ground, but, as the weeks went by, persistent problems prevented them from striking a decisive blow. The weather was against them: the prevailing wind coming from behind the Arab army was continually blowing sand in their faces. There was disunity in the ranks. As always, the Byzantine army contained a substantial contingent of Arab allies. The Arabs had never had a problem fighting each other in the past, but on this occasion it would seem that the allies' pay was in arrears and that some of them deserted to the Muslims. Like Belisarius, Vahan had to endure a constant whispering campaign at the imperial court, and in his camp, that he was planning to seize the throne. In the end though, none of these weaknesses would have lost the Byzantines the battle. What decided the issue was a clever coup by the Arab commander, who first drew the Byzantine army on by a feigned retreat, then outflanked it by night, seizing the bridge which was the only way back from the exposed position that the Byzantines now found themselves in. Realising they were cut off, the Byzantine troops panicked and lost cohesion. Hemmed in on all sides, they now died in their thousands as the Arabs pressed home their advantage. As at Adrianople in 378, the army was completely destroyed. Only scattered survivors managed to escape the encirclement. At a stroke, organised Byzantine resistance to the Arabs was at an end. From Yarmuk, the Muslims marched on Damascus, which opened its gates to them without a fight.

It seems almost incredible that at this juncture Heraclius, who had shown such energy and courage in overcoming the Persians only a few years before, now seems to have stood back like a spectator and done nothing. He played no part in the fighting at Yarmuk, basing himself far away at Antioch. After the fall of Damascus, rather than trying to retrieve the situation, he left the area and headed west. He took with him the True Cross that he had recovered from the Persians in 628, as if in open admission that all was lost. This homecoming was very different from his return from the Persian wars. When he reached Hieria, there was no delegation of torch-bearing admirers, only a ship waiting to whisk him unobtrusively across the Bosporus to the Great Palace in Constantinople. But Heraclius refused to board and returned to the Hieria palace. News of the emperor's odd behaviour prompted officials and prominent citizens to cross over in anxious delegations and to plead with him to come over and resume his duties. It was of no use. The emperor was obdurate. He sent his sons Constantine and Heraclonas across to preside in his place at Church festivals and in the Hippodrome, insisting that they return to Hieria afterwards.

Only slowly did those around Heraclius realise what was behind this apparent inertia. The emperor had developed a morbid terror of water. Drastic measures would have to be taken if ever he was to be installed in the capital once more. Instead of a ship to carry him across, a large fleet was gathered. The vessels were anchored side by side to create a bridge right across the strait. Planks were laid to form a walkway and then hundreds of shrubs and plants were uprooted and placed in pots on either side of the path. When all was ready, the emperor was persuaded to mount his horse and ride on to the bridge, the leaves of the vegetation effectively screening the sea from the imperial view. Only then did Heraclius finally arrive in Constantinople.

By then the situation in Syria had worsened considerably. The countryside was largely under Arab control and the cities, despairing of any assistance from the emperor, were surrendering one by one. Jerusalem was surrounded, but for two years, fearing a repeat of the events of 614, the citizens held out. It was the city's patriarch who brought the impasse to an end by opening negotiations with the caliph Omar. In return for promises that the Christians and their places of worship would remain unmolested, the gates were opened in February 638 and the victorious caliph rode in on a white camel. Antioch fell the following year, followed by Edessa and Daras. Early in 640, the Arab general Amr invaded Egypt and headed for the empire's second city, Alexandria. The patriarch and governor, Cyrus, was, like the patriarch of Jerusalem, hoping that a Byzantine army would come to the rescue, but with no help in sight he had to enter into negotiations with the Arabs. In November 641 he made a one-year truce with the Arabs, promising to hand over Alexandria at the end of that time. Then dispatches were sent to Constantinople imploring the emperor to send aid before the stipulated period elapsed.

That Heraclius made no move to reverse this unfolding disaster is perhaps not so surprising, for by then he was a very sick man. He was suffering from some form of dropsy that caused his stomach to swell and to place painful pressure on his bladder. It was this complaint that killed him in February 641 when he was sixty-six years old. His passing could have been the signal for a Byzantine revival but Heraclius helped to prevent that by leaving a will in which he insisted that both his sons, Constantine and Heraclonas, should be emperor, holding power jointly. The arrangement was not going to be popular. While Constantine was the son of Heraclius's first wife, Eudokia, who had died in 612, Heraclonas's mother was Martina, Heraclius's niece and second wife. The emperor's marriage to so close a relative had caused a scandal and Martina was not a popular figure in Constantinople. The general consensus seems to have been that Constantine III was Heraclius's true successor but at only twenty-nine years old the elder heir was visibly ailing even as he took the throne. He spent most of his time in the palace of Hieria where it was thought that the climate was better for his health. Nevertheless, he succumbed only four months after his father, and rumours abounded that he had been poisoned by his step-mother, Martina.

That did not end the uncertainty. Before he died, Constantine III had written letters to the army commanders, begging them to ensure that the rights of his own son, the nine-year-old Constans, were respected. During the summer of 641, units of the Byzantine army marched to Chalcedon to demand that Constans be recognised as Heraclonas's successor. Alarmed, Heraclonas and Martina had young Constans appear in public to prove that he was alive and well and they swore on the True Cross to protect and cherish him. In spite of these assurances, disturbances broke out in the city and Heraclonas and Martina had to agree to have Constans crowned as co-emperor in Hagia Sophia. The soldiers at Chalcedon, who were causing untold damage to the vineyards outside the town, had to be paid off with generous gifts of gold. Their commander received promotion and the promise of immunity from any reprisals. In the end, however, Martina and Heraclonas could only stave off their fate. Early the following year, there was a palace coup. A group of conspirators seized the young emperor and his mother and brutally sliced off Heraclonas's nose. This was not just vindictiveness, though doubtless it played a part. Physical deformity of any kind was held to be a disqualification for the imperial office and in this way the plotters prevented any chance of Heraclonas making a political comeback. They also cut out Martina's tongue, which may have been a symbolic way of marking the end of her political influence. The pair now disappeared from the record, doubtless packed off to live out their lives in a monastery somewhere. The young Constans II now reigned, carefully guided by his advisers, who were doubtless the same people who had organised the downfall of Martina and Heraclonas.

In view of these political manoeuvrings in Constantinople, it is hardly surprising that no help was sent to Cyrus in Alexandria: a large section of the Byzantine army was too busy trampling the vineyards of Chalcedon. Cyrus himself died in the spring of 642 and by September the citizens could see no point in holding out any longer. The gates were opened and the Arabs marched in. The takeover was not entirely peaceful and orderly. Several churches and the famous library burned down in the immediate aftermath of the entry of the Arabs but nevertheless most of the Monophysite population rejoiced at the change of masters. Their patriarch Benjamin emerged from hiding and returned to his see, receiving assurances from the Arab general Amr that he and his flock could practise their faith unmolested.

It was not quite the end. In 645 Constans II and his advisers belatedly sent a fleet to recover Alexandria. Since Amr had not installed a large Arab garrison, the Byzantines were able to land and seize the city without too much difficulty. Amr responded at once and marched on Alexandria with a large army. This time he found the gates closed and the walls defended so he had to mount an assault with siege engines and catapults. When a breach was made, the Muslim troops could enter and the Byzantine resistance collapsed. Manuel, the commander of the fleet, was killed and what remained of the fleet departed for Constantinople. The Byzantines were now back in the position of 620 with their eastern provinces entirely overrun, only this time they were lost forever.

In the next few years, matters were to deteriorate still further. With the coastline of Syria and Egypt now firmly in their hands, the Arabs began the construction of a fleet. Hailing from the desert and with no naval expertise of their own, they used local labour to build and largely crew the ships, and were ready to take to the water in an incredibly short time. In 649, under the leadership of the Arab governor of Syria, Muawiyah, the fleet attacked the Byzantine island of Cyprus, capturing and destroying the town of Constantia, ancient Salamis. A few years later the Arabs landed on Rhodes. Their stay was brief but they did carry off a valuable piece of booty: the remains of the Colossus, a bronze statue of the sun god Helios, thirty-two metres high. Once one of the Seven Wonders of the World, it had lain on the ground for centuries after being toppled by an earthquake in 228 BCE. It was cut up, shipped off and sold for scrap. The following year, Muawiyah struck at Constantinople itself. His fleet captured Chalcedon and prepared to make an attack across the Bosporus but was scattered by a storm before it could do so.

Sooner or later the Byzantines would have to confront the Arab naval threat head-on. During 655, Muawiyah began building another fleet at Tripoli in Syria. The preparations did not go well, for a number of Byzantine captives being held in the town's prison rioted and broke out. Charging down to the dockside, they set fire to the warehouses and equipment before commandeering several vessels and sailing off to join the emperor. Undeterred, Muawiyah continued his preparations and then dispatched his ships to attack the towns on the southern coast of Asia Minor. Constans II, now in his early twenties, was waiting with the Byzantine fleet and intercepted the Arabs off the port of Phoinix, but from the first the Arabs had the upper hand. The sea, it was said, was dyed with Byzantine blood and one of the men who had led the revolt in Tripoli begged the emperor to flee. Constans gave his cloak and robes to another man and was hustled off the flagship and on to a smaller, swifter galley, which was then rowed away from the melee. The man who had taken the emperor's cloak then stood at the prow of the flagship, leading the fight and hacking at boarders until he was surrounded and cut down. Constans arrived safely in Constantinople but with the fleet gone he must have wondered how much longer the capital would offer a safe heaven. In 626, the Persians and Avars had failed to take it because they had no ships. Now it was only a matter of time before the Arab fleet appeared once more in force in the Bosporus. Anxious eyes scanned the horizon from the Sea Walls, looking to the south from where, sooner or later, the ships would come.

CHAPTER FOUR

A World Transformed

No one who has committed himself unreservedly to his country's affairs and trusted to his own people ever came to a good end.
Pausanias (*c.* 160 CE)

Whatever the fears at the time, one hundred years after the defeat of the imperial fleet by the Arabs at Phoinix, Byzantium was still in existence – although it was a very different place from the world of Constantine and Justinian. It had shrunk drastically. Not only had the eastern provinces of Syria, Palestine and Egypt been lost but in 697 the Arabs had overrun the exarchate of Carthage, putting an end to Byzantine rule that had lasted since Belisarius's reconquest in 534. The largest remaining block of Byzantine territory was in Asia Minor, stretching from the Bosporus to the Taurus mountains. The island of Crete was still under Byzantine rule but Cyprus was a jointly ruled territory: by a treaty of 686, the Byzantines and Arabs had agreed to share its tax revenues. In the Balkans, the Byzantines had only held on to a few fortified enclaves, such as the towns of Thessalonica, Athens, Patras and Monemvasia, situated on or near the coast, from where they could be supplied or reinforced by sea. Everywhere else had been occupied by the Slavs. In Italy too, the empire had lost ground, notably when the Lombards finally captured Ravenna in 751, putting an end to the exarchate there and confining Byzantine rule to the southern areas of Apulia and Calabria and to the island of Sicily. With so much of its western territory lost, it is not surprising that the use of Latin had completely disappeared in the court and administration and that Greek alone had become the official language.

Beyond these shrunken borders, new and powerful enemies had replaced the old ones. The Sassanid Persians were gone. They had been even less

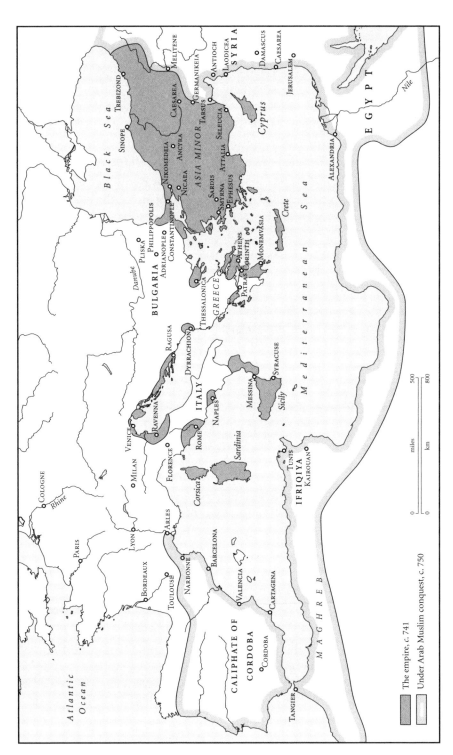

3 The Byzantine empire c. 741

successful than the Byzantines in stemming the Arab advance. After suffering a disastrous defeat at Qadisiyya in 638, they had been unable to prevent the Arabs from overrunning their empire. The last Sassanid king, Yazdgerd III, perished miserably in 652 as he tried to flee in disguise, murdered it was said by a miller who wanted to rob him of his purse and jewels. In place of the Persian empire, the Byzantine eastern frontier now marched with the Abbasid caliphate, the successor of the previous Umayyad regime. It was a gigantic superpower which stretched from Afghanistan to Morocco. Its capital at Baghdad was to become one of the largest cities of the world, with a population of over a million, and provided the setting for many of the stories in the *Thousand and One Nights*. In the Balkans, the power of the Avars had waned after their failure to take Constantinople in 626 and they had lost their hegemony over the Slavs. Their place as the dominant power in the Danube basin had been taken by another migrant Turkic tribe, the Bulgars. In the 680s, they had taken the familiar route and crossed the Danube south. An attempt by the Byzantine emperor to drive them out before they could settle and threaten the coastal areas that were still under his rule ended up as a fiasco and the Bulgars were left free to establish themselves between the Danube and the Balkan mountains. They had intermarried with the local Slavs and eventually adopted their language and became integrated with them. The Bulgar khanate that had then emerged was no mere collection of tribes but a powerful unitary state with a heavily fortified capital city at Pliska. The Bulgars were pagans, worshipping their ancestral gods, and so like the Abbasids of Baghdad were ideologically opposed to the Christian regime of Constantinople.

The drastic shrinkage of territory and the upheavals that had accompanied it had left their mark on Constantinople. The population had dwindled and was now only a fraction of what it had been in the time of Justinian. That was partly government policy: when Arab sieges threatened, many of those who were not essential for defence were ordered from the city, for with the loss of Egypt there was no easy supply of grain to feed an inflated population. Recurring bouts of plague had completed the cull. In the summer of 747 so many people died that there was an acute shortage of burial space and corpses had to be buried in vineyards and orchards. The great cathedral of Hagia Sophia still towered over the city but the days of great building projects like those of Constantine and Justinian were long gone.

Yet even though the empire was radically reduced in size and surrounded by powerful enemies, the very disasters that had befallen it had also to some extent strengthened it. The loss of the eastern provinces had, after all, put an end to the dispute over the nature of Christ since the empire now only incorporated areas that were Chalcedonian and the Monophysites were all living under Arab rule. With characteristic stubbornness, Constans II had clung to the compromise formula of Monotheletism, perhaps hoping that Egypt and Syria might yet be recovered. His son and successor Constantine IV (668–685), however, had abandoned the unloved doctrine in 681, at a specially convened ecumenical council. In the same way, the contraction of Constantinople's population had helped to calm the discord that had marked the previous two centuries. Although chariot races were still run in the Hippodrome, the factions and crowd violence were a thing of the past. The Blues and the Greens had become private clubs whose main function was to participate in imperial processions and ceremonies.

The loss of so much territory also left an empire that was more compact and easier to defend, and that was particularly true of Asia Minor. Whereas the eastern provinces had little in the way of natural defences, Asia Minor was guarded to the east by the Taurus mountain ranges. Attackers heading west would have to use one of a number of passes, such as the so-called Cilician Gates, which made it much easier to track their movements and gauge where they would be likely to strike. The route was slightly easier to the north but there the winters were very severe so that the passes would be blocked by snow for several months of the year, cutting off the route of withdrawal. Any invading army would then be faced with the grim prospect of spending the dark months marooned on the inhospitable Anatolian plateau, providing a good reason for an early withdrawal. The Arabs therefore preferred to carry their booty back to the warmer climate of Syria and to renew the fighting in the spring.

The Byzantine emperors after Heraclius sought to build on these natural advantages by reorganising the army of defence. Instead of stationing it on the frontier, it was withdrawn and distributed throughout Asia Minor. At the same time the old administrative system, where cities collected the taxes from the area round about, was discontinued or perhaps had simply ceased to function. In place of the old structure, Asia Minor was divided into seven new administrative units known as themes. Within these areas, just as in the old exarchates, the civil and military authority was merged. Each theme had its own army, and the commander, or *strategos*, was also the governor of the theme. He led the army into battle but he was also responsible for the collection of taxes and the administration of justice. However, since the tax receipts had plummeted since the days of Justinian, a new way had to be found to feed and equip the soldiers. Instead of wages, they were given grants of land, from which they were expected to equip themselves and provide themselves with a horse. They seem now only to have been paid while they were on campaign and the rest of the time the farm provided the maintenance for themselves and their families.

The stages by which this radical reform was achieved are very obscure, as there is almost no contemporary evidence for the development. The only thing that is certain is that the themes were in existence by 685 so that the credit for their creation probably belongs to Constans II and Constantine IV although it may well have carried on developing long after that. In the dark and desperate days of the seventh and early eighth centuries, the new system had a great deal to recommend it. The *strategos* had considerable independence to react without waiting for orders from Constantinople. He could gather his army to respond to an Arab raid at once. Moreover, since the armies were stationed throughout Asia Minor, they could not be bypassed by fast-moving raiders, and they provided defence wherever the Arabs might strike. Finally, although land was granted to the soldiers, it still belonged to the empire. Nothing had been alienated or lost.

The military and administrative reorganisation left its mark on the landscape of Asia Minor. The once-flourishing cities of the ancient world that had provided the backbone of the old administrative system had all but disappeared. Magnesia had dwindled till it covered an area of only about 300 by 250 metres. Pergamon, which was captured and destroyed by an Arab raid in 715, had been left as the collection of ruins that it remains today. On the other hand, a new type of city had started to emerge as the populace abandoned these sites for ones more suited to the times in which they lived. Smaller settlements were established, clustered around a *kastro*, or fortified hilltop, to which the inhabitants could flee when the Arab armies approached. One example was that at Sardis in the Thrakesion theme. The ancient, indefensible city on the plain was forsaken and the new city grew up around the acropolis, where a fortress was constructed. There was only one, extremely steep, approach to this *kastro*, as the other sides were sheer cliffs, and a bastion was built on the approach side so that attackers could be hit by arrows from concealed slits even before they got near the walls. Perhaps the most bizarre of these cities built for defence are those found in Cappadocia, in the centre of Asia Minor. There, the inhabitants used the particularly soft volcanic rock of the area to their advantage. They burrowed down and created settlements below the surface, complete with underground chapels and granaries that could provide a place of refuge when danger threatened.

It was not only the landscape of the empire that had changed, but its demography too. The Byzantines knew that human resources were every bit as important as land, and made the best use of them they could by transferring entire populations to areas where they were needed to bolster the defence. So,

Emperor Justinian II (685–695; 705–711) had removed many of the inhabitants of the frontier town of Germanikeia in eastern Asia Minor that was about to be captured by the Arabs, and had settled them in Thrace where they could help to defend the approaches to Constantinople against the Slavs. As they had done in the past, the Byzantines also brought their defeated enemies within their borders. In 688, while campaigning against the Slavs in Thrace, Justinian II took large numbers of prisoners and was joined by many Slav deserters. These he marched down to the town of Abydos on the Dardanelles and had them ferried across to Asia Minor. From there they were marched north and given lands to settle in the theme of Opsikion, doubtless in return for military service against the Arabs when needed. Similarly, the Mardaites, a Christian tribe that lived on the Byzantine border with the caliphate, were transferred to the empire's European lands. By 750, anyone travelling through the Byzantine empire would have encountered a truly multiracial society. Greek may have been the language of the government and church, but Armenian was widely spoken in Thrace and Slavonic in Asia Minor. The policy must have sometimes caused considerable hardship to those who were relocated in this way. They often had to leave many of their possessions behind because it was impossible to carry them, and it was said that some people even hanged themselves rather than be rounded up and transported to an alien land. Inevitably, there was always a danger that forcibly transferred people would harbour deep resentment at being uprooted and when the time came would not fight loyally as was hoped. In 692, the Byzantines suffered a significant defeat at the hands of an Arab raiding force when the large Slav contingent in their army deserted and fought on the side of the enemy. In a world where the young and the able-bodied were the most precious natural resource, however, the risk was worth taking.

These policies of retrenchment and reorganisation were frequently put to the test since Arab raids into Asia Minor were an almost annual event. The raids became bolder as time went on, especially after the Arabs acquired two important forward bases. One was Tarsus just to the south of the Taurus mountains, the other was Melitene, to the west of the range. Possession of the latter gave the Arabs a secure place to retire to at the end of the campaigning season without having to retreat over the mountains. Their armies would take advantage of this to spend the entire year in Asia Minor, moving from place to place, looting and plundering as they went. In 726 and 727 a force led by the caliph himself marched into Asia Minor and captured Caesarea while a raiding party was sent deeper into Byzantine territory to attack Nicaea. It failed to take the city but withdrew heavily laden with booty. Unable to stop these raids altogether, the Byzantines developed strategies for dealing with them. They adopted 'shadowing tactics'. Instead of looking for a pitched battle, they would follow the Arab armies as they retreated with their plunder towards Melitene and the Taurus mountains. They could pick off stragglers and recover some of the stolen goods. They developed an early warning system of hilltop beacons, which could alert the *strategos* of a particular theme that the Arabs were coming through one of the passes in the Taurus mountains and give him time to prepare his response. The change of plan paid off in May 740 when a huge Arab raid was withdrawing eastwards. The Byzantine commanders did not attempt to hinder the withdrawal of the main force but succeeded in cutting off two smaller contingents of the rearguard and almost completely annihilated them at the battle of Akroinon.

Such victories were doubtless heartening but they did not stop the raids and they would have been entirely in vain if the Arabs had succeeded in their ultimate goal of capturing Constantinople. In 674 they mounted a major attack on the city by sea. A large fleet sailed through the Dardanelles and occupied the town of Cyzicus, across the Sea of Marmara from Constantinople, where it was joined by an army that had marched across Asia Minor to link up with it. There it remained for several years and throughout the summer months it engaged in running battles with Byzantine vessels just off the Sea Walls. These inconclusive trials of strength might have gone on indefinitely, had the Byzantines not been able to gain the advantage with a surprise tactic. Crews of the Arab vessels must have noticed that their opponents' vessels were sporting strange, protruding pipes on their prows. They certainly would not have expected those pipes to emit a mighty roar and then shoot out a stream of fire. The flames were almost impossible to put out, burning on the water and putting any ship that they attached themselves to in danger of being swiftly engulfed.

This is the first recorded use of so-called 'Greek fire' in a naval context. The weapon was allegedly the brainchild of a Syrian Christian called Kallinikos who had fled from Arab rule to Constantinople bringing his invention with him. Exactly how the effect was produced will never be known because, for obvious reasons, it was a very closely guarded secret. It is likely that it was a mixture of ingredients which might have included sulphur, pitch, quicklime and perhaps even some crude oil, specially imported from the Caucasus where surface deposits could easily be found. How the mixture was then projected through the pipe and ignited is another mystery, although one suspects it was probably as dangerous for those using it as for those at whom it was aimed. It was probably not the kind of decisive super-weapon that transformed warfare in the twentieth century, since its users must have found it extremely difficult to score many direct hits on enemy vessels. On the other hand, it might well have had a demoralising psychological impact if the Arabs had never encountered it before and that might have influenced them in their eventual decision to withdraw the fleet. Then once more, the weather came to the aid of the Byzantines: a storm destroyed a large number of their ships as they headed back to Egypt along the coast of Asia Minor.

What really robbed the Arabs of victory in the 670s was probably not Greek fire but their failure to surround the city completely. While the fleet had fought the Byzantines out on the waters of the Sea of Marmara, the land army had remained firmly on the Asian side and does not seem to have seen much action, allowing supplies and reinforcements to be brought in through the Land Walls throughout the siege. That omission was remedied some forty years later in the summer of 717 when the Arabs launched their most concerted and dangerous attempt. A powerful army under the command of Maslama, the brother of the caliph, marched across Asia Minor to link up with a fleet that had sailed up the Aegean and into the Sea of Marmara. This time, the land army did not remain on the Asian side but crossed the Dardanelles to Europe and then marched north to the Land Walls of Constantinople. There Maslama constructed a series of earthworks parallel to the Byzantine defences, to prevent any help getting through while his fleet set up a blockade by sea. The Arabs clearly hoped to starve Constantinople into submission since there was no hope of breaching the Land Walls.

There was little that the Byzantines could do about the blockade by land but they waited for the right moment to attack by sea. On 1 September, the opportunity came. An Arab fleet of large vessels was moving up the Sea of Marmara to supply the army at the Land Walls when it found itself becalmed in the middle of the current coming down from the Bosporus and was then slowly blown backwards by wind. At once, the Byzantine fleet sallied forth from the Golden Horn, equipped with Greek fire. Since the heavily laden Arab ships were unable to flee, they were easy to approach and set alight. Some of the burning ships ran aground under the Sea Walls and some drifted helplessly across the Sea of Marmara, about twenty of them being destroyed in all. Heartening though this success was, it did not break the blockade, which continued during the winter of 717–718, and in the end it was no wonder weapon that foiled the Arabs but something far more prosaic: the challenge of providing enough to eat for the thousands of men who manned the ships and who were encamped in the trench along the Land Walls.

It happened that the winter of 717–718 was particularly severe and for some three months the earth could not be seen for a thick blanket of snow. Behind their defences, the Byzantines had plenty to live on, in spite of the Arab blockade. They had known for some years that an attack was imminent and had stockpiled food in readiness, as well as requiring anyone who had not laid by provisions to last for three years to leave the city. There was plenty to drink too, thanks to the cisterns beneath the city streets. As the weather worsened, it was the besiegers who began to run short of food. Trapped in the snowbound countryside of Thrace, the Arabs were reduced to eating the donkeys and camels that they had brought with them as beasts of burden, and when those were gone to gnawing on roots and leaves. There were even rumours of cannibalism. Great efforts were made to supply them by sea. In the spring of 718, a large fleet of over three hundred vessels arrived from Egypt, laden with arms and provisions, and headed across the Sea of Marmara. The commander of the fleet proceeded very gingerly, as he had no idea whether the Byzantine warships were in the vicinity, and as night fell he ordered the ships to go close inshore and drop anchor. During the night a large contingent of Christian oarsmen, seeing their chance, stole some small craft from the ships and rowed the remaining distance to Constantinople. Once ashore they told the emperor where the supply fleet was and as day was breaking a Byzantine flotilla bore down on it. Trapped in the bay and short of rowers, the Arab ships were an easy target, many being set alight with Greek fire or boarded and relieved of their cargoes. From then on matters went from bad to worse. Arab foraging parties who were landed on the Asian side of the strait were ambushed and massacred, while a timely alliance with the Bulgars brought an assault on Arab lines from behind resulting in thousands of casualties. By the summer of 718, it was clear that the siege had no hope of succeeding and the Arab army and fleet withdrew in August. It was the last time that the Arabs were to attempt to capture the Byzantine capital and the failure of the siege, along with the subsequent Byzantine victory at Akroinon in 740, ensured that, while the empire may have been a smaller, poorer place than in the time of Justinian, it was not going to disappear.

* * *

The survival of Constantinople and its empire was not the result only of geography, weather and impressive pyrotechnics. Some remarkably able men were in power at the crucial moment. At the time of the siege of 717–718, the emperor was Leo III (717–741). Born in the town of Germanikeia in Asia Minor, Leo and his family were among those who had been moved to Thrace during the reign of Justinian II. As a young man he had come to Justinian II's attention in 705 by presenting the emperor with five hundred sheep as he was leading his army towards Constantinople in what turned out to be a successful attempt to regain his throne from a usurper. This gesture of support impressed the emperor, who promptly took him into his service. From there, Leo rose to become *strategos* of the largest theme, the Anatolikon, in 713, and four years later he led a coup to overthrow Emperor Theodosius III and install himself as emperor. A usurper Leo may have been, but once on the throne he proved an able leader. It was he who led the defence of Constantinople against Maslama's siege at the very beginning of his reign and who led the Byzantines in their victory at Akroinon in 740. Moreover, Leo III was not just a military strong man. He knew perfectly well that security against the Arabs could not be attained on the field of battle for the caliphate was just too powerful. So, like his predecessors, he was constantly on the lookout for allies whose geographical position would enable them to do maximum harm to the enemy. During the siege of 717–718 he had brought in the Bulgars, whose territory lay behind the Arab lines, doubtless paying them well for their intervention. Even more important as a counterweight to the Arabs were the Turkic Khazars, whose lands lay in the Caucasus between the Black and Caspian seas, directly to the north of the caliphate. Like the Byzantines, the Khazars were under constant attack from their Arab neighbours and were happy to co-operate against the common enemy. Emperor Justinian II had initiated the alliance by marrying the sister of the Khazar khan. Leo III cemented it by marrying his son Constantine to another Khazar princess in 733.

Leo III was an able administrator as well as a diplomat. He introduced various internal reforms, publishing a legal handbook and introducing a new silver coin, the miliaresion. He also continued the development of the theme system for he was only too well aware of one of its major flaws. Devolving wide powers to the *strategoi* certainly gave them scope to deal quickly and effectively with Arab raids but at the same time it provided a *strategos* with the where-withal to challenge the emperor in Constantinople, something that Leo himself had done with great success. He therefore partitioned the very large Anatolikon theme to cut down the resources available to its *strategos* and to prevent anyone else from following his own example: a classic case of a successful politician pulling the ladder up after him. The measure seems to have worked, for Leo enjoyed a long reign, dying of natural causes and bequeathing the throne to his son.

Leo's son and successor, Constantine V (741–775), the second of the so-called North Syrian dynasty, was probably one of the greatest emperors ever to rule Byzantium. Sadly, the disturbed and dangerous times in which he lived have ensured that he remains a rather obscure figure. The literary records are thin and there is no surviving lifelike portrait of him, as there are in the mosaics of Justinian and Theodora at Ravenna, only the stylised busts on the obverse of his coins. They show a man with a short beard and long flowing hair, holding a cross or an orb, and looking almost identical to the coin portraits of his father. There are some hints of his character in the existing records of the time. He was very fond of watching chariot races in the Hippodrome, so much so that he had a mural of a particularly memorable race painted on to the Milion arch, a prominent landmark in the Augousteion. He was well read and literate, the author of thirteen theological works. Perhaps he liked music too and that is why he sent an organ as a diplomatic gift to the king of the Franks.

One thing that is certain about Constantine V is that he had given careful thought to how the shrunken Byzantine empire was going to survive in this new and dangerous world, sandwiched as it was between Arab expansionism and further waves of migrating tribes from Central Asia. With so much territory lost, the retention of Constantinople was more important than ever, but in the last year of Leo III's reign a huge earthquake struck the city. It brought down not only numerous churches, monasteries and statues but also several sections of the Land Walls. Repairs began at once and were completed by Constantine: the inscriptions commemorating the repairs can still be seen on some of the towers. Throughout his reign Constantine took care of his major asset, the capital city. To boost the flagging population after the plague of 747, he shipped in new inhabitants from the Greek islands. When a drought caused the cisterns to run dry, Constantine overhauled the entire water supply system. He restored the aqueduct of Valens which had been cut by the Avars during their siege of 626, bringing in hundreds of masons and plasterers from the provinces to complete the task, and so brought water flowing into Constantinople once more. The emperor's ability to transplant all these people and to feed and pay them stemmed from Byzantium's having preserved a money economy, in spite of all the vicissitudes of the previous century. Constantine V enjoyed a healthy revenue from taxes which he could mobilise to fund and carry out grand projects like this.

Vital though the capital was, Constantine V did not fall into the error of some later emperors and assume that it was the centre of everything. Like his predecessors, he was constantly moving populations around to where they were most needed to defend the borders. He is credited with settling 208,000 Slavs on the river Artanas in north-western Asia Minor and with bringing similar numbers of Christian Syrians and Armenians to Thrace and settling them in forts along the dangerous border with the Bulgars. He knew the importance of playing off one power against another to minimise the threat to his own frontier. He continued the Khazar alliance begun by his father, and Byzantium benefited greatly from the distraction provided by Khazar incursions into the caliphate during the 760s. Again, like the emperors before him, Constantine saw the value of the theme system in providing for the defence of Asia Minor without the burden of feeding a standing army, but he was well aware of the political danger presented by concentrating so much power in the hands of the *strategoi* of the themes. At the very outset of his reign, he had very nearly been overthrown by a rebellion by Artavasdos, the *strategos* of Opsikion, and had at one point been ousted from Constantinople. Only after three years of warfare had the emperor been able to turn the tables, largely thanks to the support of the troops of the Anatolikon theme. Not surprisingly, one of his first acts thereafter was to divide the Opsikion theme into smaller units to weaken it as a powerbase.

Constantine was also responsible for another measure calculated to provide a counterweight to the themes' armies in the event of another rebellion: the creation of the *tagmata*. These were a number of small elite regiments that were stationed in and around Constantinople under the direct command of the emperor alone, and they would provide him with a loyal force to take on a rebellious theme army. He seems to have fostered that loyalty assiduously by being seen to care about his men. He publicly declared that his Bulgarian campaign of 773 was a 'noble war' because there had been so few casualties on the Christian side. On another campaign, when some of his ships were wrecked on the Black Sea coast, the emperor refused to leave the spot until fishing nets had been trawled through the sea to collect as many corpses as possible for decent burial. There can be no doubt that Constantine was very popular among the men of the *tagmata* not just because of his concern for their welfare but also because he was an extremely able soldier who won spectacular victories both in the east and in the west. In 746, taking advantage of a civil war among the Arabs to go over to the offensive, Constantine led his army over the Taurus mountains into Syria, an area in which Byzantine troops had not been seen in living memory. He recaptured his ancestral town of Germanikeia but he had no intention of trying to hold it permanently because he was fighting on two fronts and his presence was needed elsewhere. The Bulgars, who had been allies against the Arabs in 718, were now looking to expand their territory and in 756 war broke out over the forts that Constantine had built to house the transplanted Syrians and Armenians and to guard Byzantine territory. When Constantine refused to pay them tribute money for the forts, the Bulgars invaded Byzantine territory almost as far as Constantinople, burning and plundering as they went. In June 763, Constantine took his revenge. Marching north along the Black Sea coast, supported by a powerful fleet, he met and crushed the Bulgar army at Anchialos in Thrace in a battle that lasted all day. He celebrated his victory with a triumphant entry into Constantinople of the kind that had not been seen since the days of Heraclius.

In view of all these achievements, one would expect Constantine V to have been remembered by the Byzantines with reverence and affection. That was not the case. The surviving historical records are all bitterly hostile, denouncing him as a limb of Satan and the enemy of Christ. Their monastic authors invariably refer to him by the insulting nickname of 'Kopronymos', an almost untranslatable epithet but carrying the meaning that Constantine's name was human excrement. When he was a baby at his christening, his detractors claimed, little Constantine had defecated in the font. The priest had not noticed the mishap and had proceeded with the ceremony, pouring the polluted water over the child's head. The senseless bile behind such stories had nothing to do with the emperor's military or administrative record but rather with his theological views. For Constantine V was an iconoclast.

* * *

During the seventh century, icons of Christ, the Virgin Mary and the saints had been credited with playing a role in saving Byzantium from its enemies. Heraclius had carried an icon of Christ into battle and the patriarch had placed the image of the Virgin and Child on the Land Walls when the Avar hordes drew near. They had become an essential part of Byzantine life. Every church, from Hagia Sophia to the lowliest country shrine, would have been decorated with such pictures, whether in sumptuous mosaic, cheaper fresco or humble painting on wood. Their role went beyond mere decoration or visual instruction. They were becoming objects of veneration in their own right and were considered capable of performing wonders. Tales circulated, such as that of a woman who dug a well hoping to find water but without success. Only when she lowered an icon of a saint down the hole did it miraculously fill up with water. Much of this was popular superstition but the political establishment realised that it could harness this reverence for pictures to its own ends. Justinian II had an image of Christ placed on his gold coinage and over the Brazen Gate, the main entrance to the Great Palace – visual symbols of divine protection for everyone to see.

Even as icons became inextricably enmeshed with the fabric of Byzantine life, there were those who had doubts, just as back in the fourth century Epiphanius of Salamis had disapproved of the image of Christ on a curtain. Those doubts were strongest out on the eastern frontier where towns like

Germanikeia regularly changed hands between Arabs and Byzantines. In those places Christians were only too well aware that in the Islamic caliphate matters were moving in a very different direction. From an originally relaxed approach to images, by the early eighth century all depictions of living things had been removed from the interior of mosques and Islamic art was concentrating instead on pattern and calligraphy. In 721 the caliph Yazid II went further and decreed that images should be taken out of churches throughout his dominions as well. Yazid's death in 724 probably prevented his decree from being carried out to any great extent but there could be no doubt now about the widening gulf between Islam and Christianity on this issue. Given that the Arabs had been so successful in expanding their domains at the expense of Christians, there were some in Byzantium who were beginning to think that the Muslims might be right and that Christians might be being punished for violating the Second Commandment's prohibition of making or bowing down to any 'graven image'.

During the 720s, reports reached the patriarch of Constantinople that two bishops in Asia Minor, Constantine of Nakoleia and Thomas of Klaudioupolis, were holding some unorthodox views on icons. Constantine had refused to bow down to them as had become customary, while Thomas had removed the icons from his church. Sharing the doubts of these clerics, once in power Leo III did not voice his dislike of icon veneration openly to start with, probably because the Arab siege of Constantinople was uppermost in his mind. By 724, however, he had among his advisers a bishop who shared his views and a man who had spent many years as a prisoner in the caliphate, and he was starting to make his disapproval known. He was moved to act further by what he considered to be a message from God. In the autumn of 726, the volcano on the island of Thera (modern Santorini) erupted, sending a dense column of smoke up into the sky and showering pumice stone across the entire Aegean and beyond. This eruption was read by Leo as a manifestation of God's anger at the growing idolatry within the empire. It seems to have been around this time that Leo ordered that the icon of Christ over the Brazen Gate be removed and a few years later he deposed the patriarch of Constantinople and replaced him with one who shared his views. That, however, was as far as Leo went. There was no attempt to rip the icons out of churches, to ban their veneration or to punish those iconophiles who held contrary views. After all, generations of Byzantines had grown up with the belief that icons were channels of God's grace, objects to be cherished and venerated. That deeply held faith could not be legislated out of existence. There had been a stark warning too of the danger of trying to impose his own views on his subjects. When a troop of soldiers had been sent to remove the icon over the

Brazen Gate, a hostile crowd had gathered. According to later tradition one of them, a woman, had pushed away the ladder on which one of the soldiers was perched as he chipped away at the icon: the unfortunate man plummeted to his death and there were several other casualties that day. Leo apparently remained content to confine his ban on icons to the court.

Constantine V, however, was different. Not just an iconophobe, sharing his father's dislike of the cult of icons, he was an iconoclast, prepared to take measures to put an end to it. This might simply have been a matter of personal conviction but there was a political dimension too. When the *strategos* of the Opsikion theme, Artavasdos, had revolted against Constantine in the summer of 741, he had deliberately fostered iconophile support, announcing once he was in control of Constantinople that icon veneration was no longer disapproved of at court. When Constantine emerged victorious in the ensuing civil war he probably regarded iconophiles as tainted with treason as well as theological error. He still moved with caution and took his time to build up support, but in 754 he summoned a council of three hundred and thirty-eight prelates to meet in the summer palace at Hieria on the Asian side of the Bosporus. After several months of deliberation, the bishops issued a series of decrees condemning the veneration of icons and those who defended it. Anyone who in future made an icon was threatened with dire punishment. Henceforth, iconoclasm was not just an opinion but an official policy.

That said, the council stopped short of decreeing that all icons and images should be destroyed and there was no wholesale destruction of works of art. Instead, removal seems to have happened piecemeal as churches and other buildings came to need renovation. One of the first to be targeted was the church of St Irene, close to Hagia Sophia, which had been damaged by an earthquake in 740. The apse of the building, where the Virgin and Child had appeared in the past, was now adorned instead with a plain cross. The church of the Virgin at Blachernae was also restored during Constantine's reign. It was a particularly well-known shrine because it housed a precious relic, the Virgin's veil, and consequently it was lavishly decorated inside with mosaics showing scenes from the life of Christ. Constantine had these chipped off and replaced with scenes from nature – trees, flowers and birds – which went back to the kind of decoration found in Byzantine churches in earlier centuries. There does not seem to have been any haste in all this. The patriarch of Constantinople, who shared Constantine's views, waited until 768 before he had the images of Christ and the saints scraped off the walls of his official residence.

Constantine's reign is so poorly documented that it is difficult to discern at this remove exactly what he was hoping to achieve. It is possible, however, that the emperor was unhappy not just about icon veneration but also about other developments in Byzantine Christianity over the past centuries and was trying to return to an earlier, simpler religion. For it was not only visual expressions of belief that were under attack, but also that other Byzantine religious phenomenon, the holy man. It is very noticeable that the most prominent opponents of Constantine V's iconoclasm were hermits and monks. Far from showing them the traditional deference, the emperor dealt with them ruthlessly. Andrew Kalyvites, who publicly denounced Constantine V by comparing him to the pagan emperor Julian and the Arian Valens, was lashed to death. Stephen the Younger, a recluse who lived on a mountain in Asia Minor, was arrested and brought to Constantinople. Constantine's *tagmata* soldiers tied a rope around his feet and dragged him through the streets until he was dead. It is possible that Constantine did not only target these holy men because they opposed his views on icons but because he disapproved of the prominent role that they had come to play in Byzantine society. He is supposed to have referred to monastic dress as 'the habit of darkness', a curious echo of the pagan Zosimus, and many of his punishments seemed to have been designed to humiliate and discredit this particular group. In the summer of 766, he rounded up a group of monks and made them parade around the Hippodrome, each holding a woman by the hand while the crowd jeered them. A favourite punishment was to shave off their beards, robbing them of what in Byzantium was considered an essential marker of manhood. Several monasteries in Constantinople were seized and converted to other purposes. The monastery of St Saviour in Chora, near the Land Walls, became a lodging house, others became barracks for the soldiers of the *tagmata*. A ruler who was so assiduous in husbanding manpower for the defence of the empire might well have looked askance at such large numbers of men opting for the religious life and so making themselves unavailable for military service.

These views were to be fatal for Constantine's posthumous reputation, for almost all the surviving records from the period were written by iconophile monks. Their authors excelled themselves when it came to recording his death. In August 775, he set out once more to do battle with the Bulgars, but long before his army reached the frontier he became unwell as sores broke out on his legs. He was taken to the port of Selymbria on the Sea of Marmara but by then he was in a fever. They carried him on to a ship for the journey back to Constantinople, and hymns to the Virgin were sung at his request, but he died before the ship reached the harbour of the Great Palace. One chronicler gleefully claimed that, as the emperor was slipping away, he cried out, 'I have been delivered to the unquenchable fire while still alive!' before going on to declare that he had reached the pinnacle of evil like the ancient tyrants. That was all written later, of course. At the time, Constantine was doubtless mourned as the great emperor he was and he was buried, as was proper, in a handsome marble sarcophagus in the church of the Holy Apostles.

* * *

While the dispute over icons called forth some of the withering scorn that the Byzantines reserved for anyone who disagreed with their religious views, the rift does not seem to have had such dire consequences for the empire as had the dispute between the Monophysites and Chalcedonians. Generally the empire held its own against its external enemies during these years and consolidated the reforms that had made its survival possible. In the end, though, in spite of all Constantine V's success and power, it was the iconophiles who won the argument, for they had always had one signal advantage. Even when the veneration of icons had been declared unsound in Constantinople, Christians further afield refused to accept the change. In Italy, where the emperor's power was tenuous at best, the pope was steadfastly iconophile. An edict was sent to him, shortly after the removal of the icon from the Brazen Gate in Constantinople, ordering him to remove all images from churches, but he refused to implement it. Instead, the pope gathered ninety-three bishops in a council of his own to endorse the role of sacred images. Leo III's representative in the area, the exarch of Ravenna, clumsily attempted to enforce compliance by sending an agent to Rome to assassinate the pope, but the plot was detected and the would-be assassin arrested. Successive popes maintained their opposition, refusing to send representatives to the council of Hieria in 754 and welcoming refugee iconophiles in Rome. Powerless to force the pope into line, the emperor took his revenge by removing Sicily and southern Italy from the pope's jurisdiction, thus depriving him of valuable revenues.

Ironically, the Christians who were safest from the iconoclast emperors and who had the greatest freedom to express their iconophile views were those living under Muslim rule. The Chalcedonian patriarchs of Alexandria, Antioch and Jerusalem all tended to oppose iconoclasm and, like the pope, refused to attend the council of 754. The most influential iconophile voice, however, was that of John of Damascus, a Christian who had held high office in the court of the caliph before entering the monastery of Mar Saba near Jerusalem. There he wrote three tracts in defence of the veneration of icons during the 730s that were to prove extraordinarily influential.

John justified the practice on the basis of two ideas. The first was derived from Plato and the Neoplatonists: the image was a symbol and mediator. He drew a distinction between the icon itself and the person depicted on it. Veneration directed towards an icon, he claimed, was not idolatry because the prayers were directed not to the wood of which the icon was made but to the saint who lay beyond it. Secondly, John went further and countered the iconoclast argument that any depiction of Christ could portray only his humanity and would implicitly deny his divinity. The counter-argument linked icon veneration to the Incarnation. Only by accepting icons, John argued, could one accept the truth of the incarnation of Christ. If you denied that Christ could be depicted in wood and paint, you denied that he could be present in flesh and bone. To reinforce his contention, he pointed to the transfiguration on Mount Tabor, when divine glory had shone around Jesus and his disciples had bowed down and worshipped him. They were not worshipping the flesh and bone of which the human Christ was composed, but the Godhead which lay beyond it, and so it was with icons. In this way, John made the case that icon veneration was not just legitimate, but essential to orthodox Christian belief.

Such arguments may have given heart to iconophiles but they had little hope of being accepted as long as Constantine V was alive, or under his son and successor Leo IV (775–780), who held similar views. Nevertheless there was still plenty of pro-icon sentiment even at the court of the iconoclast emperors. Leo IV discovered that some of the officials in his palace had been secretly praying to icons and, more worryingly, a couple of small icons were discovered in his wife's bedroom, hidden under her pillow. Empress Irene was originally from Athens, a town which had remained in Byzantine hands in spite of the Slav domination of the Balkans and which seems to have been largely iconophile. She escaped with a stern telling-off from her husband, probably because she denied all knowledge of the icons and said that they must have been put there by somebody else. Then, completely unexpectedly, in September 780, Leo IV died aged only thirty.

The late emperor's son, Constantine VI, was only ten years old, and the convention in Byzantium in such cases was that the boy's mother would become regent, assisted by a council of advisers. Irene duly stepped into this role. Given her sympathies, she must have considered this a heaven-sent opportunity to reverse official policy towards icons but she did not dare do anything openly during the early stages of her regency. Disapproval of icon veneration was still official doctrine and had many supporters, while a group at court was openly in favour of replacing Irene and her son with the boy's uncle, Nikephoros, a younger son of Constantine V. In the spring of 781, the *strategos* of Sicily revolted in favour of Nikephoros and a fleet had to be sent to oust him from the island.

Only after four years had passed did Irene feel strong enough to move. She began by writing to the pope to tell him that she wished to put an end to the division of the Church over the issue of icons and to call a general council of the Church to resolve the issue. By then a sympathetic patriarch of Constantinople, Tarasios, was in post and a fair number of the bishops seemed ready to support a return of official approval for icon veneration. On Irene's orders a council of bishops was called to gather in the church of the Holy Apostles, Constantinople's largest sacred edifice after Hagia Sophia, to discuss the issue. Representatives of the pope and the patriarchs of Alexandria and Antioch were present, and the deliberations began, with the empress and young emperor watching from the gallery. Irene had, however, reckoned without the *tagmata*. Proceedings were rapidly brought to a halt by a thunderous banging on the doors as a contingent of troops came crashing into the church with their swords drawn. Loyal to the memory of Constantine V, they threatened to kill the patriarch and anyone else who interfered with what they considered to be the orthodox faith. Irene sent her household troops down from the gallery in an attempt to restore order but the soldiers refused to leave, so the patriarch and his supporting bishops withdrew. Those bishops who remained rejoiced with the soldiers and the council was abandoned.

Clearly, this powerful body of support for iconoclasm would have to be neutralised. Word was given out that an Arab invasion was threatening. The *tagmata* were marched out of Constantinople and sent east, while troops from the themes were brought in to garrison the capital. The *tagmata* were then disarmed. Their families were ferried across from Constantinople to join them and they were told to return to their own homes, their services no longer being required. A new elite force was recruited, under officers loyal to Irene. Even so, when the council resumed, Irene very cautiously held its initial sessions in the city of Nicaea, away from possible iconoclast demonstrations in Constantinople. Three hundred and fifty prelates gathered in the main church there and the debates began anew. Obviously Irene had packed the council with iconophile bishops who knew that they were there to prepare the case for a restoration of icons, but an earnest attempt was made to build a convincing theological case. The works of John of Damascus were discussed and their arguments incorporated into the council's decrees. An examination was also made of earlier authorities to prove that icon veneration was not some innovation but had been the practice of Christians for centuries. Copies of old books that served as authorities were carefully scrutinised and compared to ensure that no one had tampered with the text or inserted extra passages. When the case was complete, the council moved back to Constantinople and held a final session in the Magnavra hall within the Great Palace. There, in 787, the decrees of what came to be known as the Second Council of Nicaea or the Seventh Ecumenical Council were publicly proclaimed, calling down curses on anyone who did not venerate 'the holy and venerable images' or who referred to them as idols. The image of Christ above the Brazen Gate was restored to its place shortly afterwards.

This emphatic voicing of the iconophile position did not end the dispute. Although there was no immediate iconoclast backlash, a generation later a series of defeats at the hands of the Bulgars led Emperor Leo V (813–820) to revoke the decrees of Nicaea in 815, believing that God was punishing the Byzantines for their idolatry. Recalcitrant monks and bishops who would not accept the change were sent into exile. One iconoclast emperor, Theophilos (829–842), went further and had a couple of monks tattooed on the forehead with a warning that they had been propagating heresy. They had to walk around with this public notice on show for the rest of their lives. More often, however, opponents of iconoclasm were simply dumped on various islands in the Sea of Marmara where they could cause no more trouble. There is little evidence of wholesale destruction of images during this second period when icon veneration was outlawed. Then the pendulum swung back as history repeated itself. When Emperor Theophilos died in 842, his son Michael III was only two. Once again a regency was formed under the late emperor's widow and once again she was a closet iconophile. Like Irene, Empress Theodora had allegedly kept icons in her bedroom and, when discovered praying to them by the court jester, had managed to avoid denunciation by convincing him that she was just playing with some dolls. Unlike Irene, Theodora was able to move swiftly and she convened another council in 843 which restored the decisions of 787, this time permanently. By now, the iconoclast cause seems to have waned and there was no backlash such as Irene had experienced when she had convened the council in the Holy Apostles. Not that it was all peace and harmony from then on. No sooner had the Byzantines agreed that the veneration of icons was orthodox doctrine than a split opened up as to how magnanimous the iconophiles should be in victory and how former iconoclasts, particularly bishops, should be treated. The patriarch and the moderates believed they should merely be ousted from their sees while the zealots demanded that they be actively punished. The disagreement rumbled on for years until another issue arose to replace it. But then there was always some kind of theological dispute going on in Byzantium: that was the way in which the political process worked.

* * *

The long dispute over icons had been an internal matter which made no difference to Byzantium's long-running struggle with the Arabs and Bulgars. When it comes to the empire's art, culture and self-perception, on the other hand, the dispute and its eventual resolution were to have a profound impact. That impact was possible because some twenty years after the restoration of icon veneration, the empire was wealthier and more secure than it had been for a century. It had been at peace with the Bulgars since 816 and in 863 the Byzantine army had won a spectacular victory over the Arabs at Poson, killing the emir of Melitene and annihilating his entire army. Thereafter Arab raids into Asia Minor dwindled and in the more settled conditions the tax revenues increased. Trade was reviving as merchants from all over the world took advantage of Constantinople's geographical position at the meeting point of two long-distance trading routes: the Silk Road from Asia and the sea routes from western Europe. Arab merchants brought spices, perfume, carpets, porcelain and jewels, as well as glassware; Italians brought timber, gold and wool; Russians wax, honey, amber, swords and fur; the Bulgarians linen and honey. Silks commanded fabulous prices in western Europe, as did furs in the Arab caliphate. Constantinople became a busy trading hub where goods from one part of the world were brought to be sold on or exchanged with those from another. Although most of this activity was in the hands of foreign merchants, the Byzantine emperor benefited by charging a customs duty of ten per cent on all imports and exports, yielding a rich and dependable income.

For the first time since the age of Justinian, the emperors now had a surplus income that they could spend on grandiose projects, and the second half of the ninth century saw something of a building boom as splendid new churches and monasteries arose in Constantinople and the provinces. During the reign of Michael III (842–867), a new domed chapel was completed within the Great Palace complex. Known as the Holy Virgin of the Pharos, due to its proximity to the lighthouse at the tip of Constantinople's promontory, it was not a particularly large or imposing structure. What impressed those who saw the chapel when it was dedicated in around 864 was the richness of its interior decoration, on which no expense had been spared. The floor was of white marble, the columns that supported the dome were of jasper and porphyry – the rare purple marble reserved for royal use – and the doors were overlaid with silver. There was a reason why this small building should be so adorned. The chapel became the storehouse for the emperors' most precious possessions, their collection of holy relics. These included the parts of the True Cross brought back by Heraclius when he retreated in the face of the Arab invasion of Syria, along with what were sincerely believed was the tunic of Christ, his Crown of

Thorns, the lance with which the centurion had pierced his side, a small phial of his blood, part of the robe of the Virgin, and the head of St John the Baptist.

The decoration of the Pharos chapel was not just expensive: it was deliberately created in accordance with the new line on images. The sacred space was dominated by two enormous mosaic figures. One was of the Virgin with her arms outstretched in the apse at the far end. The other was of Jesus Christ at the centre of the dome, looking down on the nave below. These were effectively enormous icons, focusing and channelling the worship that took place there, with a host of apostles, saints and martyrs covering the other walls. Yet it was not only the decoration that reflected the centrality of images to Byzantine theology and worship. Some eighty years later a new relic was added to the collection, having been brought back from Edessa by a victorious general. This was the Mandylion, the ancient piece of cloth on which was an image of the features of Christ that he himself had created by holding the cloth to his face. It was all the evidence the iconophiles needed for the legitimacy and orthodoxy of images, for God incarnate himself had created one. There was no longer any need for uncertainty in the face of Islam or the arguments of the iconoclasts. The Byzantines were now completely confident in their faith and the visual culture that had become inseparable from it.

Another significant project of Michael III's reign was the restoration of the mosaic of the Virgin and Child in the apse of the cathedral of Hagia Sophia. Presumably at some point it had been replaced by a simple cross as in the church of St Irene, but by the spring of 867 it had been restored along with a triumphant inscription: 'The images which the impostors had cast down here the pious emperors have again set up.' The patriarch of Constantinople, Photios, preached a sermon at the unveiling, stressing throughout the indelible link between icons and orthodoxy. Only by accepting icons, he declared, could one accept the truth of the Bible and the Incarnation. Those responsible for iconoclasm had thrown in their lot with the Arabs and could not be regarded as 'Romans' or even as Christians.

That philosophy was reflected in all the other churches built in this period, such as the five-domed Nea Ekklesia, or New Church, constructed between 876 and 880 and the church of the Myrelaion monastery in the 930s. These were not huge buildings on the scale of Hagia Sophia or the Holy Apostles and their exteriors were plain and unadorned. It was their interior decoration that was all important. The entire inside space would have been covered in visual images, whether of mosaic or paint on the walls or on wooden boards on the *iconostasis*, or screen, that divided the congregation from the sanctuary – a silent congregation looking down on the worshippers below. The church effectively became a kind of icon of heaven itself, a foretaste of what the true believer would experience in the afterlife.

So it was that in the century after his death, Constantine V's earnest attempt to steer his people away from what he had considered to be idolatry had been completely undone and the iconophiles had done their best to ensure that he went down in history as a tyrant and an unbeliever. Yet in spite of their efforts, his memory was not completely erased, and nor were his achievements in helping Byzantium to survive against all the odds. The men of the *tagmata* who invaded the church of the Holy Apostles in 786 probably did so not out of deeply held iconophobe sentiment but because they could not bear to see the work of their hero undone. By 813, Byzantium was again reeling from defeat at the hands of the Bulgars, whom Constantine V had held in check so effectively. When news arrived that the Bulgars had taken the town of Mesembria in Thrace, a panicky crowd rushed to the church of the Holy Apostles. They prised open the doors of the imperial mausoleum and fell on their knees before the tomb of the iconoclast emperor, begging him to arise and ride out against the enemy once more. Word spread in the streets that the dead emperor had been seen, mounted on his horse and galloping west to the attack. The authorities could not, of course, countenance such demonstrations. The city prefect arrived at the mausoleum and arrested the ringleaders. Later, after the restoration of icons in 843, the sarcophagus was taken out of the church and the bones of the long-dead emperor were removed and burned in one of Constantinople's main squares. This was how Byzantium repaid one of its greatest rulers who merely happened to think differently from what was ultimately to become the benchmark of orthodoxy.

CHAPTER FIVE

The Conquest of the North

[The Russians] are the filthiest of God's creatures . . . They do not wash their hands after meals. They are like wandering asses.
Arab traveller, Ibn Fadlan (922)

Tuesday 18 June in the year 860 began as any other for the inhabitants of Constantinople. The emperor and his chief advisers were absent from his capital. They had crossed the Bosporus with the army and were marching east to confront an Arab raiding force in Asia Minor. No news or warning had come in of any other threat so it seemed perfectly safe to leave to leave the city prefect in charge with only a small garrison. Business would have been carrying on as usual down on the Golden Horn, the quayside thronged with merchant galleys from all over the Mediterranean. Suddenly smoke was seen to be rising into the sky from the sea to the east: something was burning along the Bosporus and on the Princes' Islands out in the Sea of Marmara. Those who mounted the Sea Walls to find out what was going on were horrified to see that a fleet of some two hundred ships was cruising along the Asian shore, stopping occasionally to disgorge heavily armed men who waded ashore to attack the scattered and defenceless settlements. Constantinople itself was safe enough behind its fortifications but in the absence of the army and with no prior warning of what was going to happen, nothing could be done to prevent the marauders from plundering the suburbs at their leisure. Swift messengers were dispatched to recall the emperor and thereafter the only recourse was prayer. Crowds gathered at the church of the Virgin Mary at Blachernae in the far west of the city, which housed a precious relic, the Virgin's veil, believed to have helped to ward off the Avars in 626. Darkness fell and still the fires crackled in the distance. The next day, the throng was joined by the patriarch of Constantinople himself, Photios. He gave orders that the veil of the Virgin was to be taken out of the church and carried in a procession around the walls, accompanied by hymns and litanies. By the end of the day, when the relic returned to the church, the ships had vanished as suddenly as they had arrived.

As parties moved gingerly out to reconnoitre beyond the fortifications, the magnitude of the slaughter became clear. There were corpses everywhere, wrote Photios:

> There lay an ox and a man by its side, a child and a horse found a common grave, women and fowl stained each other with their blood . . . Corn-land was rotting with dead bodies, roads were obstructed . . . ravines and gullies differed in no way from city cemeteries.

But who had inflicted this massacre? It was not the old enemy, the Arabs, for the fleet had come from the north, not from the south. It was, claimed Photios, an obscure nation which previously no one had taken much notice of. No one in Byzantium, that was. Elsewhere in Europe they knew them only too well. Constantinople had been attacked by the same people who had been wreaking havoc on the coasts of Britain, France and Ireland for years, the Scandinavian Vikings. In the early part of the century, while the Danes and Norwegians had sailed west in their longships, their kinsmen in Sweden had turned east, crossed the Baltic, continued eastwards across the land mass and created a permanent settlement at Novgorod. They called themselves the 'Rhos', which might derive from a Scandinavia word for 'oarsmen' and which provided their modern name, the Russians. From Novgorod the Russians moved south-west, travelling along the river Dnieper to the hilltop town of Kiev, where they created another permanent base, ruling over the local Slavs and gradually becoming integrated with them and adopting their language. It was the Russians of Kiev who launched the attack on Constantinople in the summer of 860.

* * *

The Byzantines had not been taken unawares because they were ignorant of the existence of the Russians. For several decades, these fierce warriors had been sailing down the river Dnieper to the Black Sea and thence to Byzantium. Initially, however, they did not come with any hostile intention but to take advantage of Constantinople's opportunities for trade. They would arrive in the spring with cargoes of wax, honey, amber and fur and depart in the autumn, their ships loaded with costly silks and spices. Why suddenly they should have turned to aggression will never be known. Perhaps there was some dispute over trading rights or customs duties, or perhaps their previous voyages had alerted the Russians to the ease with which they could raid the undefended settlements along the shores of the Bosporus. Whatever sparked off the attack, it had come as a devastating surprise to the victims.

The Byzantines now had to reckon with a threat from the north along with those from the east and the west and to rethink their entire defensive strategy. Ever since Heraclius had made the decision to concentrate his forces against the Persians in 622, the Byzantine emperors had given priority to what seemed to be the greater danger from the east. After all, to that side they were facing a very large and powerful empire, first Sassanid Persia and then the Islamic caliphate. The sieges of 674–678 and 717–718 had threatened Constantinople itself, and the empire's very existence. In the west, on the other hand, Byzantine territory bordered on land held by the Slavs who, once they had thrown off Avar domination, had settled down to occupy the southern Balkans and had made little attempt to expand further. The Bulgar khanate to the north was a more unified and aggressive force but it had been very effectively held in check by the victories of the much-reviled but extremely effective emperor Constantine V. Even though the Slavs had occupied the land as far south as the tip of the Peloponnese, the Byzantines had maintained a presence in the region in fortified towns such as Thessalonica, Athens and Monemvasia. Moreover, as the eighth century went on, it looked increasingly likely that they would be able to reconquer much of what they had lost in the Balkans, something that could not even be contemplated in the case of the eastern provinces. During the later eighth and early ninth centuries, a series of military expeditions had been sent into Thrace, Macedonia and Thessaly, pushing down as far as the Peloponnese. The Slav tribes were unable to put up any concerted resistance and ultimately agreed to accept the overlordship of the emperor. By 850, all of the territory that is now Greece was back under Byzantine rule, forming a solid block of land between Constantinople and the Peloponnese. Greek-speaking settlers were brought in from southern Italy to repopulate the area and slowly Greek replaced Slavonic as the majority language. In this almost bloodless reconquest, hermits and monks were in the vanguard rather than soldiers. They wandered through the remote and mountainous area of the Peloponnese as itinerant preachers, converting the last isolated pockets of Slavs to Christianity. This success might well have reinforced the view that the west was safer than the east.

During the ninth century, however, that view of the world had to be reversed. On one hand, the threat from the east was growing weaker. The Abbasid caliphate began to develop internal problems of its own and the raids into Asia Minor grew less frequent. The annihilation of an Arab army at Poson in 863 demonstrated that the Byzantines were now better equipped to fight back and by the later ninth century a kind of *modus vivendi* had grown up between Byzantium and the caliphate. There were still cross-border raids and piratical naval attacks. During the 820s, Arab forces landed on Crete and Sicily and ultimately conquered both islands. In 904 an Arab fleet stormed and sacked Thessalonica. Damaging though these losses were, they did not threaten the very existence of Byzantium as in the days of the great Arab sieges of Constantinople. Against this backdrop of increasing security in the east, the 860 debacle had revealed a new danger from another direction.

Fifty years earlier, an even worse disaster had overtaken the Byzantines at the hands of the Bulgars. As the Byzantines had reintegrated the southern Balkans into their empire, they may well have hoped that they could do the same in the north and bring their frontier back to the Danube. So, when the Bulgar khan, Krum, made an incursion over the border and captured the Byzantine town of Serdica, Emperor Nikephoros I (802–811) decided on a robust response. In May 811, he set out to invade Bulgaria with a large army made up of both *tagmata* and soldiers from the themes of Asia Minor. Faced with overwhelming force, Krum sent envoys to sue for peace but Nikephoros was so confident of victory that he rejected their overtures out of hand. In July the invasion went ahead. The Byzantine army descended on Pliska, swept aside all opposition, captured the town and massacred the garrison. Krum's wooden palace was captured intact and was found to be stuffed with treasure, which Nikephoros duly distributed among his soldiers. The palace and town were then torched and Nikephoros's army headed south to reoccupy Serdica. That, however, meant crossing the Balkan mountains and passing through a terrain that was entirely to the advantage of the defenders. As the slow-moving columns made their way through a ravine, the vanguard discovered to their horror that the exit had been blocked with tree trunks and palisades and was held by a strong Bulgar force. By then another contingent had moved in behind the Byzantines and closed off the pass behind them.

For a time, many in the army remained unaware that they were trapped, as the officers probably made sure that the news did not spread. For two days it remained encamped in the pass waiting for Krum's next move. On the last night, the Bulgars set up a fearful din by hammering their swords on their shields and, hearing the noise through the darkness, the soldiers realised that they were surrounded by a considerable force, and a sense of dread and doom spread through the ranks. At first light the next day, the Bulgars attacked, directing their assault against the imperial camp. Within a short time the

emperor and many of his senior advisers were dead, and the fighting degener-
ated into a massacre as the Byzantine army fragmented and each man tried to
save himself. Some tried to break through to the barriers at either end which
the Bulgars had left unmanned to attack the camp. Finding it difficult to penetrate the piles of branches and tree trunks, the fleeing soldiers set fire to them.
As they rushed through the gaps left by the flames, they fell into a concealed
ditch beyond, where many were burned or trampled to death by the press
behind. Nikephoros's son Staurakios escaped but he was wounded so severely
that he died six months later. Thousands of his comrades never got out of the
ravine at all. When it was all over, Krum saw to it that the emperor's body was
located and the head cut off. It was nailed to a post and carried round for all to
see. Later, when it was reduced to just a skull, Krum had it made into a drinking
vessel, lined with silver, from which he would toast his nobles at feasts.

The annihilation of the Byzantine army in the Balkan mountains was as
great a debacle as that of Adrianople in 378 and in the short term it helped to
precipitate a second bout of iconoclasm as a panicky emperor sought to assuage
what he took to be the wrath of God over the idolatry of the Byzantines. In the
long term, it forced the Byzantines into some serious thinking, just as the
Russian attack of 860 was later to do, about how the threat from the north was
to be contained. To some extent it was merely a question of applying to these
new enemies the tactics that had saved the empire so often in the past. As in the
past, the immediate reaction to defeat was to retire behind the impregnable
defences of Constantinople. With the Byzantine army destroyed in 811, Krum
was able to march repeatedly into Thrace with impunity but his advance would
come to an abrupt halt whenever he reached Constantinople's impassable Land
Walls and he had to content himself with ransacking the suburbs. On the last
occasion, in 814, he came well prepared, having gathered 10,000 oxen to haul
up his impressive array of siege engines and catapults. He even had the thousands of waggons that carried them fireproofed with iron plates in case the
Byzantines thought to hurl down Greek fire from the walls. This time, however,
the hardware was never put to use. Krum was in the middle of overseeing the
preparations when suddenly blood started to pour from his mouth, nose and
ears. He fell to the ground stone dead, the victim of a cerebral haemorrhage,
and his leaderless army promptly withdrew.

Luck and the defences of Constantinople were also to save the Byzantines
from the Russians in 860 but they knew that they could not indefinitely rely
solely on static walls and serendipitous acts of God. Treaties would have to be
made to persuade the enemy to cease their attacks and the Byzantines had two
strong inducements to make them do so: the usual chestfuls of gold coins, and

trading concessions in Constantinople's international markets. Both Bulgarian and Russian merchants travelled to the Byzantine capital to market their goods and the promise of a lower rate of customs duty was a powerful bargaining tool. So in 816 a treaty was concluded with the new Bulgar khan, Omurtag, which was to keep the peace for many years. The Russians were rather more difficult to bring to the negotiating table. In around 907, they attacked Constantinople again. Led by the prince of Kiev, Oleg, who had united Kiev and Novgorod under his rule, their fleet cruised down the Bosporus, torching churches, monasteries and suburban settlements as it went. It was only in 911 that a treaty was finally concluded with the Russians on extremely generous terms. Russian merchants were exempted from paying the usual customs duty of ten per cent on all goods brought in and out of the Golden Horn. They were allotted a special lodging place in the suburban quarter of St Mamas, situated on the European shore of the Bosporus to the north of the Golden Horn. There they were to be supplied with six months' free lodging and, the treaty stipulated, baths whenever they wanted them. Nevertheless, the wariness with which the Byzantines viewed their trading partners was reflected in another clause. The Russians were not permitted to enter Constantinople itself, except by one gate only, unarmed, and never in groups of more than fifty at a time, accompanied by an imperial officer.

As far as Byzantines were concerned, generous treaties like this were only intended as an emergency measure. They were constantly on the lookout for the moment when the tables would be turned and the terms could be renegotiated. In the case of the Russians, that occurred in 941, when the Russian prince Igor decided to return to the old ways and launch an attack by sea. As in 860 and 907, the Russians chose their moment carefully: the Byzantine army and fleet were elsewhere and the only line of defence at sea was fifteen rotting hulks lying in the shipyard on the Golden Horn. These had to be hastily repaired and made ready for war. When the Russian vessels where anchored and their crews mostly ashore, the Byzantine ships sallied forth and started to shoot streams of Greek fire from their bows and sterns. One after another the Russian ships caught fire and their crews jumped overboard to escape the flames. Igor ordered his own ship to row away to the north, its shallow draught ensuring that it could keep close inshore where there was no likelihood of pursuit. Most of the Russians found themselves cut off before they could follow and took refuge on the Asian shore, where some months later they were mopped up by the returning Byzantine army. Now the treaty could be renegotiated and, in 944, the duly chastened Russians agreed to revised terms, losing their exemption from customs duties.

If unequal treaties were a palliative measure, Byzantine diplomatic tentacles were constantly seeking out allies who could be paid and kept in reserve to attack the Bulgars and Russians when the need arose. In the case of the Bulgars, the people who lived to the west and north and who feared the expansionist ambitions of their neighbours, the Serbs, Croats and Hungarians, were the obvious candidates. Against the Russians, the Byzantines' old friends the Khazars could be mobilised: an embassy was sent to them within a few months of the 860 attack. The perfect ally against both powers was another Turkic people that had migrated westwards across the steppes of Asia, the Pechenegs. Their territory straddled the river Dnieper, making them ideally placed both to strike against the northern borders of Bulgaria and to cut off the Russian trade route to the Black Sea. An annual 'present' of gold bullion was sent to the khan of the Pechenegs every year to buy his allegiance and to keep him in readiness for when the call to arms came.

These were, of course, exactly the same tactics that had for a long time been used to stave off the Arab threat. Constantinople's walls had saved the city in 674–678 and 717–718 and the caliphate had then often been bought off with treaties that promised the payment of annual tribute. There were trading concessions too, with a mosque even being provided in Constantinople for the use of visiting Arab merchants. The Khazar alliance had been used as a coun-terweight to the caliphate in the north for generations. During the 850s and 860s, however, a group of intellectuals in Constantinople seems to have started to ponder whether the fundamental differences between the enemies to the east and those to the west and north called for a different approach to the latter. Foremost among these revisionists was the man who as patriarch had witnessed the Russian attack on Constantinople in 860, Photios.

* * *

Although he was one of the most gifted and intelligent men of his generation, Photios was an unlikely choice for patriarch, for until his late forties he was not even an ordained clergyman. He was a member of a well-to-do Constantinopolitan family that had stuck to its iconophile beliefs during the second bout of iconoclasm, and after the restoration of icons in 843 he pursued a successful career as one of the administrators in the Great Palace. The court where Photios worked during the 850s must have been a slightly bewildering place. In theory it was presided over by Michael III but the emperor had little interest in the business of government. His chief passion in life was chariot racing, not just as a spectator but as a participant as well. He pursued his hobby not in the main Hippodrome but in the small port of St Mamas on the Bosporus, the place where the Russians were allowed to land their cargoes. There was a palace and a small racetrack in the town where the emperor and his friends could compete to their hearts' content away from the public gaze, the emperor always racing for the Blue faction. Even news of an impending Arab attack was not allowed to disturb a contest once it had begun. After dark, there were riotous parties and it was rumoured that Michael and his cronies even staged drunken and blasphemous burlesques of the Mass.

Since the emperor was so frequently away from the court and preoccupied with his own amusement, it was left to others to run the empire. To start with it was his mother, Theodora, who had been regent on his behalf since 842, assisted by Theoktistos, one of the palace eunuchs. When Michael reached the age of fifteen he began to be restless under his mother's tutelage and a faction at court headed by the empress's brother Bardas was quick to exploit his discontent. Lying in wait outside the council chamber, the conspirators seized Theoktistos as he emerged from a meeting, hustled him down to the dungeons below the palace and there did away with him. Robbed of her chief adviser, Theodora was distraught and found her position at court untenable. A few months after the murder, in the spring of 856, she called a meeting of the courtiers, handed over a set of accounts as evidence of her conscientious stewardship and then retired from public life to a convent.

After this palace coup, Michael conferred the title of Caesar on his uncle Bardas and left him to the task of administering the empire. Most of the considerable achievements of Michael's reign after 856 should probably be seen as the work of Bardas and his faction. The Byzantine army that trounced the emir of Melitene at Poson in 863, for example, was led by his brother, Petronas. Moreover, in spite of the brutal way in which he had come to power, Bardas was a patron of art: it was under him that the Pharos chapel was renovated and that work began on restoring the mosaic of the Virgin and Child in the apse of Hagia Sophia. He was also a supporter of secular higher education based on the study of the Greek classics. Centuries earlier, Basil of Caesarea and others had argued that these works, even though written by pagans, should be preserved and studied, although during the dark and uncertain days of the seventh and eighth centuries higher education seems to have fallen into abeyance. Bardas now revived the university of Constantinople, housing it in the Magnavra hall of the Great Palace and providing teachers at public expense. As emperor in all but name, however, Bardas had to take responsibility for the problems that he had inherited from his sister. One of them was the continuing rift in the church between moderates and zealots over how former iconoclast bishops should be treated. Bardas openly sided with the moderate camp: he even appointed a former iconoclast archbishop of Thessalonica to teach geometry in the new university. The patriarch Ignatios, however, fiercely opposed him and also made public criticisms of Bardas's private life, for the caesar was openly cohabiting with a woman who was not his wife. Bardas endured this challenge to his authority for about eighteen months, then in November 858 he had Ignatios arrested. He could not kill the patriarch, of course, but he had him thoroughly roughed up by his guards and dumped into the empty sarcophagus of Constantine V outside the Holy Apostles. Ignatios was left there all night in the freezing cold before being shipped off the next day to exile on the island of Lesvos.

That was where Photios came in. It is likely that he had been a member of Bardas's circle for some time, although whether he had been privy to the plot to kill Theoktistos is impossible to say. He also shared the caesar's interest in ancient Greek literature and probably was one of the teachers in the new university. He was the author of the *Biblioteca*, a collection of what can only be described as book reviews. The books in question had all been written centuries earlier and Photios was mainly interested in their style and vocabulary, for the spoken Greek language had diverged considerably from the classical idiom by his day. He could be quite scathing in his judgements. He decried the Christian Eunomius of Cyzicus (d. 393) for having 'no idea of charm and grace in style' and for producing 'pompous bombast and ugly sounds'. On the other hand, he loved the pagan Arrian, the historian of Alexander the Great, and the speeches of Alexander's contemporary, Isocrates. He was the man that Bardas wanted to run the Church in place of Ignatios, the antithesis of the fanatics that made up most of the zealot party.

There was the minor detail that Photios was ineligible to be patriarch because he was a layman, but that was soon surmounted. He was tonsured as a monk on 20 December 858, then ordained successively lector, sub-deacon, deacon and priest over the next four days. Finally, on Christmas day, he was consecrated patriarch of Constantinople. While this was an unashamedly political appointment of one of Bardas's personal friends, Photios became one of the greatest patriarchs, playing a role in almost every important development of the day. He was involved in the redecoration of churches after the victory of the iconophiles, preaching the sermon at the unveiling of the new mosaic of the Virgin and Child in Hagia Sophia in 867. When the Russians attacked Constantinople in 860 it was he who had helped to shore up morale by ordering that the Virgin's veil be paraded around the walls. Above all, he was part of a circle at the Byzantine court that thought out a new approach to dealing with the threat from the north.

At first sight men like Photios, whose education had largely consisted of reading the Greek classics and learning to write in the same highly formalised language, appear singularly unqualified for the task of understanding their neighbours. In their surviving writings they have a disturbing tendency to refer to all foreigners as 'barbarians'. For Photios the Russians who attacked in 860 were 'barbarians' and so was anyone who lived outside the borders of Byzantium or who failed to subscribe to the Christian faith as defined by the ecumenical councils. The word, however, was simply a literary convention inherited from the ancient Greeks: they had coined the word to denote anyone who could not speak Greek and whose languages sounded to them like incomprehensible 'ba-ba' noises. Educated Byzantines like Photios were not xenophobes or racists but were on the contrary well informed about the life and culture of the people around them. Photios had first-hand experience of the Abbasid caliphate, for before he had become patriarch he had been sent there on a diplomatic mission by the emperor. While in Baghdad he was reported to have made a number of firm friendships in spite of the 'dividing wall of worship'. After all, the Byzantines and the Arabs did have plenty in common: monotheistic religions derived from similar roots, large cities, a literary culture and admiration for the literature of ancient Greece.

On the other hand it was more difficult for the erudite courtiers of Constantinople to empathise with the Bulgars, the Russians and other peoples of the north. Their religion was polytheistic, with numerous angry gods who regularly needed appeasing. Krum dispatched several human sacrifices to the sky god Tangra when he was preparing his assault on the Land Walls of Constantinople. At Kiev there was a huge temple to six gods – of war, sky, light, nature and two for fertility – each represented by a carved wooden idol. The cities of Pliska and Kiev hardly compared with Constantinople or Baghdad: they were collections of wooden huts surrounded by an earthwork and wall, with the ruler's wooden hall in the middle, which was why Nikephoros I had been able to burn Pliska down so easily in 811. They had no literary culture, for their Slavonic language had no alphabet. The very appearance of these people must have been off-putting to cultured Byzantines and Arabs. A Bulgarian envoy who visited Constantinople was described as 'shorn in the Hungarian style, unwashed and girt with a bronze chain'. A kinder observer, the Arab traveller Ibn Fadlan, described the Russians as 'perfect physical specimens, tall as date palms, blond and ruddy', although he was critical of their neglect of personal hygiene and most alarmed when he witnessed a Russian funeral. According to custom, the deceased was cremated on a ship along with all his possessions – including a slave girl.

It is to the credit of Photios and his circle that they realised that the Slavs' very lack of civilisation was, in fact, a huge advantage and the key to neutralising the threat that they posed. For centuries, the Byzantines had been meeting wave after wave of migrating peoples in the Balkans and, when they could not defeat them, settling them in the empire, giving them land in return for military service and often inducing them to adopt Christianity and become integrated. The states centred on Kiev and Pliska were too large and powerful to be integrated but they could be enticed with aspects of Byzantine civilisation especially if it were subtly adapted to reflect something of their own culture.

Bardas and Photios were able to put this insight into practice when in 862 an unexpected messenger arrived in Constantinople. The envoy had been sent by the prince of Moravia, a Slav state with which, thanks to distance, the Byzantines had not had much to do in the past. He conveyed a request that missionaries be sent to Moravia to convert the people there to Christianity. The demand was not motivated by spiritual considerations alone. The small princedom was in imminent danger of extinction after the East Frankish king, Louis the German, had made an alliance with the Bulgarian khan. There was a real danger that Moravia would be divided between them and its prince was in need of an ally. Hence his request to Constantinople. Caesar Bardas and Photios decided to respond positively and agreed to the request. To lead the mission they chose one of Photios's associates and former pupils called Cyril, who was a teacher in the new university of Constantinople, along with his brother Methodios, who was then the abbot of a monastery in Asia Minor. Both were experienced missionaries, having both already taken part in an embassy to the Khazars. More importantly they were from Thessalonica, a city which had been surrounded by Slav settlements during the seventh-century invasions and where the Slav presence was still strong. The brothers had grown up bilingual in Greek and the local Slav dialect and so would, to some extent at least, be able to communicate directly with their hosts in Moravia. At some point, however, the decision was made that merely to preach to the Moravians in their own tongue was not enough: it would also be necessary to provide them with translations of the scriptures and the liturgy. Some previous missionaries had tried to do this and had transcribed Slavonic into Greek on Latin letters but that had not worked very well because there were many sounds in Slavonic for which Greek and Latin had no equivalent. In view of this difficulty, Cyril set about composing an alphabet for the Slavonic language, known as Glagolitic, which may have been developed from a script that already existed. After their arrival in Moravia, the brothers embarked on the work of translating the main offices of the liturgy, using Greek words to fill the gap where there was no equivalent in Slavonic. In the process they created a literary language, Old Church Slavonic, which was comprehensible throughout the Slav-speaking world.

As it turned out, the mission to Moravia was not a great success. The Byzantine missionaries faced the opposition of the Frankish clergy already at work there who strongly objected to the vernacular liturgy, on the grounds that only Latin, Greek and Hebrew were suitable languages in which to address the Almighty. When Louis the German invaded Moravia in 864 these opponents had military backing and the Byzantine missionaries were eventually forced to leave. Once they were gone, the pope wrote to the Moravian ruler insisting that the practice of celebrating the liturgy in Slavonic should cease. Nonetheless, the whole experience would prove very useful when it came to dealing with Byzantium's closer neighbour, Bulgaria.

* * *

Since the treaty of 816, the Byzantines and Bulgarians had remained at peace for decades. By the 860s, however, Byzantine self-confidence had returned with the spectacular victory over the Arabs at Poson and memories of the 811 debacle had faded. So when Caesar Bardas and his circle learned about the alliance that the khan of the Bulgars, Boris, had entered into with Louis the German with a view to partitioning Moravia, they took a hawkish line since it seemed to them that the alliance threatened to extend Frankish influence into an area that they considered to be rightfully theirs. In 864 they moved an army up to their frontier with Bulgaria while a fleet cruised along the Black Sea coast in support. The campaign could not have been more different from that of 811. As Krum had done before him, Boris decided not to hazard battle and offered to negotiate. His country happened to be in the middle of a severe famine and he realised that in the circumstances he would not be able to put up an effective resistance. This time the offer was accepted and no attempt was made to wreck Pliska as Nikephoros I had done. Indeed it would appear that there was no fighting or bloodshed whatsoever. The terms of the treaty are quite surprising too. The Byzantines made no demands for territory or tribute. All they asked was that Boris should renounce his Frankish alliance and accept the Christian faith. The following year, a bishop was duly dispatched from Constantinople to Pliska to baptise the khan, bringing with him a long letter from Photios full of rather patronising advice for the new convert. Work began on a church next to the khan's palace in Pliska.

All this might seem a rather meagre return for all the military preparations and expense that the Byzantines had been put to in mounting the campaign, but Bardas and Photios knew what they were doing. At Boris's baptism it was

1 Part of a monumental marble statue of Constantine from the Capitoline Hill in Rome.

2 Copper coin of Constantine from 327. On the reverse, the Chi-Rho symbol has been placed above a standard.

3 Silver ceremonial dish depicting Emperor Theodosius I and his court, probably dating from 388. Note the halo around the emperor's head.

4 Theodosius I in the imperial box in Constantinople's Hippodrome, clasping a garland to award to the winning charioteer.

5 The remains of the Serapeum in Alexandria, demolished by a Christian mob in 391.

6 A basilica-type church: Santa Maria Maggiore, Rome, built in around 440.

7 The church of St Symeon Stylites, Qalaat Semaan, Syria, erected after the hermit's death in 459.

8 The church of Sant'Apollinare Nuovo, Ravenna, completed in 504.

9 Justinian I, a mosaic from the church of San Vitale, Ravenna.

10 Justinian's cathedral of the Holy Wisdom, or Hagia Sophia.

11 The church of St Sergius and St Bacchus, one of thirty-three reconstructed during the reign of Justinian.

12 A gold coin, or nomisma, of Emperor Heraclius.

13 A reconstructed section of the Land Walls of Constantinople, which clearly shows their three-tier structure.

14 A modern icon of the Hodegetria, showing the Virgin gesturing towards Christ with her right hand.

15 The so-called 'Dark Church', Cappadocia, Asia Minor, one of many Byzantine underground structures in the region.

16 Mosaic of Virgin and Child from Hagia Sophia, Constantinople.

17 The church of Myrelaion monastery, Constantinople, built during the reign of Romanos I Lekapenos.

18 A Byzantine church at Ochrid, the town that became the seat of the archbishop of Bulgaria.

19 The cathedral of St Sophia, Kiev. The lower parts of the building date from its inception in 1037.

20 A statue of Prince Vladimir of Kiev, London.

21 The Great Lavra, Mount Athos.

22 The remains of Preslav, Bulgaria, capital of Tsar Symeon.

23 Interior of the monastery of Hosios Loukas, central Greece, dating from the eleventh century.

24 Empress Zoe, niece of Basil II, depicted in a mosaic from Hagia Sophia.

25 Emperor Constantine IX Monomachos in another mosaic from Hagia Sophia.

26 (below) Emperor Alexios I Komnenos on a coin made of billon dating from the earlier part of his reign.

27 Emperor John II Komnenos in a mosaic from Hagia Sophia.

28 The Pantokrator monastery, Constantinople, founded in 1136.

29 Mosaic of the Deesis, probably dating from the reign of Michael VIII Palaiologos, from Hagia Sophia.

30 The church of Hagia Sophia, Monemvasia, said to have been built during the reign of Andronicus II Palaiologos.

31 The church of St Saviour in Chora, Constantinople, which was restored and reconstructed in 1315–1316.

32 The town of Mistra in the Peloponnese, Greece, which flourished in the last years of the Byzantine empire.

33 Byzantium's legacy: St Sophia, Bayswater, London, completed in 1877.

made clear that the emperor Michael was his godfather and by accepting this Boris was effectively acknowledging the emperor's overlordship and aligning his country with Constantinople rather than with the kingdom of the East Franks. It was not that Boris's conversion was insincere or simply a political expedient. The khan seems to have been interested in Christianity long before the Byzantines forced his hand and he was later voluntarily to abdicate and become a monk. Nevertheless, his baptism was as much about international power politics as it was about personal religious belief. Consequently, Bardas and Photios can hardly have been so naive as to think that the ceremony would be the end of the matter. Once the immediate threat was removed Boris began to fear that he had yielded too much of his independence and undermined his authority among his own people. While some of his nobles had joined in him in adopting Christianity, others held to their traditional paganism. There were ominous rumblings of discontent over the abandonment of the Frankish alliance and the Byzantine clergy who arrived to evangelise the population were widely seen as a fifth column for the emperor in Constantinople whose aim of reincorporating Bulgaria back into his empire was well known. Within months of Boris's baptism a serious rebellion broke out and was only suppressed when Boris ruthlessly put to death fifty-two of the ringleaders, along with their children. Having survived the revolt, Boris still needed to show that adoption of Christianity from Constantinople did not entail acceptance of Byzantine overlordship. In less than a year of his conversion he was proposing that the new Bulgarian Church should not be under the jurisdiction of the patriarch of Constantinople but should have a patriarch of its own, and, when the Byzantine ecclesiastical authorities turned down the request, he cunningly sent some envoys to Rome, requesting that the pope send missionaries to replace those from Constantinople.

In the long term though, it was Byzantine influence that prevailed in Bulgaria. That was partly because Constantinople was nearer than Rome and at the end of the day it was in Bulgaria's interest to be on good terms with its powerful neighbour. In 870 Boris accepted a compromise whereby the Bulgarian Church would be headed not by a patriarch but by an archbishop who would enjoy a great deal of autonomy. More importantly, in 886 a new group of Byzantine clergy arrived at Pliska. These were the missionaries from Moravia who had been forced to leave after the invasion of Louis the German. They were all speakers of Slavonic and they brought with them the Old Church Slavonic liturgy and scriptures. Boris was delighted, for this seemed to be a version of Christianity that did not involve cultural and political submission to the emperor in Constantinople. He held discussions with their leaders, the

Byzantine monks Clement and Naum, and entrusted them with the task of preaching the new religion. While Naum remained in Pliska, Clement was dispatched to the western Macedonian town of Ochrid, where he had the unenviable task of converting and teaching the Slav population. Incredibly, by sheer hard work and force of personality, he succeeded. He preached to the local farmers but he also had new strains of fruit tree imported from the Byzantine provinces in the south to improve their lives. He trained a local clergy and may have been responsible for developing a simpler Slavonic script, the so-called Cyrillic, that was ultimately to replace Glagolitic. By the time Clement died in 916, the obscure lakeside settlement at Ochrid had become a centre for Slavonic Christian culture, a place where Greek texts were translated into Old Church Slavonic and icons painted in Byzantine style. Throughout Bulgaria the churches that were built to serve the new congregations were in the same square-domed style as those going up everywhere inside the Byzantine borders at the very same time. On the inside they were decorated with frescoes that reflected the theology of the icon, often the work of monastic artists brought in from Byzantium. Bulgaria had retained its independence but it had been absorbed into Byzantium's cultural orbit.

* * *

By the time that Ochrid began to develop as a cultural centre, Bardas and Photios were no longer at the helm. In fact, they had both fallen from power in rapid succession shortly after the baptism of Khan Boris, for while they had been immersed in the affairs of Moravia and Bulgaria a new candidate had emerged to exercise power on behalf of Michael III. Unlike Theodora, Theoktistos and Bardas, he was not from court circles but was a Thracian peasant called Basil who had come to Constantinople to seek his fortune. He found work in the house of Theophilos, a relative of Caesar Bardas, and rose to the position of chief groom. He was in attendance one evening when Bardas and Theophilos were entertaining some Bulgar envoys. As the guests became well lubricated with wine, they boasted that they had brought with them the champion wrestler of Bulgaria, to which Theophilos replied that his servant Basil would be more than a match for him. The tables were pushed back and the two wrestlers came to grips. To the astonishment of his audience, Basil lifted the gigantic Bulgar off his feet and dropped him with a resounding crash on to one of the tables.

The exploit soon came to the ears of Michael III and some time later, when Theophilos and Michael were out hunting together, Basil succeeded in recapturing the emperor's horse when it had bolted. Impressed by Basil's talents,

Michael took him into his own service and the two became constant companions. Michael took his new protégé out of the stables and promoted him to the rank of chamberlain. He even found an upper-class wife for him, one of his own cast-off mistresses. By doing so, Michael provided a leader for the faction at court which had always hated Bardas and were waiting for the moment to strike. In the spring of 866, Michael and Bardas sailed south down the Aegean with a fleet, with a view to recovering the island of Crete from the Arabs. One night, when the ships were at anchor and the emperor and caesar had landed to camp for the night, a group of conspirators, including Basil, rushed into the imperial tent where Bardas was poring over the accounts and hacked him to death. It is unlikely that all the conspirators expected that the recently promoted groom would be the one to step into Bardas's shoes, but they reckoned without the emperor. Within a month of Bardas's death Michael had adopted Basil as his son and had him crowned as co-emperor in a splendid ceremony in Hagia Sophia. In doing so, he signed his own death warrant. The co-emperor Basil and his supporters knew perfectly well that they would not be secure in his new dignity until Michael was out of the way. The following year, one September night, when Michael was lying drunk on his bed at the palace at St Mamas, the conspirators entered his room and killed him where he lay. Basil was proclaimed emperor the next morning, walking out from the Great Palace and scattering gold coins to the crowds as he passed. As Basil I, he was the founder of the Macedonian dynasty which was to rule Byzantium, directly or indirectly, until 1056.

The turn of events had left Photios very isolated, for he had been, from the first, the protégé of Bardas. After Basil's seizure of power, he had the courage to denounce Basil's murder of Michael and to refuse to allow the new emperor to take Holy Communion. Basil had, in any case, decided to get rid of him. Not only was he a relic of the previous regime but he was also an embarrassment. Many in the Byzantine Church, as well as the pope in Rome, still considered him to be a usurper because of the irregular way in which he had been appointed. So, in November 867, Basil removed him from office, imprisoned him in a monastery and reinstated the previous patriarch, Ignatios.

While Bardas and Photios might have been ousted from power, Basil I continued exactly their line of policy towards Byzantium's Slav neighbours, persuading Khan Boris to end his flirtation with Rome and to enter fully into the Byzantine orbit. During the 870s another Slav people, the Serbs, sent envoys to Constantinople asking for missionaries to be sent to convert their people. The Serbs were, of course, occupying land that had once belonged to Byzantium, but there was no prospect of recovering it, cut off as it was beyond the Bulgar khanate. Basil was therefore happy to send the missionaries and to accept the acknowledgement of theoretical overlordship which acceptance of the faith from Constantinople implied. With the missionaries went the Old Church Slavonic liturgy and scriptures, the Cyrillic and Glagolitic scripts, and the Byzantine styles of church architecture and decoration. Given that continuity of policy, it is perhaps not surprising that, during the 870s, Basil restored Photios to favour by making him tutor to his young son Leo. When Ignatios died in 877, Photios returned as patriarch of Constantinople and he remained in office until 886 when he was removed once more by Basil's son and successor, Leo VI (886–912), who does not seem to have felt any gratitude to his former tutor. It might have been some comfort to Photios, as he spent his last days in exile before his death in 893, that a kind of equilibrium now reigned in the Balkans and that he had played an important part in bringing it about.

* * *

The equilibrium, however, did not last. Even though Bulgaria had now been drawn into Byzantium's cultural orbit, that did not mean that the threat was neutralised. In fact, during the early tenth century the Bulgar khan Symeon came to present the gravest threat to Byzantium's existence since the Arab siege of 717–718. It was not that Symeon hated Byzantium. On the contrary, he loved and admired it. He knew Constantinople well because his father Boris had sent him there to be educated. He learned to speak Greek and had gained a first-hand acquaintance with the ceremonial and spectacle of the Byzantine court. He must have found Pliska a gloomy and unsophisticated place when he returned. In 893, after overthrowing his pagan brother Vladimir to become khan, Symeon set about modelling his country on Byzantium. Pliska was abandoned in favour of a new capital, Preslav, which was to be as impressive as Constantinople. Builders were brought in from the Byzantine provinces to construct a set of defensive walls and many fine churches. Of these, the most extraordinary was the great Golden Church, so called because its dome was said to be covered in gold leaf. There was a grand new palace for the khan from which Symeon issued decrees with a seal which portrayed him very much in the guise of a Byzantine emperor. Right next door was built a residence for a high ecclesiastical dignitary, for Symeon, like his father, hoped that Bulgaria would soon have its own patriarch and wanted to be ready when the moment came.

In 913, Symeon went to war with Byzantium when the annual tribute that he had extracted in an earlier conflict over trading rights was refused. Advancing to the Land Walls of Constantinople, he met little resistance, for the

Byzantines were in a period of internal political weakness. The emperor Constantine VII was a child of seven and a regency council was ruling in Constantinople. Contrary to normal practice Constantine's mother, Zoe, did not head the council. Her marriage to Constantine VII's father, Leo VI, had been deemed invalid by the Church because she was Leo's fourth wife and fourth marriages were forbidden in canon law. She was therefore kept out of the way and the regency was presided over by the patriarch, Nicholas Mystikos, a former pupil of Photios.

With the Bulgar army encamped outside the Land Walls, the patriarch saw no alternative to negotiation and he asked Symeon's terms. Interestingly, Symeon now acted just as Bardas and Photios had when they were victorious in 864. He did not demand treasure or territory but something more symbolic: that the young Constantine VII should marry one of his daughters and that he himself should be crowned emperor by the patriarch. The first demand was not unprecedented, for earlier Byzantine emperors, such as Leo III, had made similar marriage alliances with the Khazars. The second, however, was some- thing new. In 811, it had never occurred to Krum to make such a request when he had been in a similarly strong position. The insistence on an imperial coro- nation could only have come from a man who was so deeply imbued with Byzantine values that he wanted to promote himself to the top of the hierarchy of rulers. With no other options available to him, the patriarch agreed to both demands. Symeon dined with his future son-in-law Constantine VII, and some kind of coronation ceremony took place outside the walls of Constantinople. Symeon certainly considered himself to be an emperor from this moment on. He dropped the title of Khan and replaced it with that of Tsar, a Slavonic word derived from 'Caesar', and on his seals described himself as Basileus, using the Byzantines' own word for their emperor.

Having achieved his goal, Symeon withdrew to his own land, but he had underestimated the vagaries of Byzantine court politics. Within a few months of the coronation, the patriarch unwisely allowed the empress Zoe back into the palace because little Constantine had been pining for her. Once in the corridors of power, Zoe and her supporters ousted the patriarch and the empress took her rightful place at the head of the council. One of her first acts was to abrogate the terms agreed with Symeon. The betrothal of Constantine VII was broken off and Zoe's supporters put it around that the coronation had been invalid because the patriarch had at the last moment put aside the crown and put his own ecclesiastical headgear on Symeon's head: kneeling piously to receive the honour, the Bulgar ruler had somehow failed to notice. The mood in Constantinople was now very hawkish indeed and the empress decided on a military showdown to put an end to Symeon's pretensions once and for all. In the summer of 917, a large force composed of troops from the themes and the *tagmata* marched north and confronted Symeon near Anchialos on the Black Sea. The outcome was the perfect illustration of why the Byzantines generally avoided pitched battles. Although they initially prevailed, their Pecheneg allies failed to arrive because of a squabble between the commanders of the ships who were supposed to ferry them to the front. When a rumour spread that their commander had been killed, the Byzantine troops panicked and scattered, allowing the Bulgars to counter-attack and inflict a defeat every bit as catastrophic as that of 811, with virtually the entire Byzantine army being wiped out.

The victory left Symeon in control of the whole of the Balkans almost as far as the Gulf of Corinth, and free to announce that he was henceforth Emperor of the Romans and Bulgarians and that the archbishop of Bulgaria was now a patriarch. Like so many before him, however, Symeon's ambitions foundered on a combination of the defences of Constantinople and slick Byzantine diplomacy. He was well aware that he would never be able to make his claim on the empire a reality unless he took the Byzantine capital, but his victory at Anchialos had brought him no closer to that goal. Realising that he needed a fleet if he were to have any chance of taking Constantinople, Symeon sent envoys to the Arab Fatimids of Tunisia, proposing a joint attack. On the way home, however, the ship carrying the envoys was intercepted by a Calabrian vessel from southern Italy. Since they were subjects of the Byzantine emperor, the Calabrians sent their prisoners to Constantinople. There the Bulgar envoys were thrown into prison but the Arabs were treated as honoured guests. After being wined and dined they were sent home with a substantial present for the Fatimid ruler, effectively a bribe to persuade him to keep his fleet at home. Meanwhile Symeon's enemies to the north, the Serbs and the Croats, were paid to attack him and these tactics kept Symeon occupied until he was prepared to come to terms.

By then Byzantine court politics had taken another of their endless twists. The empress Zoe had fallen from power in 919 and had been replaced as guardian of the young emperor by the admiral of the fleet, Romanos Lekapenos. As we shall see in the next chapter, Lekapenos was not prepared merely to be head of the council and had himself crowned emperor, ruling alongside the legitimate Macedonian claimant, Constantine VII. It was Romanos who came to an agreement with Symeon in 924, betrothing his own granddaughter to Symeon's son Peter and recognising Symeon's title of tsar while insisting that it was a lesser honour than that of emperor of the Romans. When Symeon died suddenly of a heart attack three years later, the threat was finally removed, for his son Peter was by no means such an effective warrior. Nevertheless, the Byzantines were happy to call him tsar and send him an annual present of gold to keep him inactive.

From the Byzantines' point of view, even though Bulgaria continued to occupy territory that rightfully belonged to them, a *modus vivendi* had been arrived at which suited both sides. The Bulgars obtained security by aligning themselves with the strongest power in the region but had also asserted their independence from direct imperial rule. The Byzantines were able to vindicate their political theory that their emperors were the Roman emperors, placed on earth to guard over the whole Christian people. They now talked in terms of the emperor as the head of a family of princes. Within that family there was a strictly defined hierarchy. Obviously, the Byzantine emperor was at the top. Beneath him were his sons, followed by favoured nations who were allies and perhaps had adopted Christianity from Constantinople. Then there were friends who had an understanding with the emperor even if they were pagans, Muslims or Christians outside the Byzantine sphere of influence. The idea was developed that the Bulgars had a special place in the hierarchy. When Bulgar envoys visited Constantinople, they were given a very honourable place at table during banquets, although the placing tended to shift around depending on how cordial relations were at that moment. This careful hierarchy, backed up with ceremony and diplomatic gifts, gave the empire a kind of mystical aura in the much less sophisticated northern Balkans, providing it with a kind of spiritual authority that was every bit as compelling as military muscle.

* * *

There remained, however, the problem of the Russians. In the northern Balkans, the threat of force had helped to bring the Bulgars into the Byzantine orbit even if on two occasions, when the threat had been carried out, the consequences had been disastrous. No such threat could be levelled against the Russians, for their capital of Kiev was much too distant. In the wake of the 860 attack, efforts were made to convert them. In 874 an archbishop was sent to Kiev and Photios went so far as to boast that the Russians had become 'subjects and friends' of the empire. That proved to be very premature. There were some converts and by 944 there was a functioning Christian cathedral in Kiev, but, as long as the prince of Kiev himself remained a pagan, progress would inevitably be slow. The Byzantines made the most of the opportunity when, in 957, Olga, the widow of Prince Igor, who was ruling in Kiev as regent for her son Svyatoslav, paid a visit to Constantinople. A lavish welcome was laid on. Olga was wined and dined at a golden table with the imperial family, an open invitation to take a high place in the Byzantine hierarchy of princes. She was then baptised by the patriarch of Constantinople and departed laden down with the usual diplomatic gifts of gold and silks. In spite of all these efforts, Olga's conversion did not lead to that of the Russian people as a whole. Like the Bulgarian Khan Boris, she may have feared that taking Christianity from Constantinople would entail a loss of independence, and shortly after her visit, she invited in some Christian missionaries from Germany to Kiev. In any case, her son Svyatoslav was openly contemptuous of Christianity and once he was old enough to rule there was little prospect of further conversions.

It was under the next prince of Kiev, Svyatoslav's son Vladimir, that the conversion of the Russians finally took place. At first sight Vladimir seems a no more likely candidate for Christian conversion than his father, nor indeed for the canonisation which he subsequently achieved. By the time of his accession, he had already killed his own brother and boasted a harem of four wives and eight hundred concubines. Like his father before him, he was an enthusiastic pagan, erecting a huge new temple in Kiev, dedicated to six gods. As in the case of the Bulgar khan, Vladimir's conversion was impelled by both spiritual and political considerations. The spiritual motivations are suggested by a tale which is probably apocryphal but it may well contain a grain of truth. Around the year 987, Vladimir is said to have felt that it was time to adopt a more respectable religion for himself and his people than the paganism of his ancestors. Getting wind of this, several bands of missionaries arrived to urge him to convert to their faith. Vladimir was not particularly impressed with any of them. Islam sounded quite interesting, until it emerged that alcohol was forbidden. Judaism seemed to have little to recommend it since its adherents had lost their land and been scattered all over the world. The Christian missionaries from the pope seemed rather uninspiring, but the prince did have a long conversation with a priest who had been sent from Constantinople. Still wavering, Vladimir sent out ten trusted ambassadors to inquire into the major world religions with a view to making his choice on the basis of their report. Their first destination was the lands of some neighbouring Turks who had adopted Islam. They attended worship in a mosque but were not impressed: 'There is no happiness among them but instead only sorrow and a great stench. Their religion is not good.' The next stop was a cathedral in Germany, but Christian worship there failed to impress: 'We beheld no glory there.' Finally, the much-travelled envoys arrived in Constantinople where they were welcomed by the emperor who arranged for them to attend the liturgy in Hagia Sophia. This time it was different. The beauty and spectacle of the ceremony, performed against the backdrop of mosaics, frescoes and icons, stunned the visitors: 'We knew not whether we were in heaven or on earth. For on earth there is no such splendour or such beauty, and we are at a loss how to describe it. We only know that God dwells there among men . . .' An emotional response to the very visual nature of Byzantine religion, a result of the victory of the iconophiles, may well have influenced Vladimir's decision to accept Christianity from Constantinople.

Yet, in the end, it was probably hard-headed monetary and political considerations that played the major part in persuading Vladimir, because the Byzantines could provide certain very valuable material benefits. The Russians did not only prosper from the trade with Constantinople: their surplus warriors found lucrative employment there, and the association with a centre of wealth and power brought prestige that singled the rulers of Kiev out from their neighbours. In 987 the opportunity arose to enhance these benefits. The young Byzantine Emperor Basil II (976–1025) was facing a dangerous revolt by one of his generals, Bardas Phokas. Short of troops, Basil sent to Vladimir requesting assistance and so desperate was he that he added an additional inducement to the usual money payment: the hand of his sister Anna in marriage. Vladimir duly sent 6,000 soldiers and the rebellion was crushed. Vladimir could now marry Anna but there was a condition attached to the match: Vladimir must convert himself and his people to Christianity. It was a stiff condition but the prestige of marrying the sister of a reigning Byzantine emperor made it more the worthwhile, so Vladimir was duly baptised and dutifully dismissed the wives and concubines. In an autocratic society like medieval Russia, once the ruler had adopted Christianity, the rest was easy. Heralds were sent throughout Kiev to announce that anyone who did not go down to the river Dnieper the next day would risk seriously displeasing the prince. On the morrow, the banks were thronged, and the people, knowing what was expected of them, waded out into the water. Teams of specially imported Byzantine clergy then performed a mass baptism. Meanwhile, on the hill above the town, the great idol of Perun, god of the thunder and lightning, with its silver head and golden moustaches, was pulled down and dragged by horses to the river. Twelve men were appointed to beat it with sticks before it was tipped unceremoniously into the water where the current carried it along until it went over the falls and out of sight.

As in the case of Bulgaria, the conversion of the Russians did not mean a complete end of all hostilities between Russia and Byzantium. In 1043, Vladimir's son Iaroslav sent a fleet to attack Constantinople after a Russian merchant had been killed in a brawl there. In a repeat of the disaster of a hundred years before, Russians were worsted in the Bosporus and very few of their ships escaped. Thereafter, the two societies co-existed peacefully and the religious culture of Russia developed on very Byzantine lines. Immediately after Vladimir's conversion in 989 a new cathedral was founded in Kiev, dedicated to the Dormition of the Virgin Mary, followed by another in 1037, dedicated to the Holy Wisdom, clearly in imitation of Hagia Sophia in Constantinople. It took about twenty years to complete this church, which was built in Byzantine style, while the mosaics and frescoes inside were probably the work of Byzantine artists. Priests, sacred vessels, relics and icons were all imported from Constantinople. Inside the churches, the liturgy was celebrated in Slavonic from books written in the Cyrillic script.

Russians became frequent visitors to Constantinople and no longer just as merchants. As mercenaries in Byzantine service, they came to constitute the emperor's personal bodyguard, the Varangians, armed with their characteristic heavy axes. They also came as pilgrims, eager to venerate the numerous relics of the saints that could be found in the city's churches. The higher ranking ones might even be allowed to see the collection in the chapel of the Holy Virgin of the Pharos. For these pilgrims the experience of Constantinople was every bit as moving and inspiring as it supposedly had been for Vladimir's envoys back in the 980s. One of them, Dobrynia Jadrejkovich, who was later to become Archbishop Anthony of Novgorod, left an account of the visit he made in the year 1200. In meticulous detail, he listed all the mosaics, icons, frescoes and holy relics that he had seen. In Hagia Sophia he was shown what he earnestly believed were the tablets of the law brought down by Moses from Mount Sinai and some of the manna which dropped from heaven to the Israelites while they were in the desert. Not all the Russian pilgrims showed quite the level of respect due to the sacred place. One of them carved on to the marble balustrade in the gallery the words: 'Lord help thy slave Philip, Mikita's son, servant of Cyprian, metropolitan of Kiev and all Russia.' That, however, was all the damage that Philip did, unlike his ancestors of 870, and the very fact that he was there, that he could write and that there existed letters for him to write in, were all testimony of the integration of Russia into Constantinople's cultural orbit. In the end, Byzantium had conquered the north, not by force of arms but partly by patient diplomacy and partly by the sheer wonder of its visual and literary Christian culture. It was, perhaps, its greatest achievement.

CHAPTER SIX

Paths of Glory

We are from the Anatolikon Theme, of high-born Roman stock,
Our father is descended from the Kinnamades,
Our mother is a Doukas, of the family of Constantine . . .
Digenis Akritas

In the autumn of 904, the Byzantines were still reeling from a severe setback that they had suffered the previous summer. An Arab fleet had sailed from Syria in a daring raid on Thessalonica. The empire's second most important city was well fortified and had beaten off numerous Slav attacks by land in the past. The Arabs, however, found gaps in the defences on the seaward side, in spite of the heavy chain that had been strung across the harbour mouth. After sacking and plundering the city, they rounded up some 20,000 of the younger people and carried them off to Crete to be sold as slaves. The emperor and his advisers in the Great Palace would therefore have been cheered when news came in of a minor victory on the eastern frontier. A small Byzantine force had advanced on the ever-contested town of Germanikeia, where it had been attacked by the combined Arab forces of Mopsuestia and Tarsus. Heavily outnumbered, the Byzantines had fought bravely and driven off their enemies, returning safely home with the spoils of their raid.

The leader of the exploit was a man called Andronicus, who bore the surname of Doukas. Presumably one of Andronicus's ancestors had held the office of *doux*, or 'duke', and the name had stuck as a way of distinguishing his descendants. By the early tenth century, more and more prominent Byzantines were making use of a family name as well as a given one. Indeed the Doukas family was just one of a number of prominent clans that were emerging in Asia

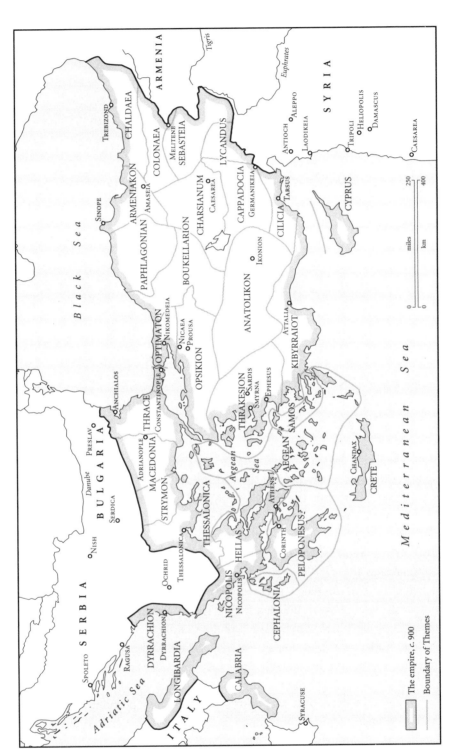

ARMENIA

Tigris

SYRIA

Euphrates

TREBIZOND

CHALDAEA

COLONAEA

MELITENE
SEBASTEIA

ANTIOCH
ALEPPO

TRIPOLI
HELIOPOLIS
DAMASCUS

LAODIKEIA

CAESAREA

SINOPE

ARMENIAKON

AMASEIA

LYCANDUS

CHARSIANUM

CAPPADOCIA

CAESAREA

GERMANIKEIA

TARSUS

CYPRUS

PAPHLAGONIAN

BOUKELLARION

CILICIA

Black Sea

IKONION

ANATOLIKON

ATTALIA

KIBYRRAIOT

OPTIMATON

NIKOMEDEIA

NICAEA
PROUSA

OPSIKION

ANCHIALOS

THRACE

Constantinople

THRAKESION

SARDIS
SMYRNA

EPHESUS

SAMOS

PRESLAV

ADRIANOPLE

MACEDONIA

Danube

BULGARIA

SERDICA

STRYMON

AEGEAN

Aegean
Sea

CHANDAX

Mediterranean Sea

NISH

THESSALONICA

CRETE

SERBIA

OCHRID

THESSALONICA

HELLAS

ATHENS

CORINTH

PELOPONESUS

SPOLETO

RAGUSA

DYRRACHION

NICOPOLIS

NICOPOLIS

DYRRACHION

CEPHALONIA

LONGIBARDIA

CALABRIA

Adriatic Sea

SYRACUSE

ITALY

miles   250

km   400

The empire, c. 900

Boundary of Themes

4 The Byzantine empire c. 900

Minor where they owned considerable tracts of land and vied with each other to mount successful raids against their Arab neighbours. Their ethos of perpetual warfare to and fro across the border gave rise to a vivid folklore telling of the exploits of these clans that eventually coalesced into an epic poem called *Digenis Akritas*, which celebrates the daring deeds of its eponymous hero in his wars against the infidel. The son of a Muslim emir and the Christian daughter of a Byzantine general, Digenis possesses all the chivalric virtues of a knight of the Round Table: loyalty to the emperor, deep religious faith and unswerving fidelity to his friends. He also has superhuman strength and can tear a lion in two with his bare hands. He defeats all his enemies and then lives out his life in retirement in a luxurious palace that he has built beside the river Euphrates. His real-life counterparts might not have had quite Digenis's strength or virtue but they too did well out of their raids into Syria.

This emerging military aristocracy could get away with these attacks because the old enemy, the Abbasid caliphate of Baghdad, was entering a period of decline. The days when the caliph himself would lead powerful raids across the Taurus mountains were gone, for there were more pressing problems nearer home. Rival Arab factions were constantly raising and dethroning caliphs and, to secure their position, reigning caliphs relied on Turkish slaves from Central Asia whom they organised into a palace guard. But, although they were completely loyal to the caliph and protected him from assassination or deposition, they did not solve the problem. The Turks were a resented minority among the majority Arab population and, as they were so completely dependent on the caliph for their wages and livelihood, they had to ensure that the present incumbent was someone who would be favourable to them and look after their interests. Consequently they had a habit of regularly overthrowing undesirable caliphs and replacing them with someone more acceptable. To political instability was added economic decline. The wealth of Mesopotamia had been based on a sophisticated system of irrigation agriculture but between 869 and 883 the African labourers who worked it were in revolt. Large numbers of troops had to be diverted to deal with the uprising, and the irrigation system and the cultivation that depended on it suffered immense damage. By 930 the caliph was virtually bankrupt and unable to pay his armies.

Weakness at the centre of the caliphate inevitably led to separatism on the periphery, exacerbated by the religious differences. In 909 an autonomous but pro-Abbasid regime in North Africa was toppled by the Fatimids, Shi'ite Muslims who did not accept the claims of the Abbasids to be the descendants of the Prophet and the rightful leaders of the faithful. It was their ruler who had alarmed the Byzantines by negotiating with Symeon of Bulgaria. The weakness

of the caliphate also radically altered the situation on Byzantium's eastern frontier. The defence of the area, and attacks on Byzantine territory, were now in
the hands of governors appointed from Baghdad. As time went by these governors became emirs, effectively independent of the caliph. By the 920s the main
power opposing the Byzantines in the east was the Hamdanids, whose independent emirate was based at Mosul and later at Aleppo. The Hamdanids were
wealthy and warlike but they could not bring the same resources to bear against
the Byzantines as the caliphate had at the height of its power.

While the rulers of Byzantium were distracted by the struggle with Symeon
of Bulgaria, it was the warlords of Asia Minor that took advantage of the opportunity in the east. The man who led the counter-attack was John Kourkouas,
whose family held land around Dokeia in the Armeniakon theme. In 919 he had
helped Romanos Lekapenos to seize power in Constantinople and his reward
was to be appointed to the relatively new post of Domestic of the Schools
(*Scholai*). This new office of commander reflected the new kind of army that
was developing in response to the opportunity. As Byzantium moved from the
defensive to the offensive on the eastern frontier, the theme armies of old were
increasingly obsolete. They were designed to parry Arab thrusts into Asia
Minor, not to carry the war into enemy territory beyond the Taurus mountains.
Their soldiers were part-time farmers, always with an eye on their livelihoods at
home. Instead, the *tagmata*, the regiments of permanent troops founded by
Constantine V, were being expanded. These soldiers were paid salaries from the
imperial treasury rather than being given land, and the improving economic
situation and greater tax returns enabled more of them to be enrolled. Increasing
numbers of those recruited into this elite regiment had been born outside the
Byzantine empire, particularly Russians, but even Arabs appear in Byzantine
service. Anemas, son of the emir of Crete, became a member of the imperial
bodyguard and died fighting for the emperor in Bulgaria in 971. The employment of what might be called mercenaries was not a mark of weakness or decline
but of the economic revival that enabled the Byzantines to buy in the best troops,
and of their extraordinary ability to absorb outsiders and to turn their bellicosity
to their own advantage. The role of the *tagmata* was changing too. They had
originally been based around Constantinople, partly as a precaution against
revolts by *strategoi* of the themes, but now they were moved out to the eastern
borderlands where they would be of more use. The Domestic of the *Scholai* was
in command of this elite force, so that Kourkouas had effective control of the
imperial armies of the east and he far outranked the *strategoi* of the themes.

During the 920s, Kourkouas mounted regular raids against the Arab towns
along the border, but he had his eye on one in particular: Melitene, which for

years had provided the Arabs with a safe haven to the west of the Taurus mountains for their raids into Asia Minor. In May 934, after Kourkouas had invaded
and subjugated the surrounding area and subjected the city to a close siege, the
governor of Melitene surrendered and opened his gates. Kourkouas handed the
city and the area round about to the emperor Romanos, who kept it as an imperial estate rather than parcelling it out to soldiers as had been done in the past.
It was more valuable now for its tax revenue, which could be used to pay more
elite troops. With Melitene secure, Kourkouas led his troops beyond the
Byzantine borders on raids into Syria. In 943, he surrounded the city of Edessa,
which lay deep in Arab territory. Realising that no relieving force was likely to
come in the near future, the inhabitants were ready to negotiate. To purchase
their safety, they offered to hand over the precious Mandylion, the ancient
cloth on which Christ himself was said to have left his image. This Kourkouas
was only too happy to accept and he withdrew over the Taurus mountains. The
relic was carried triumphantly into Constantinople in August 944 and placed
in the chapel of the Holy Virgin of Pharos. To the Byzantines, obtaining the
Mandylion was an even greater victory than Melitene. Kourkouas was the hero
of the hour and someone even wrote his biography, running to eight volumes
in length. There were some people, however, who looked on Kourkouas's
success with alarm. For while victories were being won on the eastern frontier,
events in the Great Palace in Constantinople had taken their own turn.

* * *

By the early tenth century, bloody and discreditable though its origins were,
the Macedonian dynasty had been accepted as the legitimate ruling house. So
secure was it that it survived the minority of Constantine VII, the question
mark over his legitimacy and the catastrophic defeat inflicted by Khan Symeon
of the Bulgars at Anchialos in 917. That was partly because three generations
had now passed since Basil I had seized power in 867 but also thanks to a delib-
erate policy on the part of successive emperors to make their office hereditary.
Genteel arrangements like that which brought Maurice to power through
marriage in 582 were all very well but they left too much to chance. It would be
safer to have the designated successor in place long before the previous incumbent died. As a way of making it clear who was to succeed, from the time of
Constantine V a special room had existed in the Great Palace of Constantinople
with windows that looked out on to the Bosporus. Its walls were faced with a
kind of marble known as porphyry, which could only be quarried in one remote
location in Egypt. It was deep purple – a colour associated with imperial power
since Roman times – and flecked with white crystals. The room which it

adorned was set aside as the place where the empress would give birth. That way the emperor's son could be designated a porphyrogenitos, or 'born in the purple', and as time went by the people of Constantinople in particular became convinced that any true emperor should have first seen the light of day in that room. Constantine VII, although he was the product of a fourth marriage, was still a porphyrogenitos and so, when the ambitious admiral of the fleet, Romanos Lekapenos, staged his coup in 919, he could not just dispose of him, as Phokas had of Maurice or Heraclius of Phokas. Instead, Romanos trod gingerly. Having secured Constantinople, he married his daughter to Constantine VII, thus linking his family to the legitimate dynasty. Some eighteen months later, he had himself proclaimed caesar, a lesser dignity than that of emperor. Only in December 920 was Romanos crowned emperor in Hagia Sophia and even then he did not supplant Constantine VII but reigned alongside him. Doubtless, Romanos did not expect this state of affairs to last forever. In due course, his family, the Lekapenoi, would replace the Macedonians and he prepared for that day by having his own son Christopher crowned too. But for the time being, portraits of both emperors appeared on the gold coinage, standing side by side and holding a cross. Romanos saw to it that his portrait was bigger than that of Constantine.

Expert political operator though he was, Romanos had miscalculated. His dynasty was not destined to replace the Macedonians. Everything unravelled at the end of 944. Romanos's sons, tired of waiting, overthrew their father and exiled him to a monastery. They planned to treat Constantine VII the same way and then secure the imperial crown for themselves, but when news of these developments reached the streets, the fierce attachment felt by the people of Constantinople for the Macedonian dynasty brought them rushing from their homes to intervene. An angry crowd gathered outside the Brazen Gate of the Great Palace, demanding to see that the emperor Constantine was safe and sound. Only when Constantine appeared bare-headed and recognisable did they disperse. Foiled, the Lekapenos brothers could only wait helplessly as Constantine gathered his supporters and then had them rounded up and sent into exile. Thereafter, from 945 until his death in 959, Constantine VII ruled alone and the Macedonian dynasty endured. It was Constantine himself who pronounced Romanos I's political epitaph. He may have been a successful soldier and diplomat who deserved credit for fending off the threat of Tsar Symeon but in other ways he was 'a common, ignorant fellow, and was not from among those who have been bred up in the palace'.

* * *

The survival of the Macedonian dynasty ensured the continuation of that particular outlook and mentality which had in the previous century been held by Photios, Bardas and their circle. Its proponents were usually classically educated, probably in the university in the Magnavra hall of the Great Palace, but they were by no means detached and other-worldly scholars. Their approach to the defence of the empire was, on the contrary, extremely practical. Placed as it was in the path of waves of migrating peoples, Byzantium could not purchase security by military force alone. Instead it needed to manage its enemies in a detached fashion, playing one off against another and integrating them where possible into the empire's ethos and religion. War was a distasteful necessity, to be waged only as a last resort. This outlook was codified and encapsulated in a number of handbooks compiled at the Byzantine court during the reigns of Leo VI and Constantine VII. The so-called *Taktika* of Leo VI sums up the deep distrust of all-out war and suggests the wisest alternatives:

> It is well to harm the enemy by deceit, by raids, by hunger, and to hurt them for a long time by means of very frequent assaults and other actions. You should never be enticed into a pitched battle. For the most part we observe that success is a matter of luck rather than proven courage ... You will achieve frequent victories against your enemies without actual war by making use of money. When they have other enemies lying in wait for them somewhere, an offer of money should be persuasive in getting this people to wage war on your adversaries.

Those alternatives were spelled out even more clearly in Constantine VII's own *De Administrando Imperio*, a handbook of diplomatic practice written for his son, Romanos. The handbook provides a survey of the peoples who dwelt on the empire's borders and offers advice on the best way to keep them in check. In the case of the Russians and Bulgars, the best strategy was to keep the Pechenegs on an annual retainer so that they could be called upon to attack the Bulgars across the Danube or to close the river Dnieper, the Russian route to the Black Sea, whenever the need arose. If, on the other hand, the Pechenegs were ever to turn on Byzantium, their neighbours the Uzes could be induced to attack them. Similarly, the Khazars were traditional allies but, if they ever presented a threat, then the Uzes and the Alans should be stirred up against them. These diplomatic manoeuvrings were only part of the picture. For Constantine VII and his circle, it was very important that friendly elements in the surrounding nations be encouraged and fostered and the best way to do that was to invite them to lavish receptions in Constantinople. The envoys of the Umayyad caliph of Spain, Abd al-Rahman III, who was at odds with his Abbasid rival in Baghdad, were received in 946 in the Magnavra hall which had been specially festooned with silks for the occasion. An impressive welcome was extended to Olga, the widow of Igor of Kiev, who was thinking of converting to Christianity, when she visited in 957: she was received to the sound of organ music and bags of silver coins were distributed to her retinue. Constantine VII lovingly described these occasions in his handbook on imperial ceremonial. Such largesse also had its role in military campaigns. Constantine counselled that expensive silk garments should always be carried with the army so that they could be given as gifts once the fighting was over and the treaty made.

This practical, if unheroic, outlook of the educated elite of the capital had already proved its worth, helping to bring about the development of the Slav alphabet and liturgy, the conversion of the Bulgars and the Serbs, and the widening of Byzantium's cultural orbit beyond the empire's frontiers. On the other hand, it did tend to promote a very Constantinople-centred view of the world. It was developed and held by a small group based in the Great Palace who shared a common educational background. For them Constantinople was the only centre of authority, learning and culture in the empire, and they often looked with well-bred disdain on those who hailed from outside its walls. Those members of the circle who found themselves posted to distant regions of the empire bemoaned their fate and longed for the day when they could return to the bright lights of the capital. A clergyman who was sent to be bishop of the small town of Synada in Asia Minor around 1000 complained bitterly in a letter to the emperor Basil II about the basic conditions that he had to endure, with a lack of good wine high on his list of grievances:

> We do not grow olive trees; nobody grows them in the Anatolikon theme. Our region knows no viniculture for we are situated at a considerable alti-tude. Instead of wood, we use zarzakon, a specially prepared dung, a thing most vile and evil smelling for fuel; and all things needed by people, whether healthy or ailing, we import either from the Thrakesion Theme, from Attaleia or from Constantinople itself.

Such an outlook, and the erudite pragmatism of Constantine VII's handbooks, could not contrast more strongly with the aggressive ideology of the frontier and the military clans as expressed in *Digenis Akritas*. The divide even extended to grammar and vocabulary: while Constantine VII wrote in the archaic and stilted idiom of the Magnavra palace university, the epic poem was expressed in homely, everyday Greek. In short, by the mid tenth century, a certain gulf had started to grow up between capital and provinces. The provincial warlords were extremely mistrustful of Constantinople and the imperial court there, with its elaborate ceremonial and strict hierarchy. It was, as one nobleman counselled his son, to be avoided like the plague. Much better to stay out in his powerbase in the provinces:

> If you have your own land, fortified places or estates of which you are the owner and governor, do not let yourself by seduced by gold, by honorific titles or by great promises of the emperors . . . For in the eyes of the emperor and of all, you will remain a considerable personage, honoured, esteemed and noble, so long as you and your children and the children of your children remain in possession of your land, and of your power.

The Macedonian emperors and their circle of advisers in Constantinople felt, in turn, considerable distrust of the warlords of Asia Minor, in spite of their victories on the frontier. Just as Belisarius had been feared by Justinian and the *strategoi* of the themes by Leo III and Constantine V, so in the early 900s successful generals like Andronicus Doukas and John Kourkouas were looking suspiciously like potential usurpers. With immense wealth from their estates in Asia Minor and in command of large armies which would follow wherever they led, they were in a position to topple the Macedonians any time they chose. Those suspicions were well founded because it was not long before a provincial magnate made the attempt.

When the seven-year-old Constantine VII had succeeded in 913, Constantine Doukas, the son of Andronicus, had moved his troops up to the capital. Admitted by night through the Land Walls into the city by his supporters on the inside, he had marched in a torchlit procession towards the Hippodrome, his men proclaiming him emperor as they went. When they reached the gates of the stadium, however, they found them locked and barred. The people of Constantinople, ever loyal to the Macedonian dynasty, had moved to bar the usurper's way. Doukas's master of horse, confident that he could clear the rabble easily enough, led a squad forward to prise the gates apart, but no sooner had a gap opened than a spear came flying out and killed him on the spot. Foiled, Doukas switched his attention to the Brazen Gate and tried to break into the Great Palace. There he encountered a squad of palace guards who put up a stiff resistance. Doukas cantered around encouraging his troops but he forgot that he was not out on the plains of Anatolia: his horse lost its footing on the cobblestones and threw him to the ground. As he lay unconscious, someone sliced off his head. Slippery ground had saved the dynasty, but Doukas had come uncomfortably close. It was only a matter of time before someone else made another attempt.

When the coup came in 919, however, it was not a member of a prominent military clan who seized power: although admiral of the fleet, the usurper Romanos Lekapenos was the son of an Armenian peasant. Once in power, not only did Romanos keep the Macedonian dynasty in place, he was also something of a poacher turned gamekeeper. Neither a military aristocrat like Doukas nor one of the highly educated elite of the capital, he could therefore take a dispassionate view of the relations between the capital and the provinces and reach his own conclusions. While at first he honoured and promoted John Kourkouas following his run of victories in the east, he ultimately became suspicious of him. A few months after Kourkouas's triumphant return from Edessa in 944, he was abruptly dismissed as Domestic. It was not just the Kourkouas family that worried Romanos. He had noticed that many of the powerful families of Asia Minor were building up very large landed estates, partly by buying up the land from the local peasantry. The more land they acquired, the greater their powerbases became, and Romanos took steps to stop them. In 922 he introduced a law designed to prevent the lands of poor peasants in Asia Minor falling into the wrong hands, ordering that, if for some reason a peasant wished to sell his lands, his relatives and neighbours were to be given first option to purchase. Only if these were unwilling or unable to buy was anyone else to be allowed to. The law did not work well. There was a hard winter and a famine in 927–928 and during that time many aristocrats bought up the land of desperate peasants very cheaply since no one else could. Romanos responded with a new law which was enacted in 934 and which ordered that land that had been bought for less than half the just price was to be returned without compensation. If bought for more than half its value, the land was to be returned and the purchase price repaid over a period of five years. The same concern was probably partly behind Romanos's decision, after Kourkouas took Melitene in 934, that the town and the area round about should become imperial property: he did not want it to be quietly usurped by the local warlords.

Much as he disliked his father-in-law, after the downfall of the Lekapenoi Constantine VII continued the policy. He reinforced Romanos's legislation with a series of laws of his own, lamenting that 'We have received word of the destitution and indigence among the people in the Anatolikon theme and of their oppression at the hands of the powerful . . .' It was probably Constantine too who reversed what for centuries had been one of the prime characteristics of the theme system, the merging of civil and military authority. Henceforth the *strategos* was only to command the army, and civil matters were placed in other hands. Since members of the powerful families had come to monopolise the office of *strategos*, it was another way of clipping their wings. The irony was that, just as Romanos I and Constantine VII were enacting these stern measures, they also depended on the very same families who were objects of their fears both to defend the empire's borders and to keep them on their thrones. That need ensured that not only were the military clans not suppressed, but that one of them would rise to a position of dominance.

* * *

When Constantine VII had overthrown the sons of Romanos Lekapenos in January 945, he had not relied solely on the support of the people of Constantinople but had been careful to surround himself with prominent military men. One of them was a certain Bardas Phokas whose family, like those of Doukas and Kourkouas, was a wealthy Asia Minor clan that had for centuries battled it out with the Arabs along the border. Phokas was a useful man to have around in a crisis. He had distinguished himself in the defeat of the Russian attack on Constantinople in 941 when he had led a troop of horsemen in a charge on some Russians who came ashore to forage, and had wiped them out to a man. Now it was Phokas and the other soldiers who struck the decisive blow for Constantine VII – it was they who arrested the Lekapenos brothers while they were dining in the Great Palace. Naturally Constantine rewarded his supporters well once he was firmly in sole control. The post of Domestic of the *Scholai* went to Bardas Phokas while his sons Nikephoros, Leo and Constantine became *strategoi* of the Anatolikon, Cappadocian and Cilician themes. As a result of these appointments, the Phokas family effectively controlled the Byzantine army in the east.

As it turned out, Bardas Phokas was something of a disappointment in his new position and his tenure of the office of Domestic was marked by a minor reverse that he suffered near Germanikeia in 954. He accidentally ran into a raiding party commanded by the Hamdanid emir of Aleppo, Sayf al-Dawla, and was unable to keep control of his troops, most of whom fled. Bardas himself would have been captured had his bodyguard not rallied around him and hustled him away. In the melee he received a deep cut on the forehead and he carried the scar for the rest of his long life. His son Constantine, *strategos* of the Cilician theme who was present at the engagement, did not manage to escape and died in captivity in Aleppo some years later. Bardas's reputation never really recovered from the setback. Someone quipped that he was a fine commander – provided he was serving under someone else. The fortunes of the Phokas family were to be revived, however, by Bardas's other sons

Nikephoros and Leo, both very able soldiers indeed. Two years after his father's defeat, Leo intercepted Sayf al-Dawla's army as it returned from a raid, someone having provided him with details of the route it would take. Trapping the Arabs in a narrow pass, he massacred large numbers of them. His brother Nikephoros, who replaced his father as Domestic of the *Scholai*, also had a run of successes against the Hamdanids, but his reputation was made further to the west when he pulled off the greatest Byzantine military success for a century.

Ever since a group of Arab corsairs had invaded and occupied Crete in the 820s, the Byzantines had yearned to get the island back. Not only was it a wealthy and fertile island, but thanks to its geographical position it was the ideal launch pad for seaborne raids against Byzantine coasts and islands in the Aegean, something of which the Arabs had taken full advantage. Several attempts had been made to reverse the occupation but all had ended in miserable failure. The commanders of the failed expeditions had not been able to overcome the logistical challenge of ferrying a large enough army by sea, along with its horses, then of landing it safe and ready to fight. After Constantine VII died in 959, his son and successor Romanos II (959–963) decided that a renewed attempt must be made and entrusted the task to his Domestic, Nikephoros Phokas.

In the spring of 960, Nikephoros assembled his army at Phygeia to the south of Ephesus. Morale was good, for Nikephoros was an extremely popular commander with a reputation for looking after his men. On campaigns, he shared their privations and hardships. Once, having given orders for the construction of a fortress on a hill, Nikephoros himself carried the first heavy building block up the slope, ordering every man in the army to do the same. No wonder that his troops adored him and nicknamed him the 'White Death of the Saracens'. He was hardly a charismatic figure though. Short and stooped, with bushy black eyebrows and a hooked nose, he was described by one of his enemies as 'someone you would not want to meet in the dark'. Nor was Nikephoros one to purchase popularity by sharing the rough jests of his soldiers. On the contrary, even in a society where religious belief was taken so seriously, Nikephoros stood out for his piety. He was given to praying all night standing up and would always sleep on the floor on the night before receiving the sacrament. The calling of a soldier was, he thought, an unworthy one and he longed to become a monk. Indeed, he planned to take monastic vows as soon as the campaign on Crete was brought to a successful conclusion. While the preparations for the invasion were going ahead, he sailed across the Aegean to the promontory of Mount Athos in northern Greece, where he sought out the spiritual counsel of the reclusive hermit, Athanasius.

For all his religious ardour, Nikephoros had not neglected his military duties. He had thought very deeply about tactics and strategy: indeed he had even written a book on the subject. He put his knowledge and experience into his preparations for the Cretan expedition. Everything was ready and the army was embarked on to the waiting ships. The approach of such a large fleet could hardly have been kept secret and the Arabs were waiting on the coast, ready to attack when the invaders were at their most vulnerable as they disembarked. Nikephoros, however, had planned for this precise situation. He had equipped his vessels with ramps so that once close inshore these could be lowered and both the infantry and cavalry could disembark fully equipped, mounted and ready to fight. The Arabs were so astonished that they held back and it was the Byzantines who launched the assault, driving the Arabs back behind the walls of their main town, Chandax. During the winter of 960–961, the Byzantines were able to occupy most of the island, leaving the Arabs closely surrounded and besieged in Chandax.

Inevitably, once news of the success reached the Great Palace, it received a mixed reception. Naturally there was jubilation that it looked as if Crete was going to be retaken, but rumours also started to fly that the great general would use his victory to make a bid for the throne. The emperor's chief minister, the eunuch Joseph Bringas, who dominated every administrative department, was particularly apprehensive and urged Romanos II to recall his dangerous subordinate. Fortunately, Romanos did not act on Bringas's advice and in March 961 the walls of Chandax were breached in a full-scale assault and Crete was returned to Byzantine rule.

After ensuring that the newly conquered island was garrisoned and secure, Nikephoros returned to Constantinople with part of the fleet. He made a triumphant entry into Constantinople and the spoils of the victory, ranging from armour and shields to gold coins and carpets, were put on public display in the Hippodrome. Part of the proceeds was dedicated to founding a new monastery, known as the Great Lavra, on Mount Athos under the superintendence of the hermit Athanasius. Nikephoros may even have been planning to join the brethren there but he was given no peace to do so for Romanos II almost immediately posted him to the eastern frontier. While a large portion of the Byzantine army had been absent in Crete, Sayf al-Dawla had taken advantage by raiding into Asia Minor. Nikephoros's brother Leo had intercepted him and driven him off but now Nikephoros arrived to extract full punishment. A full-scale invasion of Syria went ahead and the Hamdanid capital of Aleppo itself was taken and sacked before the Byzantines withdrew.

The energy and effectiveness of the Phokas brothers could hardly have been more in contrast with the state of affairs in the capital. While his father had been most at home in a library, the young Romanos II was most interested in having a good time with his circle of friends. He was encouraged in this by his chief minister, Bringas, who preferred to have the emperor out of the way so that he could run matters himself. That might well have been a costly mistake. During Lent in 963, Romanos went hunting in the countryside outside Constantinople but was clearly very unwell when he came back. Within a few days he was dead, the victim of some kind of seizure. The sudden demise of the young emperor had not been expected or planned for. The patriarch of Constantinople, Polyeuktos, at once stepped in and declared that Romanos's sons were now legitimate joint emperors, but Basil II was only a small child and Constantine VIII still an infant. The empire was back in the same situation that it had been in 913. The widow of the late emperor, Theophano, became regent along with the patriarch and Bringas, but everyone knew that in this situation it was almost inevitable that some military strong man would attempt to seize power as Romanos Lekapenos had in 919. The empress deeply disliked and mistrusted Bringas and clearly thought that if there was going to be a military takeover, she ought to be on the winning side.

It would seem that Theophano sent a message to Nikephoros Phokas, begging him to come to Constantinople. He arrived within a month of Romanos's death, bringing with him the booty from the sack of Aleppo which he ostentatiously deposited in the public treasury. For the next few weeks, nothing happened. The empress Theophano continued to act as regent for her sons and Bringas was left to run the administration. Nikephoros Phokas lived quietly at his house in Constantinople while Bringas eyed him warily. One evening in early summer, as Bringas was preparing to sit down to dinner, there was a knock on the door of his house and it was announced that the distinguished general himself was paying a visit, accompanied by only one bodyguard. Bringas was so astonished that he could think of no course of action other than ushering Phokas into a side room for a private conversation. There, Phokas showed the eunuch the hair shirt that he was wearing under his tunic and assured him that he had no desire whatever to be an emperor, only a monk. Bringas seems actually to have believed the story and even apologised to Phokas for thinking ill of him. A few days later, the general left the capital to rejoin his army.

It is quite possible that Phokas had been genuine in his protestations but Bringas overplayed his hand. Repenting of what he considered with hindsight to have been his gullibility in accepting Nikephoros's assurances, Bringas sent secret letters to some of Nikephoros's subordinates, including the general's nephew John Tzimiskes, promising rewards and promotion if they would arrest their commander. He had reckoned without the loyalty that his enemy enjoyed among his troops: Tzimiskes and the others simply passed the letters to Phokas. His hand forced, Nikephoros allowed himself to be proclaimed emperor by his troops at Caesarea on 2 July 963 and then began the march on Constantinople. The tidings of his approach caused pandemonium. The usurper's father Bardas, along with other relatives, fled to sanctuary in Hagia Sophia, while Leo, dressed as a workman, managed to escape from the city through one of the water pipes and rushed to join his brother. Nikephoros had, however, sent a bishop on ahead of him, armed with letters to the patriarch and leading citizens, promising that if they accepted him as emperor, he would safeguard the rights of the young representatives of the Macedonian dynasty. There were many at court, not just the empress, who considered that the best way forward would simply be to accept Nikephoros as emperor. Prominent among the eunuchs was Basil Lekapenos, an illegitimate son of the late Romanos I, who had been castrated as a child to ensure that he did not later attempt to seize the throne. Enrolled among the administrators of the Great Palace, he had long been a rival of Bringas. Lekapenos armed 3,000 members of his own household and launched an attack on Bringas's house and those of his supporters and it was Bringas's turn to flee for sanctuary. On 16 August, Nikephoros arrived by ship and made his entry into the city through the Golden Gate in the Land Walls to shouts of 'Receive the divinely crowned Nikephoros!' While his partisans seized Bringas and hustled him off into exile, the great general rode to Hagia Sophia for his coronation as Nikephoros II (963–969). A month later he legitimised his position by marrying Theophano and thus becoming the stepfather of her two boys. The arrangement was as it had been under Romanos I Lekapenos, with Nikephoros II and Basil II both displayed on the coinage but with the older man as the undisputed ruler of the empire.

* * *

With one of the leading families of the military aristocracy now in control of the empire, the cautious tactics of Photios and Constantine VII were firmly off the agenda. The war in the east was prosecuted relentlessly. During 965, Tarsus was captured and Cyprus, which for centuries had been jointly ruled by the Arabs and Byzantines, was now returned to sole Byzantine rule. The Hamdanid emirate of Aleppo was forced to accept the overlordship of the emperor and in 969 the great city of Antioch, which had been lost to the Arabs three hundred years earlier, was returned to Byzantine rule. These campaigns were conducted in a fervent religious atmosphere, reminiscent of Heraclius's Persian war. Nikephoros II even went so far as to demand that the patriarch should declare that soldiers who died fighting against the Arabs were martyrs for the faith, although he did not get his way. The run of victories cemented Nikephoros's almost legendary status in the army and inhabitants of Asia Minor seem to have thought highly of him too. During his reign a fresco was painted in a church in Cappadocia, showing him with Theophano and his father and brother, with an inscription: 'Lord preserve our pious rulers always . . .' There was no mention of young Basil II or of his brother Constantine VIII.

It is significant though that Nikephoros enjoyed much lower esteem in Constantinople than he did in the provinces, especially after the first heady days of his accession in 963. Among the educated courtiers of the palace, the new emperor's confrontational policies must have seemed as dangerous as his manners were rough and ready. They must have cringed at his lack of diplomatic finesse, for he had a gift for caustic repartee which he exercised freely on the ambassadors of foreign countries which had displeased him in some way or another. The envoy of Bulgaria heard their tsar dismissed as a 'leather-gnawing ruler who is clad in a leather jerkin'. A bishop who came to Constantinople on behalf of the German emperor was told that his master's troops did not know how to fight because they were too busy filling their stomachs. The bishop complained that he had not been treated in this way on his previous visit when Constantine VII had been at the helm. Indeed he had departed laden with gifts. The palace officials had to explain:

> The emperor Constantine, a mild man, one who always stayed in the palace, made the nations friends of his by that sort of thing. Nikephoros instead . . . is one eager for combat, he avoids the palace like the plague . . . he is one who does not make the nations friendly to himself by paying them, but by terror and the sword he makes them subject to himself.

The emperor did have one staunch supporter among the palace administrators in the person of Basil Lekapenos, who had succeeded the ousted Bringas as head of the administration. Lekapenos and his circle doubtless shared the Constantinopolitan outlook of the Macedonian dynasty, but they perceived the value of Nikephoros's military victories and were well aware that he had the great virtue of having no heir. His only son had died some years before when he was accidentally struck by a spear during a military exercise. The emperor was now in his late fifties and it seemed unlikely that his marriage to Theophano would result in a child, so there was little apparent danger of his trying to supplant the Macedonian dynasty with his own clan. The current arrangement therefore suited all parties.

Outside the palace and on the streets of Constantinople, on the other hand, the soldier emperor was cordially hated for the way that he put the needs of his troops before those of the rest of his subjects. When he had entered Constantinople to be crowned emperor in 963, many soldiers took the opportunity to plunder the houses of the citizens, rich and poor alike. The new emperor had made no attempt to curtail or punish this behaviour, casually remarking that it was 'hardly surprising if a few misbehave in such a large body of men'. To supply and pay his ever-larger armies, Nikephoros requisitioned supplies whenever he needed them and instituted new taxes. He even resorted to the particularly low trick of tampering with the gold coinage. For centuries, the nomisma had been the standard Byzantine gold coin, weighing 4.55 grammes. Now a new lighter coin, the tetartaron, was introduced with the nomisma remaining in circulation alongside it. Nikephoros decreed that payments to the treasury, such as taxes, should be made with the nomisma but his own expenditure was with the tetartaron. He therefore made a net profit in gold on every transaction.

The volatile people of Constantinople soon made their feelings plain. On one visit to the capital, while riding through the streets, Nikephoros was jeered and pelted with mud and stones by the crowd. Two women, mother and daughter, climbed on to the roof of their house and lobbed rocks at him from there. Nikephoros rode on regardless, looking neither to left nor to right and by nightfall the tumult had died down. The insult did not go entirely unpunished. Someone had been careful to make a note of the house where the two women lived. The next day they were arrested, taken outside the city and summarily burned to death. For all his insouciance, Nikephoros too was worried. He ordered a stout wall to be built around the Great Palace, perhaps remembering how a popular demonstration had helped bring down the Lekapenoi in 945. Separated though he was from the populace by his wall, Nikephoros still had the common touch and he could take a joke. He once came across a grey-haired man who was trying to enlist as a soldier and suggested to him that he might be too old to serve. 'Not at all,' replied the man, 'I'm even stronger now than when I was young.' In the past, he said, he had needed a donkey to carry one nomisma's worth of grain but now he could carry two nomismata's worth on his own shoulders. It was a sly dig at Nikephoros's inflationary policies but, to his credit, the emperor saw the funny side.

Ironically, in the end Nikephoros did not fall victim to the Constantinopolitan mob but to a member of his own class. The warlords of Asia Minor may well have expected that, once on the throne, Nikephoros would repeal the legislation that hindered them from acquiring land property. The new emperor was sympathetic but largely left the laws in place. Now that he was safely on the throne, it was hardly in his interest to encourage the aggrandisement of potential rivals. Certainly when a plot was formed, its leader was Nikephoros's formerly loyal lieutenant and nephew, John Tzimiskes, who had served alongside him in many of his campaigns and was a descendant of the great John Kourkouas. Like his uncle, Tzimiskes was of diminutive stature but had a reputation for courage that bordered on rashness: he had on several occasions single-handedly charged an entire contingent of the enemy. In the autumn of 969, Tzimiskes received a message summoning him to Constantinople. The message was from Nikephoros but the emperor had sent it at the behest of his wife, Theophano, who had told him that the recently widowed Tzimiskes needed to be found a suitable wife. On arrival, Tzimiskes found that Theophano had something else in mind. She begged him to rid her of her boorish and excessively pious husband and take his place as emperor. Tzimiskes readily agreed, suggesting that there were prior grievances, and the plot was hatched.

The supposedly secret plan was soon widely known in palace circles and attempts were made to warn Nikephoros. One evening he found a note in his bedroom identifying Tzimiskes as a potential assassin. A few days later while he was attending church, a priest handed him a cryptic letter, saying 'Prepare yourself, O Emperor, for no small danger is being prepared . . .' For some reason he failed to act on these tip-offs. One night in December, Tzimiskes and his confederates arrived by boat in the harbour of the Great Palace and were hauled up through one of the windows by supporters on the inside. By now Basil Lekapenos knew about the plot, but sensing which way the wind was blowing he took to his bed, pretending to be unwell. Even Nikephoros himself suspected that something was afoot that night and sent a note to his brother Leo asking him to come to the palace with a band of armed men. But Leo was busy playing dice with his friends and was having a winning streak. He stuffed the note under his cushion and went on with the game. Thus the conspirators reached Nikephoros's bedroom unchallenged and found the door left unlocked. On entering, though, they found the bed empty. Retreating in confusion, they assumed that the plot had been betrayed until one of Theophano's servants arrived to reassure them that all was well: Nikephoros was in the room but it was his habit to sleep on the floor in preparation for the monastic life that he still craved. Crowding back into the bedroom, the conspirators found the slumbering emperor on the far side of the bed. They woke him with a savage kick and one of them brought a sword down on to his unprotected head. Nikephoros still managed to cry out for help, so they sliced off his head and held it out of the window where those coming to the rescue could see that they were too late. At Tzimiskes's command, late the following day, the body was dumped in a coffin and taken to the church of the Holy Apostles for burial in an empty sarcophagus. Only much later did someone, well aware of Theophano's role in the plot, add an epitaph to the tomb in memory of 'Nikephoros, who vanquished all but Eve'.

* * *

Back in the Great Palace, even before dawn had broken, Basil Lekapenos had miraculously recovered from his illness and presented himself to the new ruler, who rewarded him by confirming him in the position he had enjoyed under the previous regime. All members of the Phokas family in the city were rounded up and bundled on to ships bound for various islands in the Aegean. Leo Phokas ended on Lesvos, no doubt bitterly regretting that prolonged dice game. Tzimiskes and his followers then strode off to Hagia Sophia, confident that his accession would be sealed with a coronation. They reckoned without the aged patriarch Polyeuktos, who appeared and barred the way, declaring that a man who had just murdered his kinsman was not fit to enter, let alone be crowned emperor. Negotiation was called for. John protested that he was not a murderer, for he himself had not actually struck the blows that had dispatched his uncle. Nor was he even the instigator of the plot – that had been the empress, Theophano. He accepted that he must do penance for his part in the crime and promised that he would distribute everything he owned as a private citizen to the poor. Polyeuktos gave way and agreed to crown him but not to sanction a marriage with Theophano. John's erstwhile ally was now an obstacle to power and he had her seized and sent off like Nikephoros's relatives to a secure island. She did not go quietly. She had to be dragged from Hagia Sophia where she had sought refuge and in the scuffle she managed to land a punch on Basil Lekapenos's head. The two men who had killed Nikephoros were also exiled, which must have seemed a poor reward for their loyalty to Tzimiskes. John I (969–976) was duly crowned emperor on Christmas day and he took over his predecessor's role as protector of the two legitimate child emperors, Basil and Constantine.

As for the population of Constantinople, they accepted the coup as they had never liked Nikephoros anyway. John eased his usurpation by marrying Theodora, a daughter of Constantine VII and the aunt of his young charges. This move was very popular among the people of Constantinople because it kept power within the Macedonian dynasty. A lavish show was also laid on in the Hippodrome and John found himself rather popular in the capital. Ribald songs circulated in the streets about the disgraced Theophano and her *amours* and life went on as normal. It was in the provinces that opposition to John's takeover emerged. Not surprisingly, the Phokas family were dismayed at the downfall of their kinsman and had hatched a plan to reassert their grip on power. In the summer following John's coup, another Bardas Phokas – Leo's son, and nephew of the ill-fated Nikephoros II – succeeded in escaping from his place of exile at Amaseia in the Armeniakon theme and made his way to his family's powerbase at Caesarea where he was proclaimed emperor by the troops. Unable to leave Constantinople, John delegated the task of dealing with the threat. His late wife had been a member of the Skleros family, another of the military clans, and he now gave his brother-in-law, Bardas Skleros, command of the eastern army. Skleros soon had Phokas surrounded in a fortress, compelling him to surrender and sending him off into a more secure exile on the island of Chios.

* * *

The Phokas family may have been completely ousted from power, but the policies pursued by the new emperor and his Skleros allies were virtually identical. The military aristocracy remained firmly in charge and the aggressive wars continued. An unexpected sequence of events, however, ensured that John's initial campaign as emperor was not waged in Asia Minor or in Syria but in Bulgaria. By the treaty made with Tsar Symeon back in 924, the Byzantines had agreed to recognise his title and to make him an annual present of gold coins, the idea being that, in return for the present, the Bulgars would prevent Turkic peoples from the Steppes from raiding Byzantine territory. Symeon's son Peter had signally failed to do this, so in 966 Nikephoros II had stopped the payments. When war consequently broke out, Nikephoros moved his troops up to the frontier and captured some Bulgarian fortresses, but, remembering the fate of his predecessor and namesake in 811, he was reluctant to proceed any further and in any case a campaign in the east against the Arabs demanded his attention. Instead, Nikephoros decided to fall back on the kind of tactics that the military aristocracy had largely abandoned in favour of direct military confrontation. He decided to pay someone else to teach the Bulgars their place. An envoy was dispatched with 1,500 pounds of gold to the Russian prince Svyatoslav at Kiev.

This Svyatoslav was the son of Igor and Olga, and father of that Vladimir who was later to bring about the conversion of the Russians to Christianity, although Svyatoslav himself remained staunchly pagan until the end of his life. He was a formidable warrior who had recently crushed the old allies of Byzantium, the Khazars, and in the summer of 968 he led his army into Bulgaria in accordance with Nikephoros's request. So devastating was the incursion that Tsar Peter hastened to come to terms with the Byzantines and even to abdicate in favour of his son, Boris II. Then, the following year, what had seemed to be a signal success for Byzantine cunning and diplomacy unravelled with terrifying speed. During his raid, Svyatoslav had not failed to notice the prosperity and fertility of the land between the Danube and the Balkan mountains or the weakness of Bulgarian resistance. When summer returned he invaded again on his own account and this time with a much larger force. The Russian army crossed the Danube unopposed and headed straight for Symeon's old capital of Preslav. The Bulgars barricaded themselves behind the city walls, then made a sally against the attackers, with some success. The Russians, however, responded by mounting a full-scale assault on the city, which breached the defences and allowed them to storm in. With Preslav gone, Bulgarian resistance collapsed. Tsar Boris was now a prisoner of Svyatoslav and the Russians quickly occupied the rest of the country. Only Philippopolis held out and, when it did fall, a vengeful Svyatoslav had many of the defenders impaled. Within the space of a few short months, the Byzantines had seen a weak and unthreatening Christian neighbour replaced by a strong and pagan one.

This unwelcome outcome might well have convinced John Tzimiskes that neither diplomacy nor 'other means' were applicable on this occasion and he began to make preparations for all-out war, just as the regency had against Symeon in 917. Throughout the winter of 970–971, he stockpiled weapons and food supplies at Adrianople and readied a fleet that could support the army on the Black Sea and the Danube. In April, he took a hand-picked band of 5,000 men and crossed the Balkan mountains while the bulk of the army, led by Basil Lekapenos, followed on behind. This vanguard moved so swiftly that the Russians were taken completely by surprise and the first they knew of the emperor's campaign was when news arrived that he would shortly be before the walls of Preslav. Some 8,000 Russian soldiers were outside the city walls engaged in training exercises as the Byzantine army drew close and they fled ingloriously back behind the fortifications. Shortly afterwards, the main body of the Byzantine army arrived and the attack on Preslav began in earnest. On 13 April the Byzantines stormed into the town, but a large contingent of Russians refused to accept defeat and barricaded themselves inside Tsar Symeon's fortified palace. Emperor John decided that the easiest solution was to smoke them out. Fires were started all around the building and burning arrows were fired in through the windows. This certainly had the desired effect: some Russians came running out, others died in the flames. But the fires also devastated what had once been Symeon's showcase city, destroying the

Golden Church and the fine buildings that he had hoped would rival Constantinople. Tzimiskes celebrated Easter among the ruins.

Svyatoslav had not been in Preslav when it fell and he now moved towards the city with his main army, hoping to reverse the coup. A series of pitched battles were fought around the town of Dristra from which ultimately the Byzantines emerged victorious. By that time, thousands of Russians had died and Svyatoslav realised with great reluctance that he would have to extricate himself from his Bulgarian entanglement. He therefore sent a peace envoy to the emperor John, offering to give up Dristra and evacuate Bulgaria. These terms John accepted, for he was anxious to bring the campaign to a conclusion. The opportunity was taken to renew the old trading treaty, allowing the Russians to bring their wares to Constantinople as they had done in the past. The Russians then marched out and began the long trek back to Kiev. Most of them never made it. The Pechenegs were lying in wait on the Dnieper and pounced on the weary Russians without warning. Svyatoslav was among those killed.

Having pulled off a victory of rare completeness and occupied the whole of Bulgaria, John had to decide what to do with it. During the campaign he had made public pronouncements that his quarrel was with the Russians, from whom he had come to liberate the Bulgarians. When Preslav had fallen, the Byzantines had freed Boris II and his family. The emperor treated them kindly and released any other Bulgarians he had captured in the course of the campaign. It soon became clear, however, that he had no intention of handing Bulgaria back to its former rulers. The land between the Balkan mountains and the Danube had been Byzantine territory in the past and it would be so once more. It was announced that Preslav would henceforth be known as Ioannopolis, that is 'city of John', in the emperor's honour and a Byzantine governor was installed. The hapless Boris had to accompany the emperor back to Constantinople and take part in a ceremonial victory parade through the Golden Gate in the Land Walls to the cathedral of Hagia Sophia. He was publicly divested of his crown and royal regalia which were then placed on the altar of Hagia Sophia as offerings to God. Instead the former tsar was left to live in comfortable retirement in Constantinople and was provided with a mean-ingless title so that he could take part in ceremonies and processions.

Almost immediately John turned his attention to the Syrian frontier, where events had been moving very fast. In 969, the Fatimids of North Africa had moved east and captured Egypt, robbing the Abbasids of one of their richest provinces and setting up their own Shi'ite caliph in opposition to the one in Baghdad. Later the same year, their armies moved into Syria and Palestine, threatening to bring their power up to the Byzantine border. Fifty years earlier, a Byzantine emperor and his advisers might have seen in the situation boundless possibilities for gaining concessions by playing Abbasid off against Fatimid. Not so John Tzimiskes, who exploited the uncertainty to attack the cities of the region. His most daring raid began in the spring of 975. Marching deep into Syria, the Byzantine army burned and pillaged as it went. The town of Heliopolis was captured and sacked after a few days' siege but John was perfectly happy to achieve much the same result by extortion. He was soon within sight of Damascus, in territory where the Byzantine army had not been seen for centuries, but the people there had no desire to share the fate of Heliopolis. They came out to meet the emperor with gifts of money, horses and mules. In return for recognition of Byzantine overlordship and a payment of annual tribute, the city was spared and the emperor moved on. After receiving tribute from Beirut, Tripoli and other towns, John pressed south into Palestine during September, marching as far south as Caesarea.

John's high-handed annexation of Bulgaria and his aggressive campaigns of naked extortion in Syria and Palestine could not be more in contrast to the earlier policies that the Byzantines had pursued. There was the same atmosphere of righteous warfare that had attended the campaigns of Nikephoros II. When he returned to Constantinople from Bulgaria in triumph in 971, John was careful to make sure that the Hodegetria icon of the Virgin Mary headed the procession in a chariot while he rode behind on a horse, thus modestly attributing the victory to God. Shortly afterwards, John had the imperial portrait removed from the copper coinage and replaced with that of Christ. In the east, John's campaigns were accompanied by a search for holy objects and relics. The sandals of Christ and some of the hair of John the Baptist were found. At Beirut, an icon of the crucifixion of Christ was found: it had supposedly once bled real blood after having been stabbed by a Jew with a spear. As the army drew close to Jerusalem in 975, John even began to toy with the idea of liberating the Holy Sepulchre which had been under Muslim rule since 638.

But, even as John was carrying all before him, the nature of Byzantium meant that he had constantly to be looking back over his shoulder at what was happening in Constantinople, the centre of political power. What might Basil Lekapenos be planning, now that young Basil II was approaching manhood and ready to enter into his inheritance? The emperor was deeply disturbed too, when his columns were passing through fertile agricultural land that had recently been conquered from the Arabs, to learn that most of it had now become the property of Lekapenos. All the money spent on the campaign and all the hardships his men had endured had served only to increase the wealth and powerbase of the very man who had the wherewithal to dethrone him. It was considerations such as these which probably explain why John did not attempt to capture Jerusalem, a feat that was to be left to the First Crusade in 1099. Instead, in the autumn of 975 John headed back to Antioch and then took the road to Constantinople. When his army reached the vicinity of Prousa in western Asia Minor, the emperor stopped off to stay at the house of a prominent nobleman for a few days. A cup of wine was handed to him which he drank off heedlessly, feeling secure in the home of his loyal subject. The next day, the emperor was found to be most unwell, with a disturbing numbness in his limbs that the physicians were unable to diagnose. Rather than stay put, John decided that he must reach his capital at all odds, so his bodyguard rode with him through the bleak early January landscape towards the Bosporus. When his ship docked at the Great Palace, he was at once taken to his bed chamber where he made anxious enquiries about whether his tomb was ready. He died on 10 January 976 and many believed that he had been poisoned on the orders of Lekapenos. It is just as likely, though, that he fell victim to the ever-present scourge of medieval armies, dysentery.

The unexpected death of John I opened up a huge gulf of uncertainty, for no one had given much thought to who would rule the empire once he was gone. Would another warlord take power and rule on behalf of the legitimate Basil and Constantine? Would Basil Lekapenos take on that role and thus gain access to the power from which his castration formally barred him? Or would the Macedonian dynasty reassert itself as it had in 945? Perhaps the most burning question of all was whether Byzantium would continue the aggressive frontier wars or would return to those other ways of securing its borders that had stood it in such good stead in the past.

CHAPTER SEVEN

The Long Shadow

For [the Phokas family] held perpetual dominance,
I daresay, until we came on the scene.
Land Law of Basil II (996)

Of the three groups contending for power in 976, the Macedonian dynasty must have looked the least likely to succeed. It had now been many years since an effective emperor of the ruling family had actually directed affairs of state and some observers might have assumed that it would shortly die out or be elbowed aside. They were wrong. The Macedonians were to shape Byzantium's destiny for another eighty years. They were to preside over a further extension of the empire's borders and a period of relative peace and prosperity. They were also to widen the gulf between Constantinople and the provinces that was to lead to another of the desperate crises that were a recurring feature of Byzantine history. The survival, the expansion, the peace, the prosperity and to some extent the eventual crisis were all the work of the man who ruled the empire for fifty years and whose long shadow dominated it for another fifty thereafter: the gloomy tyrant, Basil II (976–1025), known as the Bulgar slayer.

* * *

Back in 976 it had naturally been assumed, especially in the armies of Asia Minor, that the power vacuum left by the death of John I Tzimiskes would be filled by some other warlord or other who would step forward to take up the role of emperor and protector of the legitimate rulers, Basil II and his younger brother Constantine VIII. The obvious candidate was Bardas Skleros, brother-in-law of the late Emperor John. Skleros had an outstanding military record.

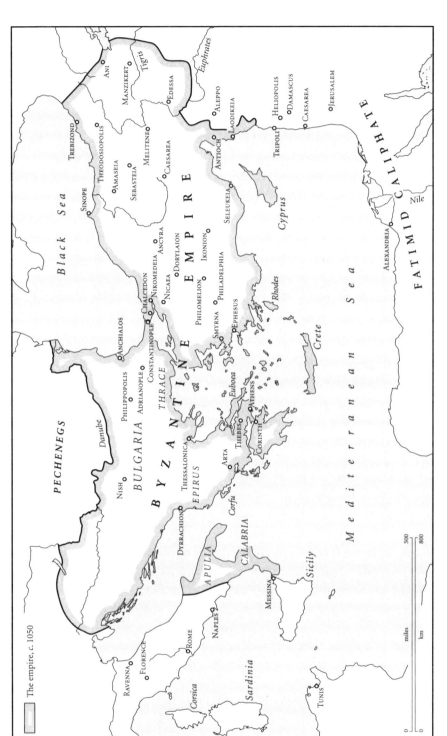

The empire, c. 1050

PECHENEGS

Danube

Black Sea

ANI
MANZIKERT
Tigris
EDESSA
Euphrates
ALEPPO
LAODIKEIA
HELIOPOLIS
DAMASCUS
CAESAREA
JERUSALEM

TREBIZOND
THEODOSIOPOLIS
AMASEIA
SEBASTEIA
MELITENE
CAESAREA
ANTIOCH
TRIPOLI

SINOPE

Nile

FATIMID CALIPHATE

ANCHIALOS
PHILIPPOPOLIS
ADRIANOPLE
CHALCEDON
CONSTANTINOPLE
NIKOMEDEIA
NICAEA
DORYLAION
ANCYRA
IKONION
PHILOMELION
PHILADELPHIA
SMYRNA
EPHESUS
SELEUKEIA

Cyprus

Rhodes

Crete

Mediterranean Sea

ALEXANDRIA

NISH
THESSALONICA
THRACE
BULGARIA
BYZANTINE EMPIRE
EPIRUS

Euboea
ATHENS
THEBES
CORINTH

ARTA
Corfu
DYRRACHION
CALABRIA
APULIA
MESSINA

Sicily

NAPLES
ROME
FLORENCE
RAVENNA

Sardinia

Corsica

TUNIS

miles   500
km   800

0

5 The Byzantine empire *c.* 1050

He had served with distinction in Tzimiskes's campaign against Svyatoslav, where he was credited with having sliced a Russian in two in single combat. It was he too who had put a stop to the younger Bardas Phokas's bid for the throne in 970. The post of Domestic of the *Scholai* having been divided, he now held the rank of Domestic of the East and had all the credentials for a strong man to fill Tzimiskes's shoes.

In Constantinople, where loyalty to the Macedonian dynasty was strong among the city's population, many people thought otherwise. They had hated Nikephoros II and only accepted John I when he had married into the Macedonian family. Many courtiers in the palace agreed with those popular sentiments and felt that it was time for the dominance of the warlords to come to an end. Significantly, the most powerful man at court, Basil Lekapenos, the great-uncle of the two young emperors, had come to agree with them. Even though it was he who had been instrumental in bringing Nikephoros Phokas to Constantinople in 963, Lekapenos now moved to end the dominance of the warlords. Ostensibly acting in the name of the young emperors, he had Skleros relieved of his command and sent off to the eastern frontier to command a few border regiments instead. The eighteen-year-old Basil and his younger brother Constantine were proclaimed rulers of the empire, with Lekapenos the undisputed power behind the throne.

Astute though Lekapenos was, he had gravely underestimated how much support Skleros had in Asia Minor. The disgruntled former Domestic departed for the east and, after having made sure that all his close relatives were safely out of Constantinople, had himself proclaimed emperor by his retinue in the castle of Charpete. Volunteers flocked to his banner and, by rounding up all the local tax gatherers and relieving them of their takings, Skleros ensured a healthy revenue to fund his campaign. His local connections meant that he was on good terms with the neighbouring Arab emirs across the border and they too provided him with men for his army. Armies were dispatched against him and it was over a year before the road to Constantinople was open, but by the time Skleros marched into Nicaea, less than 200 kilometres from the capital, Lekapenos was in desperation. He had to find someone effective to deal with Skleros or face total ruin, but the only people with the military skills to do so were as dangerous as the usurper himself. That was a risk he had to take and he decided to recall the man whom Skleros had brought to heel in 970, Bardas Phokas, who was still languishing in exile on the island of Chios. Like his illustrious uncle, Bardas was signally lacking in personal charm, with a dour and gloomy disposition. On the other hand, he was an experienced soldier and had an imposing physical presence. It was said that his shout could make an entire army tremble and that he could kill a man with one blow of his hand. Transferred from Chios to Thrace by a fast ship, he was promoted to Domestic and sent over the Dardanelles to do battle with Skleros.

For a year, the two titans slugged it out on the plains of Asia Minor, with Skleros generally having the upper hand. When the two sides met halfway between Ankara and Caesarea in March 979, it soon became apparent that Skleros's troops were pushing Phokas's off the field. Having decided that a glorious death was better than an ignominious defeat, Phokas set spurs to his horse and charged directly at Skleros himself. In the brief clash, Skleros managed to chop off the ear of Phokas's horse but Phokas dealt his opponent a blow on the head with his mace before riding off. Skleros's attendants laid him down to help him recover from the concussion but they failed to tether his horse. This distinctive steed went charging through the ranks of Skleros's army, riderless and covered in blood. The soldiers drew the obvious conclusion that their commander had fallen and they fled the field. When Skleros recovered he realised that all was lost and fled to Arab territory, ultimately reaching Baghdad where he threw himself on the mercy of the Abbasid caliph. Almost by accident, Bardas Phokas had saved the day for Lekapenos.

The powerful eunuch was now supreme in Constantinople while on the eastern frontier Bardas Phokas as Domestic ruled the roost. In the tradition of his ancestors, he mounted regular raids over the border into Arab territory, extorting money from undefended cities and enriching himself and his men in the process. This delicate equilibrium was only disrupted when a new and very unexpected participant entered the fray: the young emperor Basil II. During his teens and early twenties Basil, like his father Romanos II before him, had lived a free and easy life, taking no interest in politics, enjoying the good things that limitless wealth and power could provide, and leaving Lekapenos to run the empire. Just as Bringas had done with Romanos II, now Basil's great-uncle had carefully encouraged him in these pursuits, the better to keep him out of government. From the time of the defeat of Skleros, however, Basil started to take an interest in what was going on and began to demand that he be allowed to take on his rightful role. In 980, when some ambassadors arrived from Baghdad to negotiate what was to be done with Bardas Skleros, Basil insisted on receiving them in person, although Lekapenos would keep butting into the conversation. After some years of enduring this tutelage, in 985 Basil one day abruptly informed his great-uncle that he was dismissed, that his vast landed properties were confiscated and that he would be taken into exile. Basil even decreed that a monastery that Lekapenos had piously established should be demolished so that no trace of his former power should remain. Almost overnight, the eunuch had lost everything and his career was at an end.

The stroke was bold but risky. Basil had deprived himself of his most experienced and reliable adviser and he would now have to prove that he was able to run the empire himself. There was ample opportunity to do so, for almost as soon as John Tzimiskes had died the Bulgars had risen in revolt against their incorporation into the empire. With the Byzantines distracted by the Skleros revolt, the Bulgar leader Samuel had taken Preslav and by 985 he had conquered as far south as Larissa in Thessaly. In the summer of 986, Basil II led his army out of Constantinople to retrieve the situation, but his first command ended in a fiasco when he fell into the classic Bulgarian ambush in one of the passes through the Balkan mountains. The army had to fight its way out and was compelled to leave most of its equipment behind.

This reverse was just what Bardas Phokas needed. The empire was clearly heading for destruction in the hands of a witless boy. A man of maturity and experience was needed to take the helm. The following summer, for the second time in his life, Phokas was proclaimed emperor at Caesarea. The Phokas name still held its magic and many of the leading families threw in their lot with the usurper. Even his old adversary Bardas Skleros decided to return from exile in Baghdad to join the rebellion on the promise of being made Domestic once Phokas was in possession of Constantinople. Phokas welcomed him at Caesarea but then wisely had him locked up in a castle. The man was just too dangerous to have on the loose.

The odds on Basil II's survival were now slim indeed, for he had the majority of the nobles of Asia Minor and their followers ranged against him. But Basil was a Byzantine. Hopeless odds against myriad enemies were in his blood and his one trump card was control of Constantinople. That gave him command of the ample resources of the treasury and he looked around for allies whom he could pay to come to his rescue. It was at this point that he contacted Vladimir, the son of Svyatoslav, who was now ruling the Russians at Kiev, and offered a generous subsidy and the hand of his sister Anna in marriage in return for military aid, an agreement that was to bring about Vladimir's conversion to Christianity. With 6,000 sturdy Russians behind him, the young emperor's cause began to prosper. He crushed a force led by Phokas's brother at Chrysopolis in 988 and the following spring came face to face with the usurper himself at Abydos. As with the downfall of Skleros, the battle was decided by an unexpected stroke of fortune rather than any military prowess. Phokas had decided that the easiest way to end the matter was to kill or capture his rival. So he personally led his best troops in a charge up the slope to where Basil and his brother Constantine were standing. The rebel was nearly there, scattering the opposition as he went, when suddenly he reined in his horse and rode to one side. He rather unsteadily dismounted and then slowly lay down on the ground. By the time his men reached him, he was stone dead. No one ever knew what had killed him. Some said he had been hit by some projectile: Basil's brother Constantine even claimed that he had thrown it. There were also rumours that Phokas's servant had been bribed to poison him. Others attributed it to the intervention of the Virgin Mary, whose icon Basil had clutched to his breast throughout the entire encounter. Whatever the cause, with its head removed, the rebellion crumbled with minimal casualties on either side.

Basil marched triumphantly with his army through Asia Minor, reaching Antioch in November 989 and receiving the surrender of Phokas's brother Leo. Skleros too fell into his net, after escaping from prison and briefly attempting to revive his own bid for the throne. In this case, Basil was inclined to be merciful, especially as Skleros was now getting on in years. He was given the title of Kouropalates, was allowed to retire honourably to his estates in Asia Minor, and his supporters were not to be persecuted. Basil insisted that they meet to ratify the agreement and, on the appointed day, Skleros presented himself at Basil's camp. The two men sat down to drink wine in the emperor's tent, Basil making a point of taking a sip from Skleros's cup before handing it to his guest: the fate of Phokas can hardly have been far from either of their minds. The young man then turned to the older and asked his advice. How could he keep the empire free from the kind of civil strife that had plagued it ever since 976? Skleros very frankly advised the emperor to rein in the power of his own class:

> Cut down the governors who become over proud. Let no generals on campaign have too many resources. Exhaust them with unjust exactions, to keep them busied with their own affairs.

The interview was at an end. The would-be emperor departed and Basil never saw him again. The advice Skleros had given, however, lingered long in the emperor's mind. Almost from the beginning there had been some tension between Byzantium's monumental capital and the periphery. The political theory that dictated that no one could be emperor unless he possessed Constantinople was a powerful incentive for the ruler to remain there and delegate the defence of the frontiers to someone else. That of course then led to the danger that a popular and victorious general would return at the head of his army either to dethrone his sovereign or to reduce him to a puppet, as

Romanos I, Nikephoros II and John I had. In response to the dilemma, Basil II now seems to have developed a unique and very personal way of governing. On the one hand, he would take over the leadership of the armies, the first Macedonian emperor to do so since his great-great-grandfather Basil I, and beat the warlords of Asia Minor at their own game. He would even imitate their martial outlook and their contempt for the court in Constantinople and its ceremonies. When giving audiences he took to wearing a simple purple robe with a few jewels, rather than the gorgeous array of silk and gems favoured by his predecessors. Intellectuals like Photios were not welcome in the Great Palace during his reign and he insisted that all memoranda be drafted in plain and straightforward language. But that was only one side of the coin. On the other was an uncompromising insistence on his legitimacy as a porphyrogenitos that was every bit as strident as that of his forebears. That insistence, along with his takeover of military leadership, would justify and underpin the emperor's all-out assault on the power and privileges of the military aristocracy.

When it came to leading the Byzantine armies, after the initial debacle of 986 Basil proved to be an unexpected success, although it is noticeable that he waged his campaigns in a very different way from the military aristocracy and with a different end in view. On the Syrian frontier, he put a stop to the raids across the frontier on Arab towns and there is no hint of fervour for war against the infidel that had been so prominent under Nikephoros II and John I. Instead Basil contented himself with defending the position already achieved and particularly with countering the threat posed by the Fatimid regime of Egypt, which aimed to oust the Byzantines from northern Syria altogether. In 995, while campaigning in the Balkans, Basil received news that the Fatimids were threatening the old Hamdanid capital of Aleppo. He marched east at lightning speed with 17,000 men, arriving in Antioch weeks before anyone had hoped to expect him. After a series of sharp encounters, in 1001 the Fatimid caliph al-Hakim agreed to a truce and hostilities largely came to an end. There was expansion in the east during Basil's reign but it was at the expense of Christians rather than Muslims and it was largely achieved not through conquest but by treaties. The neighbouring Armenian kingdoms were becoming ever more fragmented by civil war and Turkish incursions on their eastern borders, and their rulers increasingly looked to the Byzantine emperor for protection and aid. One of them was David, who ruled Tao, a principality on the Black Sea between Armenia proper and Georgia. He had helped Basil II against the revolt of Bardas Skleros and in 990, since he had no heir, he made a will leaving his lands to the emperor. When he died in 1000, Basil II turned Tao into the Byzantine theme of Iberia. Other rulers followed suit, sometimes swapping their Armenian lands for estates in Asia Minor and some grand Byzantine court title. By the end of Basil's reign, the frontier extended beyond Lake Van, further east than it had ever been.

If Basil's wars in the east were defensive and limited, in the west he went all out to recover the territory lost to the empire since 976 with the revolt of Bulgaria, but here again his tactics were different from those of his two predecessors. While John Tzimiskes had conquered Bulgaria in a lightning campaign over a matter of months, Basil took years over the task, fighting a relentless war of attrition. Every year, when commitments in the east allowed it, he would lead his army deep into Bulgar territory, burning and looting as he went. Later generations credited him with defeating a Bulgar army and blinding all 15,000 captives, except for a selected group who lost only one eye and were then charged with leading their sightless comrades home. The story is almost certainly a myth: the blinding of 15,000 men would have disabled a significant proportion of the able-bodied population of Bulgaria, yet no contemporary made any mention of it. Even so, the tale does bear witness to the grim resolution with which Basil slowly ground Bulgaria down. The long drawn out saga finally came to an end in the summer of 1018 when the Bulgar leaders laid down their arms and the land south of the Danube was once more placed under Byzantine rule.

Basil had proved that he could match the military aristocracy in the field, even if his methods and goals were rather different from theirs, but that was not enough. Their threat to the dynasty in Constantinople had to be neutralised permanently. The emperor waited until his position was secure enough and then set about implementing the advice of Skleros, to the letter. In the summer of 995, as Basil was marching back to Constantinople through Asia Minor following the campaign in Syria, he was approached by a delegation from a small village. They complained about a certain Philokales who they claimed had used his wealth to buy up all the land in the village and in the surrounding area, turning it into his private estate. Basil promptly had the land confiscated and returned to the villagers while Philokales's grand country house was demolished to the foundations. Moving on, the emperor and his retinue were cordially welcomed in Caesarea at the house of Eustathios Maleinos, one of the wealthiest of the Asia Minor gentry. Basil accepted the hospitality but he remembered only too well that it had been in that same house that Bardas Phokas had been proclaimed emperor nine years before. At the end of his stay, the emperor proposed to Maleinos that he might like to return with him to the capital, couching the request in terms that made a refusal impossible. Once in Constantinople, Maleinos found himself immured in comfortable house arrest and there he remained for the rest of his life. On his death, his estates were confiscated.

It was not only individuals who were targeted as Basil launched his campaign, but an entire class. Back in Constantinople that winter, the emperor introduced a new law portentously entitled 'New Constitution of the pious emperor Basil the Younger, by which are condemned those Rich Men who amass their wealth at the expense of the poor'. Introduced on 1 January 996, the law extended the old policy of strictly restricting the acquisition of peasant land, ruling that any land acquired illegally since 922 was now liable to restitution without compensation. Further legislation in 1004 changed the way that the main tax paid by the peasantry, the Allelengyon, was collected. In the past any shortfall on the part of one individual had had to be made up by the other members of the village community but now it was to be made up by any great landowner in the district. The reasoning behind the law is clear enough: it inflicted a financial blow on the magnates, while the emperor had greater security for the collection of the tax. Moreover, by shifting the burden from the peasantry, it made it less likely that they would be forced by poverty to put themselves under a powerful patron.

This aggressive policy towards some of the most powerful figures in the empire was hardly likely to pass without protest. A delegation of clergy and monks led by the patriarch of Constantinople begged the emperor to relent, but to no avail. Revolt was slow in coming but when it did it was led by the Phokas family. They may have been defeated in their bid for the throne in 989 but they were still wealthy and influential. Basil made no secret of his aversion for them, going so far as to refer to them specifically in his law of 996 as among the worst offenders for accumulating wealth and land. In 1021, while Basil was distracted by a campaign in Armenia, one Nikephoros Phokas, son of the ill-fated Bardas, joined with another Asia Minor magnate called Nikephoros Xiphias and proclaimed himself emperor. This Phokas seems to have shared the family trait for physical unloveliness, being popularly known as 'Crookneck', but his surname was enough to attract widespread support in Asia Minor. In the event, his bid for power was short-lived because he was assassinated at his camp when he fell out with his fellow conspirator Xiphias. Without Phokas, the rebellion fell apart, giving Basil the excuse to confiscate the estates of all those involved.

Brief and unsuccessful though the rebellion was, it shows that, even towards the end of his life, Basil II's rule could be seriously challenged in Asia Minor, and he was never entirely secure in that part of the empire. His powerbase was in Constantinople where, as the representative of the Macedonian dynasty, he could rely on the loyalty of the population. Not that he courted popularity. He never stooped to the scattering of largesse with which emperors before and after purchased the adulation of the crowd, and all the loot from his campaigns and proceeds from his confiscations disappeared into the vaults below the Great Palace. He made no attempt to cultivate the image of the virtuous Christian prince and was apparently happy to be feared rather than loved. Nor did Basil try to curry favour with the administrators of the Great Palace. He earned a reputation for ignoring their advice and brutally punished any whom he suspected of disloyalty. He was alleged to have personally beheaded one of his officials and to have had an imperial chamberlain who had tried to poison him fed to the palace lions. The mystique of being a porphyrogenitos of the Macedonian dynasty was enough to allow him to act exactly as he wanted.

It was not only his military prowess and the support of the people that allowed Basil to rule largely unchallenged. There was one thing that he was happy to spend his money on and that was perhaps the deciding factor. Just as he had purchased the help of Russian troops against Bardas Phokas in 989, Basil needed foreign mercenaries to provide a reserve of troops if ever one of his generals staged a revolt and attracted the loyalty of the armies. His preference was for Armenians and Russians, Christians whose countries were within the orbit of Byzantine cultural influence, and military manuals of the day make it clear that they composed a significant part of the army. In this Basil was acting exactly as Constantine I, Justinian I and Constantine V had before him, turning the vast human resources from beyond the frontiers to his advantage.

Then one December evening in 1025, shortly after having made the appointment of a new patriarch of Constantinople, Basil II died, having ruled so long that there was almost no one alive who could remember when he was not on the throne. Enigmatic to the last, he was buried, on his own instructions, not in the church of the Holy Apostles in Constantinople like most of his predecessors but in the village of Hebdomon outside the city walls where there was a small palace and a church dedicated to St John the Evangelist. It was as if in death as in life, Basil wanted to distance himself as much from the administrators of the Great Palace as from the magnates of the provinces. His epitaph, which he himself may have written, proclaimed that he had 'kept vigilant through the whole span of my life guarding the children of New Rome'. It was not an idle boast but he had left a mixed legacy: a full treasury and expanded borders but also a sullen and resentful provincial aristocracy.

* * *

Basil II was succeeded by his brother, Constantine VIII. In theory, Constantine had been emperor ever since his father's death back in 963, ruling jointly with Basil, but he had been completely sidelined first by Nikephoros Phokas and John Tzimiskes and later by his brother, who had no desire to share power. Basil had ensured that Constantine had ample scope for hunting, bathing and his favourite hobby of cookery, but gave him no political role and assigned him only a meagre guard of honour. That Constantine should now, aged well into his sixties, suddenly be in command of the empire was the result of an extraordinary omission on the part of Basil II. He had spent a lifetime striving to ensure that the Macedonian family ruled from Constantinople without the interference of the warlords of Asia Minor, yet he had never married or sired an heir to take his place. Constantine did get married, to a lady called Helena Alypia, and they had three children, all girls. The obvious course of action would have been to find them suitable matches so that the dynasty would be perpetuated. One of them, Zoe, was engaged to the German emperor Otto III but, when she arrived in Italy on her way to the nuptials, she received news that he had died, so she promptly sailed back to Constantinople. Thereafter nothing whatever seems to have been done and by 1025, all three women were still unmarried and were entering into middle age. The eldest, Eudokia, had in fact taken religious vows and entered a convent. Perhaps Basil's omission is understandable. If his nieces were to marry within the empire it would have had to have been to someone of wealth and position: to someone among the very group that the emperor most feared.

By the autumn of 1028, however, the business of providing for the succession could no longer be put off. Constantine VIII fell ill and he anxiously did what Basil had always avoided by consulting with his courtiers on the best course of action. Clearly some prominent individual would have to be brought in to take over, as Maurice had been back in 582, but at least the transfer could be stage-managed by the administrators of the Great Palace so that they could choose a candidate who would not sacrifice their interests and those of the Macedonian family to those of the army and the distant provinces. Above all they wanted to avoid a successful general who could use his standing with the troops to impose himself on them. So while they did consider Constantine Dalassenos, an able soldier who had wide estates in the Armeniakon theme, he looked rather too like a potential Nikephoros Phokas and was rejected. In the end they decided on a certain Romanos Argyros, who was distantly related to the Macedonians, held the office of governor of Constantinople and looked a great deal less threatening. The process by which he was made emperor was hasty and clumsy. He was summoned to the palace and informed by the courtiers that he must divorce his wife and marry Constantine's youngest daughter, Theodora. The ambitious Argyros was happy enough to comply but after his wife had been safely consigned to a nunnery and the patriarch had been leant on to give his sanction, Theodora refused to go through with the ceremony. The middle daughter, Zoe, had to be prevailed upon. Constantine VIII died three days after the wedding and Argyros was proclaimed emperor as Romanos III (1028–1034).

The nuptials ushered in a period of nearly thirty years when a series of emperors ruled by virtue of their association with the niece of Basil II. Zoe herself generally took little part in politics. While her husband ruled the empire, she busied herself in her suite of rooms in the palace distilling new and exotic perfumes. She installed charcoal braziers in her bedroom for this purpose and was so obsessed by her hobby that she was completely indifferent to the stifling heat they generated in the summer months. She is one of the few Byzantines, along with Justinian, of whom we have both a realistic portrait and a first-hand description. Her portrait is a mosaic that still survives in the cathedral of the Holy Wisdom. It appears to be remarkably flattering for a woman who must have been in her late sixties when it was made, but it is confirmed in a description left by someone who knew her quite well, the courtier Michael Psellos:

> Her eyes were large, set wide apart, with imposing eyebrows. Her nose was inclined to be aquiline without being altogether so. She had golden hair, and her whole body was radiant with the whiteness of her skin. There were few signs of age in her.

When Romanos drowned in his bath in mysterious circumstances in 1034, Zoe immediately married again, this time taking a husband of her own choice, one of the commanders of the palace guard, a man many decades her junior with whom she had probably been having an affair before Romanos's demise. The new incumbent reigned as Michael IV (1034–1041) until he succumbed to the epilepsy from which he had suffered all his life. There followed a brief period when the nephew of the late emperor ruled as Michael V (1041–1042) after being adopted by Zoe as her son. His reign came to an abrupt end when he attempted to thrust his adoptive mother aside and establish himself as emperor in his own right. The loyalty of the Constantinopolitan populace towards the Macedonians was undiminished and rioting broke out in the streets of Constantinople. Michael V was forced to flee the palace and Zoe returned in triumph. After a few months of ruling alongside her sister Theodora, in the summer of 1042 Zoe married her third and last husband, Constantine Monomachos, who then became Constantine IX (1042–1055).

Although the period 1028 to 1055 saw four emperors come and go, continuity was provided by the bureaucrats of the Great Palace. While Basil II had preferred to rule largely without advice after the downfall of Basil Lekapenos in 985, the decades after his death saw the return of the powerful figure behind the throne. The first was a eunuch who came from the Black Sea coast of Asia Minor and who was known as John the Orphanotrophos because one of his jobs was to look after Constantinople's orphanage. He had worked in the Great Palace under Basil II, and the great emperor's successors found him far too useful to be dispensed with. Everyday administrative details could simply be delegated to him and his zeal and attention to detail were legendary. He would sally forth from the palace on his horse at a moment's notice and turn up anywhere in the city where he was least expected. Woe betide any official who had neglected his duties when the piercing eyes of the eunuch went over the accounts. Most terrifying of all was his ability to get uproariously drunk at parties while still remaining alert and listening to every word that his subordinates said while in their cups. The next day, hung over and embarrassed, they would be reminded of their indiscretions by their superior, himself apparently unaffected by the previous evening's revels. John's star rose even higher when in 1034 the palace guard Michael married Zoe and became emperor as Michael IV, since he was the eunuch's brother. When Michael became increasing unwell, John effectively ruled the empire. But, in the end, the Orphanotrophos too slid off the greasy pole of Byzantine politics: he was dismissed from office by the callow and short-reigned Michael V and sent off to a monastery. As soon as he became emperor in 1042 Constantine IX had him blinded, an effective if brutal way of preventing any resuscitation of his career. The once powerful eunuch died shortly after.

Before long the palace came to be dominated by another powerful *éminence grise*. Michael Psellos was not a eunuch but he had gained entry to the imperial civil service by virtue of his silver tongue. When first interviewed by Constantine IX, he later claimed, the emperor was 'affected by a strange feeling of pleasure' and felt a strong desire to embrace the young man. It is unlikely that the emotion was a sexual one, for the emperor's needs in that direction were met by his numerous mistresses, but rather Constantine had recognised that Psellos would be very useful to him. He made him his chief adviser. Psellos drew up official correspondence, gave public speeches presenting and justifying Constantine's policies and was generally, he said, 'entrusted with the most honourable duties'. It was a role he maintained almost unbroken until about

1075 and in that period he had almost as much influence on policy as any emperor. He left his own account of his life and work in a set of memoirs which, highly partisan though they are, provide an extraordinarily detailed insight into life in the Great Palace.

Under this regime of short-reigned emperors and powerful administrators, things now reverted to the way they had been in the days of Constantine VII, and policy was formed by a group whose outlook was firmly centred on Constantinople, whether they were aristocrats like Romanos III and Constantine IX or of humble origins like Michael IV and Michael Psellos. They deeply distrusted open war as an instrument of policy and soon abandoned the aggressive expansionism of the past. There were a few campaigns beyond the borders. In 1030, when the emir of Aleppo threw off his allegiance to Byzantium, Romanos III marched into Syria, but the expedition was not a success. The army was attacked and scattered by the Arabs, and Romanos had to make an undignified retreat back to Antioch. There was an attempt to conquer Sicily in the 1030s and in 1045 the Byzantines annexed the Armenian city of Ani, which had been bequeathed to the emperor by its ruler. Thereafter, however, the instinct of the regime was for consolidation. Wars tended to be defensive, as in 1041 when a revolt in Bulgaria was put down and in 1043 when a Russian attack on Constantinople by sea was beaten off. Instead treaties were made with potential enemies. Since 1001 Byzantium had observed a truce with the major Muslim power on its eastern border, the Fatimid caliphate of Egypt, and in 1027 the truce became a formal treaty. In 1045 peace was made with the Russians. Prince Iaroslav's son, Vesvolod, was married to a daughter of Constantine IX by a previous marriage and there were no further attacks on Constantinople from Kiev.

Parallel to this curtailment of military commitments was the reorganisation of the provinces to allow the capital to exert greater control over the administration of the themes. Originally, the *strategos* had administered both civil and military matters but during the tenth century his role had been confined to military matters. Civil affairs, including law suits, had been entrusted to a local judge. In the 1040s, a kind of ministry of justice was established in Constantinople to supervise the activities of these local judges. There was also a rethinking of the military role of the themes. Designed to counter Arab raids deep into Asia Minor, the theme armies had become largely redundant once those raids ceased, with the salaried *tagmata* becoming the backbone of the Byzantine army. In the middle of his reign, Constantine IX decided to disband the army of the theme of Iberia in Armenia and to require its 50,000 peasant farmers to pay taxes in money in lieu of military service, a useful boost to the treasury.

In short, ruling circles in Constantinople were reverting to the old Byzantine technique of achieving security by means other than war, particularly the judicious use of money. The rich diplomatic gift made a comeback. Foreign dignitaries who visited Constantinople were plied with presents of gold, silver and silk garments and with proposals to sign up as allies of the emperor. Basil II's parsimony and dislike of ceremony and display were abandoned. Both Romanos III and Constantine IX built vast new monasteries in Constantinople, lavishing public money on the interior decoration. This was not mere profligacy. Romanos and Constantine were raising the empire's prestige with wealth, art and beauty, a tactic that had worked so well in helping to convert the Russians. It was still working now. In 1045, a Pecheneg leader called Kegen visited Constantinople, where he was baptised. He was given the title of patrician and three castles along the Danube frontier. A monk was sent back with him to baptise Kegen's 20,000 followers in the river. Like Basil II, the new regime eagerly recruited mercenaries whom they could control and keep under their own command, although they were now increasingly western Europeans, particularly Normans and Scandinavians, rather than Russians and Armenians.

These policies were not unreasonable and by no means unprecedented but there was one group with whom they were not going to be popular: the military aristocracy of Asia Minor, who had been largely excluded from the decision-making process since 989. To them the grandiose building projects in Constantinople were sheer prodigality and the treaties with foreign powers no more than cowardice. They knew perfectly well, too, that the reform of the provincial administration had another motive beside efficiency. By supervising local judges more strictly from Constantinople, the bureaucrats in the Great Palace could ensure that they were not in the pocket of the *strategos*. The aristocrats also resented the recruitment of mercenaries from outside the empire. As one of them warned the emperor:

> If foreigners are not of royal descent in their own country, do not invest them with great honours nor entrust to them high offices. For in doing so you will not help yourself in any way, nor will you please your own officers who are of Roman origin.

For the fact was that those who ruled Byzantium under the long shadow of the late Basil II shared his deep mistrust of the warlords and were acutely aware of the danger of another Phokas rising up to challenge them. It was Constantine VIII who finally crushed the family altogether, having the grandson of Bardas Phokas arrested on a trumped-up charge and blinded, but the successors of

Basil II were aware that it was dangerous to alienate the warlords completely. So, to start with, a few concessions were made. On his accession in 1028, Romanos III repealed Basil II's Allelengyon law of 1004 which had made the aristocrats responsible for making up the shortfall in tax receipts in their districts. It was hardly a radical move, for both Basil II and Constantine VIII had contemplated doing so, but in this way Romanos aimed to signal his good intent. He also released those people who had been imprisoned for failure to make their Allelengyon payments, and recalled from exile Nikephoros Xiphias who had been involved in the revolt of 1021–1022. In the long term, however, the gulf between the provincial and Constantinopolitan view could not be bridged. There were further plots and punishments. In 1029 the *strategos* of the Thrakesion theme, Constantine Diogenes, was arrested for treason and committed suicide by throwing himself from a tower. By the 1040s tensions had built up to a dangerous level.

* * *

The outbreak came when the regime in Constantinople handed out to one of the empire's most successful generals the kind of treatment Basil II had meted out to Philokales and Maleinos in 995. Although he had not been born into the military aristocracy but had risen through the ranks, George Maniakes looked every inch the warlord. Like Bardas Phokas, he was extremely tall with a thunderous voice that could easily make itself heard above the din of battle. He had come to prominence in 1030 after the Arabs had routed the army of Romanos III and sent him scuttling back to Antioch. As *strategos* of the theme of Teleuch, Maniakes had ambushed an Arab contingent that was returning from the victory, capturing 280 camels laden with plunder. The following year, he had captured Edessa and in 1038 he was sent to southern Italy with a view to recovering Sicily from the Arabs. Over the next year he retook much of the eastern coast of the island, including the city of Syracuse.

News of these successes received a mixed response in the court at Constantinople. Maniakes was recovering lost territory but John the Orphanotrophos can hardly have forgotten that Nikephoros Phokas's conquest of Crete had quickly been followed by his march on Constantinople and seizure of the throne. When a letter arrived from his brother-in-law, who was serving in Maniakes's army, warning him that the general was planning to seize the throne, John did not hesitate. He had Maniakes relieved of his command and brought back to Constantinople as a prisoner. On this occasion Maniakes was lucky. After the family of John the Orphanotrophos had lost power in the riots of 1042, Empress Zoe had Maniakes released and sent back to Italy to resume his command. But the seeds of mistrust had been sown and, when Maniakes heard that his estates in Asia Minor had been plundered with impunity by one of his neighbours who had connections at court, he began to contemplate revolt. Constantine IX, by now emperor, got wind of the plot and dispatched an official called Pardos to relieve Maniakes of command once more. But it was too late. By the time Pardos arrived, Maniakes had already been proclaimed emperor and his troops, who were fanatically loyal to their commander, set on Pardos as he rode into the camp and killed him. There was now no going back. Maniakes marched with his army to the sea, crossed the Adriatic and marched on Constantinople.

At first it looked as if Maniakes would pull off the same feat as Nikephoros Phokas in 963. That he did not was the result of a stroke of luck reminiscent of the sudden demise of Bardas Phokas in 989. In February 1043, as it marched east, Maniakes's army encountered a force sent from Constantinople to block its path. The imperial troops had little hope of success, because the very name of Maniakes struck terror into their hearts, and after a confused melee they started to beat a hasty retreat. Then, as they did so, a stray arrow hit Maniakes, who was leading the pursuit, in his right side. He fell from his horse and bled to death before help could reach him. Deprived of its leader, the revolt evaporated. Constantine IX was to enjoy a similarly charmed life throughout his reign. Another military revolt in 1047 reached the Land Walls of Constantinople and while Constantine was on the battlements inspecting the defences an arrow whistled close by his head. But this attempt on the throne also fizzled out when it was clear that no one on the inside was prepared to let the rebels in through the Land Walls. For the time being, the military men were kept out in the cold.

* * *

There were two developments that allowed the successors of Nikephoros Phokas to return to power. The first was the renewal of the threat to the Byzantine frontiers. This was partly another legacy of Basil II. His annexation of Bulgaria had removed the empire's buffer state and given it a border with the Pechenegs on the Danube. In the past, the Pechenegs had been a useful ally to turn on the Bulgars or Russians but now it was Byzantine territory that lay in the path of their attacks. Their raids had started in 1027, and by the 1040s had become so intense that Constantine IX and his advisers resorted to the tried and tested method of allowing the Pechenegs to settle on imperial land in the former Bulgaria in return for military service. Unfortunately, the Pechenegs did not like the territory they had been given and in 1048 they moved south, across the Balkan mountains, on to land that the Byzantines had no intention of giving them. Fighting dragged on for several years, with the Byzantine army chasing the Pechenegs round the Balkans, all to no avail. Realising that this was an unwinnable war, in about 1053 Constantine had to make a thirty-year truce with the Pechenegs on most disadvantageous terms and to accept their settlement south of the Balkan mountains.

The worsening situation in the Balkans was paralleled by threats elsewhere from enemies that the Byzantines had not encountered before. In southern Italy, the departure of George Maniakes in 1043 opened the way for Normans. Kinsmen of the Normans who were later to conquer England, they had arrived in southern Italy in 1018 to fight as mercenaries for a Byzantine rebel. They soon fell out with their employer and began to seize parts of the area for themselves. On the other side of the empire, in newly annexed Armenia, a similar danger was posed by the Seljuk Turks. Like the Pechenegs, the Seljuks were a nomadic people who had originated on the steppes of Asia and who had migrated down into north-eastern Persia. They had converted to Islam and by the middle of the eleventh century had become a major power in the Muslim world. In 1040, under their leader Tughrul, the Seljuks had won the battle of Dandanaqan, giving them control of a large swathe of Central Asia and Persia. This area bordered on Byzantine territory in Armenia and during Constantine IX's reign Turks along that border starting making damaging raids into Byzantine territory.

In this new world where defence had suddenly replaced expansion, provincial noblemen ceased to look like potential rebels and more like heroes, rising to the occasion while the government in Constantinople was entirely ineffective. In 1048, after a Seljuk force had sacked the Armenian town of Artze, they attacked the Byzantine army that had come to relieve the town. The commander, a Georgian prince called Liparit, whom Constantine IX had enrolled to fight the Turks, was surrounded and captured. On the right wing, however, the Byzantines fared much better. Kekavmenos Katakalon, governor of Ani and a veteran of George Maniakes's Sicilian campaign, routed the Seljuks and pursued them until nightfall. A similar incident occurred a few years later when the Pechenegs ambushed a retreating Byzantine column in the Balkan mountains. While most of the Byzantine troops scattered, making easy targets, one officer, Nikephoros Botaneiates, kept his contingent together. For eleven days they fought off Pecheneg attacks, allegedly without food or sleep, before finally reaching Adrianople and marching into the city in good order.

While gallant officers like Katakalon and Botaneiates were proving their worth on the field of battle, a second development robbed the regime in

Constantinople of its figleaf of legitimacy. The Macedonian dynasty was coming
to its natural end. Zoe died in 1050 and, when her husband Constantine IX
expired five years later, there was some uncertainty as to who would succeed. A
number of courtiers were in favour of elevating some high-ranking bureaucrat
to the throne but among others attachment to the Macedonians remained
strong. The last niece of Basil II, Theodora, was still alive and it seemed only
natural to many that she should exercise her birthright and rule the empire. So
for eighteen months the old royal family enjoyed its last days of power before
Theodora developed a bowel complaint and died. A few days later, the eunuchs
and courtiers of the Great Palace announced that an elderly courtier of the
Bringas family would succeed as Michael VI (1056–1057). They had unashamedly chosen from among their own group and they could hardly have expected
their choice to go uncontested.

* * *

The break came during Holy Week the following year, 1057. It was customary
at that time for the emperor to distribute annual payments to his officials,
counsellors and administrators. He would sit at a long table in one of the halls
of the Great Palace and the office holders would be called in in descending
order of rank. They were paid in gold coins so some of the higher officials
brought servants with them to drag away their heavy sacks. Since there were
many hundreds of names on the civil list, the ceremony went on for several
days. The new emperor Michael VI conducted the proceedings as usual but the
payments were, it was noticed, considerably more generous. Michael, after all,
owed his promotion to the throne entirely to the officials of the palace who had
chosen to put him there and he was not ungrateful.

Then the moment came for the military honours to be distributed. A
number of prominent commanders had travelled to the capital to receive their
due. One of them was Kekavmenos Katakalon, who had driven off the Seljuk
raid of 1048. John and Constantine Doukas represented one of the older military families, and also present was Isaac Komnenos, who held land around
Kastamon in Asia Minor. As they filed in, Michael Psellos was standing behind
the emperor and he noted what happened next. The largesse heaped on the
palace bureaucrats was not extended to the soldiers. Not only was there no
promotion or salary increase but the emperor also berated the commanders for
failing in their duty against the Seljuks and Pechenegs and accused them of
trying to use their positions for personal advancement.

Stunned and humiliated, the generals left the room. They sought out
Michael VI's chief adviser, Leo Paraspondylas, and demanded that he change

the emperor's mind, but they found no comfort there either. They stalked out of the palace and across the Augousteion to Hagia Sophia to discuss their next move. It was there that the plan to rebel was hatched, the only point of disagreement being who was to lead the rebellion. Katakalon seemed the obvious candidate but he was unwilling. In the end they settled on Isaac Komnenos and they left the city without further delay. About a month later, Isaac was proclaimed emperor at Gounaria on his estates in Asia Minor.

Michael VI had precipitated the very thing that ruling circles in Constantinople feared most and, if he hoped that Isaac Komnenos would conveniently drop dead as Bardas Phokas and George Maniakes had done, he was to be disappointed. Komnenos and his army marched west to Nicaea, put to flight a force sent to oppose them and then marched into Nikomedeia. Michael VI tried to negotiate, sending a delegation led by Psellos to offer Komnenos the succession to the throne after Michael's death. The rebel leader would have been happy to accept these terms but as it turned out he did not have to. In Constantinople crowds had been gathering in the streets and opposition to Michael VI was being orchestrated by the patriarch. When he realised that he lacked support even among his own advisers, Michael abdicated. Two days later, Isaac Komnenos entered Constantinople to a tumultuous welcome from the populace who, now that the Macedonians were no more, were happy to give a chance to a soldier from the provinces.

With Constantinople secure, Isaac acted very wisely to avoid the kind of opprobrium that Nikephoros Phokas had attracted. He quickly paid off his soldiers to forestall any temptation on their part to loot the homes of the citizens, and withdrew them to Asia Minor. There was no witch hunt against the supporters of the previous regime who had striven so long and hard to keep the soldiers out of power. Psellos, who had expected to be arrested, was received in a friendly way by the new emperor and confirmed in his post in the administration. But nobody could doubt that things were going to be different from now on. Isaac signalled the change in his first issue of gold coins. Contrary to previous practice, the emperor was displayed standing and holding a drawn sword: the new master meant business.

* * *

Like many of those who have been in opposition for a long time, Emperor Isaac and his military supporters probably underestimated the difficulties of reversing the policies of the previous regime. The priority was obvious: re-establishing the defences of the empire, whose weakness the recent Seljuk, Norman and Pecheneg invasions had so starkly exposed. That would need money and the treasury was depleted at the time of Isaac's takeover. Within weeks he had implemented a drastic programme of cutbacks on expenditure, reversing the high spending of his predecessors. Honours and pensions awarded by Michael VI were rescinded, gifts to the Church were cancelled, prestigious building projects were halted. The chief losers in the new austerity were the courtiers and officials of the palace but even Michael Psellos, one of their number, was prepared to admit that the cutbacks were necessary. The problem was that Isaac moved rather too fast and so provoked a vocal opposition to his reforms among the clergy and people of Constantinople, just as Nikephoros Phokas had. But while Phokas had at least been adored by his soldiers, Isaac was fair-minded enough to extend his cutbacks to military salaries, causing resentment in that quarter too.

Had Isaac pulled off a spectacular victory all would have been well, but in the months after his accession things only seemed to get worse. In the spring of 1059, a Seljuk raiding party laid siege to the town of Melitene, which had once been such a bone of contention in the cross-border war against the Arabs. Most of the civilian population wisely got out before the net closed but those who were left when the town did fall a few weeks later were mostly put to the sword. A Byzantine army pursued the attackers as they withdrew with their plunder but it did not engage them and instead allowed them to pass safely back to their own territory. It was hardly the kind of robust response that Isaac's drawn sword had promised. A few months later, Isaac had his chance to deal a blow when a group of Pechenegs crossed the Danube into Bulgaria. He led out the army in person in the style of Basil II, but unfortunately the raiders withdrew almost as soon as the emperor appeared on the scene. On the march back to Constantinople the Byzantine army got caught in a torrential rainstorm. As it attempted to ford a swollen river many men were swept away to their deaths. Within a few weeks of his return to the capital, the dejected and depressed Isaac fell ill of a fever and his life was despaired of. His death would be a signal for a rush for the throne by every prominent soldier in the empire. Desperate to avoid that, the courtiers persuaded Isaac to abdicate there and then in favour of another of the conspirators of 1057, Constantine Doukas.

As Constantine X (1059–1067), Doukas took a rather less head-on approach than Isaac had. Indeed even though he was a scion of one of the oldest military families, he does not give the impression of being a soldier emperor at all. Eager to court popularity, he restored many of the honours and pensions that Isaac had taken away as well as granting new ones. He announced that he had a great concern for the administration of justice and spent a great deal of time hearing civil suits. When it came to the crisis on the borders, he fought shy of

confrontation and never once led out an army in person. He resorted instead
to diplomacy, renewing the treaty with the Fatimids in 1063, well aware that
the regime in Cairo was as fearful of the Seljuks as he was. But the run of disasters continued. In 1060, a Seljuk raiding force plundered the city of Sebasteia
unchallenged for eight days, and four years later the Seljuk sultan, Alp Arslan,
invaded Byzantine Armenia and sacked the city of Ani, which the Byzantines
had taken over only twenty years before. Incredibly, Constantine's response
was deliberately to keep the army short of funds. Sebasteia had fallen so easily
because it had no garrison. The Turks had at first hesitated to attack the city
because, from a distance, the domes of the churches looked like the tents of an
occupying army, but once they realised that it was completely undefended they
simply marched in.

The fact was that, in spite of his military background, now that he was
emperor in Constantinople, Constantine X saw things in a different light. He
was acutely aware that now that there was no longer a universally recognised
legitimate dynasty, there was nothing to prevent any successful soldier from
mounting exactly the kind of coup that had unseated Michael VI. The next
time, Constantine and his family would be the victims. He was, therefore,
consciously or unconsciously, following the advice of Bardas Skleros to Basil II
to 'let no generals on campaign have too many resources'. At the end of the day
the divide was not between the civilians and the soldiers but between the needs
of a metropolitan centre and those of the far-flung and newly acquired provinces. It was that divide that was to lead to disaster.

* * *

In December 1067, Michael Psellos was summoned to an interview with the
empress. Constantine X had died the previous May and since then the empire
had been ruled by the usual regency council, composed of Constantine's widow,
Eudokia, his brother John Doukas and Psellos, on behalf of his son Michael
VII, who was only in his early teens. 'You must be aware', said the empress
Eudokia, 'of our loss in prestige and the declining fortunes of our empire.' That
Psellos could hardly deny: the Seljuks had recently attacked Caesarea, a city
that was not in Armenia but deep in Asia Minor, far from the frontier. Even so,
he temporised, fearing that the empress's solution was likely to be unpalatable,
and suggested that some thought should be given to the matter. This elicited
only a laugh. The empress announced that a decision had already been
made and that she intended to provide leadership by remarrying. Her choice
had fallen on Romanos Diogenes, a Cappadocian aristocrat and son of the
Constantine Diogenes who had killed himself in 1029 after being charged with

treason. His military record was impeccable and during the previous reign, as governor of Serdica, he had inflicted several defeats on the Pechenegs. Thus Eudokia hoped to provide the strong military emperor that Isaac I and Constantine X had failed so signally to be, ruling alongside the legitimate emperor Michael VII, just as Nikephoros II Phokas had ruled alongside Basil II and Constantine VIII. The marriage took place on the first day of 1068 and Diogenes was proclaimed emperor as Romanos IV (1068–1071).

The new emperor certainly made a drastic change of course. Treaties and tribute were once again off the agenda in favour of direct military confrontation. Like Heraclius before him, Romanos made the decision to deal with his eastern enemies first and aimed to inflict a knockout blow on the Seljuk Turks. As soon as he was established, he gathered a large army and set out for eastern Asia Minor. His very presence was enough to ensure that there were no Seljuk raids that year but he failed to get to grips with the enemy, who withdrew whenever he was in the area. The following year, he followed in the footsteps of John Tzimiskes and invaded Syria, probably to ensure that Byzantium remained a player in the Seljuk–Fatimid rivalry over the emirate of Aleppo. That, however, did not prevent the Turks from invading Byzantine territory and sacking Ikonion.

By this stage one can detect some frustration on Romanos's part that all-out victory had eluded him. He knew perfectly well that on that victory depended not only the security of the frontiers but his own political survival, because he had many enemies in Constantinople. When Eudokia had negotiated her marriage with Romanos, she had deliberately left her brother-in-law John Doukas and Michael Psellos in the dark, knowing perfectly well that they would see Diogenes' promotion as a threat both to the rights of the young Michael VII and to their own position at court. Psellos had been a personal friend of Constantine X and had helped to engineer his accession as emperor, so that his political future was intimately connected with that of the Doukas family. Were Romanos to fail, Psellos and his Doukas allies were waiting in the wings to oust him. That was why, in the spring of 1071, the emperor marched into eastern Asia Minor once more, seeking a complete military victory like that of 971 in Bulgaria.

At first the campaign went well. Romanos successfully recaptured the Armenian town of Manzikert. When his scouts reported the presence of a Turkish army under the command of the sultan Alp Arslan himself, Romanos felt confident enough in his larger force to reject the sultan's peace overtures and he ordered an attack on the Turkish army. At first the Byzantines seemed to be winning. The Seljuks wavered in the face of their attack and withdrew precipitately. The emperor led the pursuit until nightfall but ended up being cut off with his bodyguard from the rest of his army. After putting up a fierce fight, during which his horse was killed under him, and warding off his enemies for hours with his sword, he was taken prisoner. Darkness then fell and the battle of Manzikert, fought on 26 August 1071, came to an end. The encounter has gone down in history as a catastrophe but it was in fact nothing of the kind. There was very little pitched fighting and relatively few casualties on either side, certainly nothing on the scale of the severe losses inflicted on the Byzantines by the Bulgars in 811 and 917. Most of the Byzantine soldiers escaped. Indeed, one of Romanos's officers, Andronicus Doukas, son of the disgruntled John Doukas, encouraged them to withdraw to safety even before the emperor had been captured. Naturally the supporters of Romanos regarded his action as treachery but it could also be seen as a sensible move to prevent further losses. The capture of the emperor was certainly a blow but the sultan released him after only eight days and allowed him to return to his army: Alp Arslan was far more interested in returning to Syria to pursue his war against the Fatimids. The supposed catastrophe was therefore merely an unfortunate and embarrassing reverse.

It was the events that followed the battle that constituted the disaster, and this arose from the mismatch between capital and provinces. At the end of August, messengers started arriving in Constantinople bringing confused reports of the defeat, some announcing that Romanos was dead, others that he was captured. In the circumstances, Psellos and the Doukas family, who had never wanted Romanos to be emperor anyway, declared that Michael VII should now rule in his own right, as he was old enough to do so. The Varangian guard gathered around the young man and started to bang their shields together as they proclaimed him sole ruler. Then a few days later more messengers arrived in the capital: Romanos was not in fact dead and was no longer even a prisoner – he was reunited with his troops and marching westwards. The Doukas family could, of course, have accepted this and allowed Michael VII to return to his subordinate position but this they were unwilling to do and so orders were immediately sent out to the provinces that Romanos was no longer to be acknowledged as emperor. For all his experience and prestige, Romanos IV quickly lost the civil war that followed. In May 1072, his forces were put to flight by Andronicus Doukas near Adana. Rather than prolong the hopeless struggle by trying to hold the town, Romanos surrendered on the promise of his personal safety. Doukas promptly reneged on the undertaking and had the deposed emperor blinded, the operation being carried out so brutally that Romanos was dead within a few months.

It was an undisputable victory for Michael VII and his supporters which meant that he was now secure as sole emperor in Constantinople. In the past that would have been enough but now the decades of alienation between capital and provinces came home to roost. Many of those who had been loyal to Romanos IV refused to accept the sovereignty of Michael VII and created their own independent lordships in Asia Minor. A French mercenary called Roussel of Bailleul, who had served in Romanos's army during the Manzikert campaign, mutinied and led off the four hundred troops he was commanding to set himself up as an independent ruler in the Armeniakon theme around Amaseia. The local inhabitants, despairing of effective protection from distant Constantinople, paid their taxes to him instead and so purchased a local force to protect them against Turkish raiders. Philaretos, an Armenian who had also been with Romanos IV at Manzikert, took over Edessa and much of Cilicia. In 1077, Nikephoros Botaneiates, the commander who had saved his men in the Pecheneg ambush in 1047, was proclaimed emperor and began to march on Constantinople. Later in the same year another general, Nikephoros Bryennios, declared his candidature for the throne at Adrianople.

These internal upheavals inevitably meant that the defence of the borders began to break down and Turkish raids into Armenia and Asia Minor resumed. These were not orchestrated by the Seljuk sultan himself but by his subjects living along the border, over whom he had little or no control. Finding that they were not opposed, they no longer withdrew after their raids but began to settle on the land, particularly on the Anatolian plateau. One group, led by a man called Danishmend, seized the city of Sebasteia and took control of the area round about. Another band, under Süleyman ibn Kutulmush, a cousin of Alp Arslan, marched into western Asia Minor, where they were recruited by Nikephoros Botaneiates to aid him in his bid for the throne. Having taken Nicaea, Botaneiates handed it over to Suleyman to govern, allowing the Turks to establish themselves there too. By 1080 the emperor in Constantinople had effectively lost control of almost the whole of Asia Minor apart from a few small coastal enclaves.

In the wake of such a drastic loss of territory, recriminations and mud-slinging were inevitable. The supporters of Romanos blamed the Doukas family for treacherously overthrowing the gallant soldier emperor. Psellos and the Doukas family accused Romanos of rashness and military incompetence. Some looked further back and remembered how Zoe's third husband Constantine IX had disbanded the theme army of Iberia and spent money instead on a splendid new monastery in Constantinople. Doubtless all these people played their part but the process had been set in train long before. At

the end of the day, however, whatever his qualities as a soldier and his achievements in the field, it was Basil II who had begun the alienation of Asia Minor
from the capital, crushing the very class who provided its defence and leading
them to resent the centre of power that sucked in resources but provided little
in return. In time, Byzantium was to display its almost legendary ability to
come back from the brink, but the uneasy relationship between Constantinople
and its hinterland was to persist for the remainder of its existence.

CHAPTER EIGHT

The Enemy Within

During the reign of Manuel, beloved of God, the Latins had found great favour
with him – a reward well deserved because of their loyalty and valour.
William of Tyre, *c.* 1130–1186

A century after the defeat at Manzikert, the Byzantine empire was not only still in existence but was flourishing. The western provinces of the empire that had once taken so long to recover from the Slavs and Bulgars were now prospering. Towns such as Athens, Thebes and Corinth had become centres for manufacturing and commerce and were expanding fast. Ports like Thessalonica and Dyrrachion were enjoying a boom in trade. The empire had also recovered much of the territory in Asia Minor that it had lost in the last decades of the eleventh century. Nicaea, Smyrna and Amorion were once more under Byzantine rule, as was most of the Asia Minor coastline, the most fertile and developed part of the region. Most prosperous of all was the city of Constantinople where trade was flourishing as never before, bringing in a healthy stream of taxes, duties and customs dues to the imperial treasury. The Golden Horn was thronged with merchant vessels and the conspicuous display of wealth in the streets was a source of comment and wonder from visitors. Once again Byzantium had displayed its extraordinary ability to bounce back from the worst of disasters.

Political stability had been restored after the upheavals and near anarchy of the 1070s. A new imperial dynasty had established itself, the Komnenoi, the same family of Asia Minor warlords that had provided the short-reigned Isaac I. At Easter time in 1081 Isaac's nephew had seized Constantinople and had then gone on to enjoy a long reign as Alexios I (1081–1118). He had had no

legitimacy whatsoever at the time that he seized power apart from his marriage
to a member of the Doukas family. It was only that he got to Constantinople just
ahead of another would-be emperor whom he then had to buy off with titles and
lands. The stigma of being a usurper was never quite erased, and Alexios's reign
was marked by constant plots and attempted coups. By the time he died, however,
the family had come to be accepted as the royal dynasty. Power passed almost,
although not entirely, seamlessly to an adult son John II (1118–1143) who had
been born in the purple chamber, the first time this had happened since 959.
When John died on campaign in Syria in 1143, his son Manuel succeeded,
though again there was some slight irregularity: Manuel I (1143–1180) was the
youngest son and he had to imprison his elder brother to ensure his own succession. In comparison with the upheavals of the late eleventh century, however, the
period 1118 to 1180 was one of internal peace and harmony and the inhabitants
of Constantinople now accorded the same aura of legitimacy to the Komnenoi
as they had to the Macedonians for so long. When a son was born to Manuel in
1169 it was an occasion of great rejoicing, as it would ensure no return to the
days when a general might march his troops on Constantinople to seize power.
Moreover, like Basil II, the Komnenoi led the armies on campaign themselves,
so reducing their reliance on dangerous underlings.

The new imperial incumbents left their mark on the cityscape of
Constantinople with new buildings springing up alongside Hagia Sophia,
Justinian's column and the church of the Holy Apostles. In the centre of the city,
a new church and monastery had appeared. Founded by John II and his wife
Irene in 1136, the Pantokrator was partly designed to provide a mausoleum for
the deceased emperors of the Komnenos family. A mortuary chapel dedicated
to the Archangel Michael, beside the main church, became John and Irene's last
resting place. No expense was spared on the marble pavement and the mosaics
but the Pantokrator was not only built to flatter the vanity of an emperor. Like
many Byzantine ecclesiastical institutions, it also played a social function, in
this case by housing a hospital where the poorer residents of Constantinople
could receive treatment for free. With his usual attention to detail, John II drew
up a foundation charter for the monastery which spelled out precisely what
kind of treatment the hospital was to dispense. It was to specialise in fractures,
ophthalmitis and stomach disorders, and a proportion of its beds were to be set
aside for women, who would have female doctors to attend them. John's father
Alexios had established a similar complex at the far eastern tip of the city.
Known as the Orphanotropheion, it fed and housed thousands of severely
disabled at the expense of the state and provided a school for orphaned children. The imperial residence had changed too. The Komnenian emperors had

largely abandoned the Great Palace and moved to Blachernae. Situated at the northern end of the Land Walls and overlooking the Golden Horn, the palace there provided a much more comfortable living space and gave easy access to the countryside of Thrace where the emperors could pursue their favourite pastime of hunting. Manuel I had the whole complex rebuilt on a grand scale, inserting a grand throne room and long, colonnaded galleries, their walls overlaid with mosaics depicting his many victories.

It was not only the landscape of Constantinople that had changed by the 1170s but its demography as well. The city had always been cosmopolitan, with Arab merchants, Russian pilgrims and Pecheneg mercenaries all thronging its streets. But now one group of outsiders had become more prominent than any other. These were the people that the Byzantines referred to rather vaguely as 'Latins'. They were Christian western Europeans, hailing from all over the continent, from Scandinavia, Normandy, England and Flanders in the north to the city states of Italy in the south. They were most in evidence in the strip of land alongside the Golden Horn, Constantinople's commercial quarter. Here the Venetian, Genoese and Pisan merchants had their houses, wharves and warehouses. But they were to be found elsewhere too. In the palace of Blachernae they now made up most of the emperor's personal Varangian guard, once the preserve of the Russians. When the emperor marched out of the city on campaign, Latins likewise constituted a significant proportion of his army, with Normans and others from what is now France predominating. In many ways, their presence brought huge benefits and they could claim a large part of the credit for the empire's survival and recovery after the disasters of the 1070s. Yet in the end these western Christians were to prove something of an enemy within and they were to inflict on Byzantium a catastrophe far greater than those which it had weathered in the past.

* * *

It was not that the Komnenoi were solely responsible for bringing the Latins to prominence in Byzantium. The process had begun decades before. Where Basil II had relied on the Russians to see off challenges from the military aristocracy, his successors had become aware of the martial qualities of the westerners and recruited them on a large scale as mercenaries. They had helped Constantine IX Monomachos to survive a serious military revolt in 1047 and by the 1070s Latin mercenaries had come to compose a considerable proportion of Byzantine armies in the field. Hence, as an army commander, it was only natural that Alexios Komnenos should find himself leading large numbers of Latin troops, and, when he made his bid for the throne in early 1081, they were the soldiers that he led towards Constantinople. As was always the case, Alexios's advance came to an abrupt halt at the Land Walls and the army camped outside them as various means of getting into the city were considered. Bribery was an obvious route but Alexios was informed that two stretches of wall were held by the Immortals, a regiment of Byzantines, and the Varangian guard. It was well known that both were renowned for their fidelity to the reigning emperor and could not be suborned. Another section, however, had been entrusted to the Nemitzoi, a regiment of Latin mercenaries that might be tempted by the prospect of some bonus pay. One of Alexios's Latin soldiers was sent forward under cover of darkness to parley with the leader of the Nemitzoi, who lent over the battlements cautiously to exchange words. It was this man who on 1 April 1081 opened a gate in one of the towers to allow Alexios's troops to pour into the city. Once they were in, Alexios completely lost control of them and both his Latin and Byzantine soldiers spent the day looting churches and private houses. The new emperor had to spend the first forty days of his reign under a strict regime of penance, imposed by the Church to atone for these outrages, wearing a hair shirt under his imperial robes and sleeping on the floor with a stone for his pillow.

In spite of the unfortunate end of the episode, the fact remained that Alexios had come to power partly through the help of the Latins. Not surprisingly they became even more visible in Constantinople during his reign. An English monk who visited Constantinople in around 1090 was astonished when one of the palace guards suddenly addressed him in his native language. As well as providing his guards, Latins were also to be found among Alexios's closest counsellors. In a treaty that he signed in 1107, six of the eight other signatories from the imperial court had Latin names such as Geoffrey of Mailli. He was right to trust them for it was largely with Latin help that Alexios was able to remain in power and to reverse the desperate situation that the empire found itself in at the beginning of his reign.

By 1081, the empire had almost lost control of the whole of Asia Minor. The southern area of Cilicia had fallen under Armenian rule while most of the rest, as far west as Nicaea, was under the control of various bands of Turks. Imperial rule lingered in isolated outposts such as Antioch but that too was to fall to the Turks in 1084. In the Balkans, the Pechenegs remained unsubdued and liable to attack Byzantine towns and villages at any time, while the whole of southern Italy had been lost to the Normans. Matters deteriorated further in the summer of 1081 when the Norman ruler of southern Italy, Robert Guiscard, launched an invasion of the Balkans across the Adriatic, laying siege to the port of Dyrrachion and threatening to march east towards Constantinople.

In this situation the usual recourse to Latin mercenaries was risky. Normans, who had often been recruited in the past, might have a conflict of loyalty if sent against Guiscard. Alexios therefore recruited several thousand troops from among the Turks of Asia Minor and ferried them across to Europe, but he also targeted those Latins whom he knew to have no love for the Normans. One obvious group were the Anglo-Saxon exiles who had fled from England in the wake of the Norman conquest of 1066 and a contingent of them was with Alexios's army when it clashed with that of Guiscard at Dyrrachion in October 1081. If these English mercenaries were hoping to take revenge for the battle of Hastings, they were cruelly disappointed. The Byzantine army was swept from the field and, although Alexios was not captured as Romanos Diogenes had been at Manzikert, he had to flee ignominiously from the field with Norman horsemen in hot pursuit. Many of his English soldiers were not so lucky. They took refuge in a church but the Normans showed no respect for sanctuary, setting fire to the place and burning it to the ground along with everyone inside.

Holed up behind the walls of Constantinople, the emperor put out diplomatic feelers towards other Latin allies, particularly the German emperor Henry IV whom he knew to be at loggerheads with the Normans of Italy. His envoys made an offer of 144,000 gold nomismata if Henry would strike at Guiscard's lands in Italy. Henry took the money but was to prove an unreliable ally. He did not invade Italy until 1084 and then his objective was Rome rather than the Normans, but at least his threat forced Robert Guiscard to return across the Adriatic, leaving his son Bohemond in charge of the war against Alexios. Another western ally had a more direct impact on the Norman invasion. Situated at the head of the Adriatic, the maritime republic of Venice was ideally placed to use its fleet to cut off the flow of men and supplies to the Norman bridgehead in the Balkans. It was, moreover, in its interest to come in on the Byzantine side because it had no desire to see one power in possession of both shores of the Adriatic. Venetian attacks on Norman fleets bringing over supplies and reinforcements undoubtedly hindered the invasion, which slowly lost momentum in the face of dogged resistance. In 1085 the Normans withdrew.

Latin help was also instrumental in putting an end to the old scourge, the Pechenegs, who were still at large and untamed in the Balkans. During the harsh winter of 1090–1091 they raided as far as the suburbs of Constantinople and for weeks no one dared venture outside the Land Walls into the snow-bound countryside. The following spring, Alexios marched out against them in force. His army included five hundred knights that had been sent to him by the count of Flanders and another Latin contingent that had arrived from Rome, as well as representatives of another Steppe tribe, the Cumans. On 29 April at Levounion in Thrace, this mixed force inflicted a devastating defeat on the Pechenegs, virtually wiping out their entire force of several thousand. The day after the battle, the victors had to leave the area hastily because of the stench of so many corpses. In Constantinople the relieved populace sang jubilantly in the streets: 'All because of one day, the Pechenegs never saw the month of May!'

Given that Latin help had been instrumental in bringing Alexios to power and defeating the Normans and Pechenegs, it is hardly surprising that he continued to seek more and more recruits and allies from that quarter. Unlike his predecessors, who contented themselves with attracting passing pilgrims, Alexios cast his net wider and sent out embassies to ever more distant western countries, to the king of England, the count of Flanders and even the pope in Rome. The recruitment drive was all the more urgent because, now that matters had been resolved in the western half of the empire, Alexios and his advisers were planning to recover territory in the east and to drive the Turks out of land that they had occupied in the aftermath of Manzikert. In doing so, Alexios may have subtly altered the traditional way in which allies and mercenaries were recruited. Generous amounts of gold were, as ever, offered but it is possible that other inducements were subtly added. Stress might well have been laid on the fact that, while the Byzantines and Latins were Christians, the Turks in Asia Minor were not. Fighting against these 'infidels' for the Christian emperor would therefore be a righteous cause which might well attract a spiritual, as well as the usual material, reward. Alexios's envoys may even have made mention of Jerusalem which, although it lay far outside Byzantine territory, exercised a potent hold on the Latin imagination as the place on earth closest to heaven. None of this can be proved for there is no record of exactly what it was that the Byzantine envoys said. But if they did make this kind of case on the instructions of the emperor then Alexios was partly responsible for what happened next.

* * *

In the spring of 1096, news arrived in Constantinople that several large Latin armies were being formed and that they would be marching east to join up at Constantinople before crossing the Bosporus to do battle with the Turks and forge on to liberate Jerusalem. Even if Emperor Alexios had dangled spiritual rewards and the prospect of a pilgrimage to the Holy Land in his recruitment drive, it is unlikely that he had envisaged a response on such a huge scale. What he could not have known was that his embassy to Pope Urban II in the spring of 1095 was to have unexpected repercussions. The pontiff took the Byzantine envoys' appeal for help against the Turks of Asia Minor to heart and the following autumn, when he was in France, he preached a rousing sermon to a huge congregation of knights and noblemen. Urging them to head east to help Byzantium and then capture Jerusalem, he promised that anyone who took part in the expedition would have their sins forgiven and that if they died on the campaign they would be admitted immediately to paradise without any need to atone for their wrongdoings in purgatory. It was this offer that prompted the mass response to the pope's appeal and led to the launch of what has come to be called the First Crusade.

To Alexios and his advisers in Constantinople the approach of these vast armies was the cause of some alarm and perplexity. On the one hand they were coming purportedly to help the empire against its enemies, but on the other they looked suspiciously like some of the many other invaders who had crossed the Byzantine frontiers over the centuries. After all, among the ranks of the crusaders were to be found men who had fought against Byzantium in the past, such as Bohemond of Taranto, the son of Robert Guiscard. Moreover, the sheer size of the approaching armies posed huge logistical problems, leading to fears that they would plunder the towns and villages they passed on their route to provide themselves with food. The emperor therefore fell back on a mixture of the tried and tested tactics by which the Byzantines had always diverted the bellicosity of one potential enemy against another. When the armies reached Constantinople, Alexios invited their leaders to the palace of Blachernae where he showered them with the usual gifts and flattery, but at the same time he took steps to ensure that the forthcoming offensive would be to Byzantine advantage. He insisted that the crusaders swear an oath that they would return to him any towns they conquered that had formerly been in Byzantine territory. When they requested that he accompany them to Jerusalem, however, he politely excused himself. Doubtless privately the emperor considered this to be a foolhardy enterprise and likely to end in disaster. All he could do was take as much advantage of it as he could before that happened.

Once the armies had been supplied and ferried over to the Asian side of the Bosporus, Alexios did exactly that. When the crusaders energetically laid siege to Nicaea in the spring of 1097, Alexios opened negotiations with the Turkish defenders and persuaded them to surrender the city to him. When the crusaders marched east on the next stage of their campaign, crushing a Turkish army at Dorylaion, Alexios took advantage of the diversion to send an army south to recover Smyrna and the Aegean coast. Within a few years some of the most fertile and prosperous parts of Asia Minor were again under Byzantine rule. By that time the crusade army had long moved beyond Byzantine territory, capturing Antioch in 1098 and finally Jerusalem itself in the summer of 1099. The establishment of the principality of Antioch and the kingdom of Jerusalem meant that Byzantium now had Christian neighbours in the east on what had once been Muslim territory. So, at first sight, the energy and bellicosity of the Latins had once more brought great benefits to Byzantium.

Ironically it was at this very moment of triumph that the seeds of doubt began to be sown in Constantinople as to just how beneficial the Latins actually were. While the passage of the First Crusade had allowed the Byzantines to recover western Asia Minor, the crusade leaders had not remained true to their oath to return to the Byzantines all towns that had once belonged to the empire. It had taken the crusaders nearly a year to capture the city of Antioch from its Turkish garrison, during which time they had been reduced to virtual starvation. Emperor Alexios had left Constantinople with an army to come to their aid but had turned back when he had received news that a huge Turkish army was approaching. Thus, when the city was finally secured in June 1098, the leaders felt in no hurry to hand it over to the emperor. When they moved on to attack Jerusalem, Bohemond of Taranto seized Antioch and garrisoned it with his own men, establishing a principality that was to last until 1268. Alexios first protested and then sent troops by sea to try to prevent Bohemond from occupying the land round about, but he could not dislodge the Latins from Antioch. His Christian allies had effectively robbed him of one of the most important Byzantine cities, leading some people in Constantinople privately to question the competence of Alexios's handling of the First Crusade.

Similar doubts were raised about another Latin power that Alexios had brought in as an ally: the Venetians. Their fleet had certainly helped to bring about the defeat of the Normans in the 1080s, but had the emperor not perhaps paid too high a price for their intervention? As well as the usual gold, silks and titles, the Venetians had received something much more valuable in view of their interest in the maritime trade between Constantinople and the west. Their merchants were henceforth allowed to traffic all manner of merchandise in all parts of the Byzantine empire without having to pay the standard ten per cent customs duty. They also received property along the Golden Horn in Constantinople, measuring approximately half a kilometre in length and containing three landing stages, which was to form the basis of their own commercial quarter. It became a kind of Latin enclave whose inhabitants were not answerable to the Byzantine authorities. Not surprisingly these concessions caused some resentment among Alexios's subjects not least because they still had to pay the taxes from which the Venetians were exempt. 'Their immoderate enrichment', complained one, 'quickly elevated them to boastfulness.'

Had customs duties and ownership of Antioch been the only matters at issue, then it is unlikely that relations with the Latins would have grown into such a topic of debate. There was, however, another element that greatly complicated the issue. While both Byzantines and Latins were Christians, there was a growing perception on both sides that the other had fallen into error. In 1054, three papal legates had visited Constantinople and had become involved in a dispute with the patriarch. The main issue was one of authority. The patriarch resisted the ever more strident claims of the pope to authority over the whole Church, including that of Constantinople. There were matters of divergent practices, such as whether to use leavened or unleavened bread in Holy Communion. Finally, and most serious, there was a dispute over the wording of the Nicene Creed. The western Church had added the word *Filioque* ('and [from] the Son') to the Latin version of the Creed, giving the reading: 'We believe in the Holy Spirit, the Lord, the giver of life, who proceeds from the Father and the Son ...' The Byzantines regarded the addition as illicit and possibly heretical. When no agreement was reached, the three papal legates had marched into the cathedral of Hagia Sophia and placed on the altar a letter excommunicating the patriarch.

The events of 1054 certainly did not represent a complete break between the Byzantine and western Churches but the First Crusade was to exacerbate and emphasise the differences. When Bohemond took over Antioch, one of his first actions was to expel the city's Byzantine patriarch and replace him with a Latin, and the same happened in Jerusalem where the new Latin masters chose a patriarch of their own. Alexios continued to appoint his own patriarchs of both cities who resided in Constantinople. With two parallel hierarchies now in existence, the Byzantine and western Churches were effectively in a state of schism. In the medieval world, where religion was so central to everyday life, the schism did not just involve squabbling bishops but the whole of society and had important political repercussions. When Bohemond launched an attack on Byzantine territory in 1107, in revenge for Alexios's attacks on Antioch, he told the pope that he was justified in doing so because the Byzantines were schismatics. He thus created a dangerous precedent for future Latin aggression, fuelling the anxieties of those who questioned how beneficial the Latins were.

Some of these anxieties were shared by Alexios's son and successor John II, and he probably also judged it politically expedient to be seen to be firm with the Latins. So on his accession he refused to renew the concessions granted by his father to the Venetians and on two occasions, in 1137 and 1142, he led his army eastwards in the footsteps of Nikephoros Phokas with a view to vindicating the Byzantine claim to Antioch and reasserting his suzerainty over the

Armenian principality of Cilicia. In both enterprises he failed. The Venetians had no intention of losing their hard-won tax immunity. A fleet on its way to assist the crusader kingdom of Jerusalem was ordered to attack the Byzantine ports and islands in the Aegean. This it did to such devastating effect that John had no choice but to capitulate and to renew the treaty on the same terms that his father had given. In Antioch, the successors of Bohemond were happy enough to admit John's theoretical lordship over the city whenever he was in the vicinity with his powerful army but they found excuses to delay handing it over, until on the first occasion he had to withdraw and on the second he suffered a fatal injury while out hunting. Besides, John discovered how dangerous the religious issue made it to act against Antioch. When the pope heard that John had ejected Latin bishops from towns around Antioch and replaced them with Byzantines, he issued an angry encyclical letter calling on all Latins in the Byzantine army to desert or face eternal damnation.

The prospect of mass desertion of his Latin troops was a particularly worrying one for John because, in spite of the tough stance over Venice and Antioch, he was every bit as dependent on the Latins as Alexios had been. As in the case of his father, they had played a role at his accession: it was because the Varangian guard accepted John as the legitimate heir rather than his sister Anna and her husband Bryennios that he had been able to gain entry to the palace and seize control. John was a very able general but Latin troops played a prominent role in his victories. His defeat of the Hungarians in 1128 was achieved with the help of a force of Italian horsemen, and when he charged into battle against the Pechenegs in 1122 he was surrounded and protected by a Latin bodyguard wielding heavy axes. Moreover, whether John was aware of it or not, he and his empire benefited from the presence of the Venetians. Within a very short time, quite apart from the international trade they pursued in the capital, they had come to dominate the internal maritime commerce of the empire, shipping foodstuffs, oil and wine from the Peloponnese and Thessaly to Constantinople. They were a vital link in the capital's food supply chain. So the problem of the Latins remained. They were useful but dangerous, and, while over the centuries Byzantium had successfully absorbed wave after wave of invaders and had turned their energies to the empire's benefit, these people were different.

* * *

That was the situation at the accession of the third emperor of the Komnenian line, Manuel I, in 1143. The new ruler was very unlike his father and grand-father. Alexios I and John II come across as dutiful and competent but rather unimaginative. Their response to the ever greater prominence of the Latins had been to resort to the old tactics of plentiful gifts and overawing the 'barbarians' with magnificence. Manuel was a very different personality, possessed of intellectual curiosity and considerable personal charm. He did not view the Latins just as useful tools as his predecessors had but actively liked them and admired aspects of their culture. He is said to have written to the king of England, Henry II, asking for information about his realm and people. He liked to take part in western-style tournaments and it was probably under his influence that aspects of western dress such as broad-brimmed hats and breeches caught on for a time among the Byzantine aristocracy. As well as relying on Latin mercenaries in his armies, he attracted western intellectuals to his court to work as secretaries and advisers on western affairs. He was most unhappy that the Byzantine and western Churches were now divided by the schism and did everything he could to encourage dialogue with a view to healing the breach. Thus it was that he earned his reputation as 'the friend of the Latins' both in Byzantium and in the west.

Manuel's liking for the Latins and his better understanding of the way their minds worked directly informed his policy towards his Latin neighbours. He came to realise that the traditional tactics, successful though they had been in the past, needed to be subtly altered when dealing with Christian western Europeans. Given that they had their own Christian ideology that placed the pope and the defence of Jerusalem much higher than Constantinople and the Byzantine emperor, there was no point in trying to present Byzantium to them as God's kingdom on earth. Instead, Manuel sought to present his policies and actions in a way that was acceptable to western opinion. While he was as resolute as his father had been in maintaining the Byzantine claim to Antioch, he made sure that he did so in a way that would not provoke an outraged reaction from the pope. He waited until the prince of Antioch gave him a pretext by attacking the Byzantine island of Cyprus and then led his army to Syria in 1159. With much of western opinion against him, the prince was forced to capitulate and accept Manuel's overlordship and the reinstatement of the Byzantine patriarch. Manuel also gained much kudos by paying for the restoration of the church of the Nativity in Bethlehem. So acceptable did he make himself, in fact, that at one point the pope offered to crown him emperor of the west.

Manuel's pro-Latin stance should not be overstressed. He by no means loved and trusted all Latins. At the time that the Second Crusade passed through Constantinople on its way to the Holy Land in 1147, Manuel seems to have shared fears that the French and German armies might turn on the Byzantine capital. There was, moreover, one group that he heartily detested and that was the Venetians. The antipathy arose from an incident which took place in 1149 when the Byzantines and Venetians were allied in an attempt to retake the island of Corfu from the Normans of southern Italy. The siege of the citadel of the main town had dragged on for some months and the besiegers were becoming bored and frustrated. One day a fight broke out among the Byzantines and Venetians in the town's marketplace. Having got the worst of it, the Venetians retreated to their ships but exacted their revenge by taking the imperial galley in tow. Below the decks they discovered purple robes and a crown which they placed on an African, who they then mockingly acclaimed as emperor. All this was done in full sight of the Byzantines and their emperor on the shore and Manuel considered the burlesque a deadly slight not only on his position but also on his dark complexion. The matter was patched up for the time being but it made Manuel only too ready to listen to those who said that the time had come to deprive the Venetians of their favoured trading position. In 1171 Manuel suddenly had Venetian merchants all over the empire arrested and their property confiscated. For the rest of his reign they were largely excluded from the Constantinopolitan trade, but after Manuel's death his successors brought them back and compensated them for their losses. Like other Latins, they were just too useful.

Manuel's pro-Latin reputation should be qualified in another respect. He was as open to any outsiders who he believed were friendly and beneficial to the empire. The Seljuk Turks were a good example. Left reeling by the passage of the First Crusade, they had now made the town of Ikonion the centre of their Asia Minor sultanate. Both John II and Manuel I fought wars against them and pushed back their western frontier, but these were not crusades. There were long periods when the emperor and the sultan were at peace and Turkish mercenaries were as prominent in the Byzantine armies as were the Latins. When the Seljuk sultan Kilidj Arslan II visited Constantinople in 1161, he received a magnificent welcome. He stayed for eighty days and even took part in a procession to Hagia Sophia. The sultan and his retinue were being given exactly the same treatment as that given to the Russian delegation in the tenth century which was allegedly so impressive that it recommended Prince Vladimir to accept Byzantine Christianity. Indeed Manuel later proposed that the ceremony for accepting Muslim converts into the Church should be changed so that they did not have to abjure the 'god of Muhammad'. In short, Manuel was an emperor who believed strongly in the old tradition of bringing all kinds of outsiders into the fold of Byzantine culture and political thought.

It is therefore very striking that, as Manuel's reign went on, there was a rising voice of criticism of his approach to outsiders. At the time of the 1161 visit of Kilidj Arslan there were murmurings that it was inappropriate for an infidel to take part in Christian ceremonial. An earth tremor that shook Constantinople during the visit was taken as evidence of divine displeasure. There were similar rumblings of discontent over the privileged position enjoyed by some westerners, and complaints that Manuel preferred them in his service over Byzantines. One courtier who was trying to secure a post in the administration for his uncle claimed that there was unfair competition from 'those of barbarian tongue'. Undue favours to foreigners was only one of the charges laid at Manuel's door by his subjects. The courtier and historian Niketas Choniates recorded that many people mocked him for 'nurturing inordinate ambitions and setting his eyes upon the ends of the earth'. Manuel's foreign policy was certainly ambitious, for he seems to have entertained hopes of conquering southern Italy and Egypt and of being recognised as emperor of the west as well as of the east. None of these hopes was fulfilled and in 1176 Manuel suffered a serious setback when in a renewed war against the Seljuks his army was cut to pieces at the battle of Myriokephalon. There was vocal resentment of the heavy taxes that were levied to pay for these enterprises and of the unscrupulous tax farmers who had the job of collecting them. There was also anger at the way the money was spent, often on gifts to foreign rulers to persuade them to ally themselves with the empire.

Yet, when Manuel died in September 1180, after a long reign of thirty-eight years, there was a genuine sense of loss. He was buried in the side chapel of his father's Pantokrator monastery and the decision was made to mark his memory by placing in the same chapel a precious relic, the red marble slab on which the body of Christ had been placed after the crucifixion. Manuel had ordered it to be brought from Ephesus to Constantinople in 1169 and, when the ship had docked in the harbour of the Great Palace, the emperor had personally carried the slab on his back up to the chapel of the Virgin of Pharos where the rest of the relic collection was housed. It was an unprecedented honour for it to be removed to the Pantokrator. The honour seemed all the more appropriate with hindsight when contemporaries like Choniates looked back and concluded that 'when the wise helmsman had been cast overboard, the ship of state sank'.

* * *

After Manuel's death the political instability and provincial separatism that had been kept at bay for decades by the Komnenian emperors returned to haunt Byzantium. The upheavals were partly the result of Manuel leaving a minor as his heir, his son Alexios II, who was only eleven. The usual regency was formed under his mother, the empress Maria, and, as a porphyrogenitos, no doubt young Alexios hoped that his aura of legitimacy would protect him from any attempt by a military strongman to repeat his great-grandfather's coup of 1081. Sadly, it could not protect him from his own kinsman, Andronicus Komnenos.

A cousin of Manuel I, Andronicus had spent the years 1143 to 1180 in a constant round of rebellion and rehabilitation. His plotting and intrigue had led to his being incarcerated for nine years in the dungeons beneath the Great Palace until he managed to escape by smuggling a wax impression of the keys out to his supporters. He had spent his later years in exile until being forgiven and allowed to return a few months before Manuel's death in 1180. Even then he was not welcome in the capital but resided quietly in his castle on the Black Sea coast of Asia Minor. He was, after all, now advanced in years and might have been expected to live out his days in peaceful retirement. When news arrived that the regency in Constantinople was deeply unpopular, however, Andronicus could not resist the challenge. He gathered an army made up largely of local recruits and marched on the capital. As had been the case with his forebear Isaac Komnenos in 1057, Andronicus found that a popular uprising in the streets had prepared the way for him and in April 1182 the gates were opened for his army to march in.

Up to this point, Andronicus's coup had followed a standard pattern but a difference now emerged. Initially, like the usurpers of the tenth century, Andronicus ruled alongside the legitimate Alexios II, but, after a year or so, gauging that he was securely lodged in the public mind as emperor, he had his young charge and his mother secretly disposed of. Both were strangled and Alexios's corpse was placed in a lead casket which was then thrown into the Bosporus to hide the evidence. Several other members of the Komnenos family met similar fates. Not since Phokas's slaughter of Maurice and his family in 602 had a usurper so completely eradicated all connections with his predecessor. It cannot have taken too long for the population of Constantinople to realise that something must have happened to the young porphyrogenitos but they probably accepted the change partly because Andronicus himself was a member of the imperial family and partly because once he was in power he made it his avowed aim to rein in the hated tax collectors. Certainly no one protested openly when he had himself crowned as Andronicus I (1183–1185).

On the other hand, there was one body of opinion that was not so easy to gull. Thanks to an event that took place when Andronicus arrived in Constantinople in 1182, opinion in the Latin west regarded Andronicus's coup with dismay and horror. Once the usurper's soldiers were through the gates of the Land Walls and in the city, they joined with a mob of Constantinopolitans in marching on the Italian quarters along the Golden Horn. There were few

Venetians in the city at that time as a result of Manuel I's expulsion in 1171, but other Italian merchants, Genoese and Pisans particularly, were just as much resented for their commercial privileges. Many of them realised what was about to happen and fled to their ships but those who could not run were left to face the onslaught. The mob broke into a Latin hospital and killed the patients in their beds; pregnant women and children were murdered in the street. Among the victims was a priest from Rome who was visiting Constantinople on Church business. It is unlikely that Andronicus ordered the massacre as he had nothing to gain from it nor was he particularly 'anti-Latin'. Like all his predecessors he employed Latin mercenaries and negotiated commercial treaties with the Italians. It was he, in fact, who came to an agreement with the Venetians that allowed them back into the city with their old privileges after their expulsion by Manuel. But, even if the outrage of 1182 had not been authorised from the top, it sent Byzantium's image in the Christian west plummeting and it never quite recovered.

That was only the first of many disasters during Andronicus's short reign. Even more damaging was the renewal of tension between the emperor and the provincial aristocracy. The loss of Asia Minor and the economic and military revival under the Komnenoi had for a time put an end to the frequent rebellions of disgruntled army commanders, but now they began once more. No sooner was Andronicus established in Constantinople than he discovered that most of the cities of Asia Minor, under the leadership of the Vatatzes family, were refusing to accept his authority. The revolt was brutally crushed in the spring of 1184 but Andronicus now became increasingly paranoid, believing that any prominent person with wealth and land was likely to be plotting against him. Going far further than Basil II had done, he had a huge portrait of himself painted on an outer wall of a church in the centre of Constantinople. He was depicted in peasant garb, holding a sickle, thus stating his claim to be on the side of the poor against the powerful. He boasted to his sons that he would rid them of giants, so that after he was gone they would have only pygmies to rule over. A reign of terror followed. Even Andronicus's closest supporters were not safe. In May 1184 he ordered two noblemen who had assisted him in his rise to power to be stoned until they were unconscious and then impaled. Their crime appears to have been to have provided pledges for the good conduct of a friend under suspicion of treason who had then fled the city. Not surprisingly, many prominent individuals who lived in Constantinople did not wait for the heavy tread of Andronicus's guards coming to arrest them but fled abroad, to the Norman ruler of Sicily or to the court of the Ayyubid sultan Saladin who, having overthrown the Fatimids, now ruled Syria and Egypt.

Outside Constantinople, Andronicus's reign of terror had an even more unfortunate effect, giving impetus to provincial separatism. During 1184, one of Andronicus's relatives, Isaac Komnenos, a former governor of Cilicia, crossed with a force of soldiers from Asia Minor to Cyprus. There he produced forged imperial letters appointing him to the governorship of the island. Once in control, he revealed his hand and had himself proclaimed emperor. Isaac's ultimate goal was to reach Constantinople itself but his revolt had the effect of separating Cyprus from the empire. He ruled it independently until 1191 when it was invaded and taken over by the king of England, Richard the Lionheart, who was on his way to join the crusade in the Holy Land. The island was never again under Byzantine rule.

Andronicus's reign of terror came to an abrupt end in September 1185. Some of his henchmen went to the house of a wealthy young nobleman called Isaac Angelos to arrest him for treason. Knowing that arrest meant certain death, Angelos mounted his horse and charged out, killing one of the group and then galloping through the streets to Hagia Sophia. There he declared himself emperor and the Constantinopolitan mob which had remained passive while Andronicus had disposed of Alexios II now rallied to the cause of Isaac. Seeing the way things were going, Andronicus attempted to flee from Constantinople but was captured and brought back. He came to a violent end, lynched in the Hippodrome by the incensed crowd.

The accession of a new emperor and dynasty in the person of Isaac II Angelos (1185–1195) did not put an end to the separatism or instability. Isaac had been on the throne for less than a year when he began to lose control of Bulgaria. This did not come about as the result of a nationalist uprising to reverse the humiliating national disaster of 1018 but out of the dissatisfaction among the local nobility with their place in the imperial hierarchy and resentment of high taxation. Moreover, at the outset the leaders of the revolt were not Bulgars at all but Vlachs. Early in 1186, when Isaac II was at Kypsella in Thrace, he was visited by two Vlach brothers, Peter and Asen. They made the kind of request that Byzantine rulers were only too used to hearing. They offered military service in the Byzantine armies in return for a reward, in this case some estates in the area of the Balkan mountains. When the request was turned down, the brothers became angry. In the heated exchange that followed Asen was struck in the face by one of the emperor's relatives. They rode off, vowing revenge and, exploiting the discontent among the Vlachs at a recently imposed tax to pay for the emperor's wedding, raised and led an army against Preslav. The Byzantine army soon responded and drove the Vlachs over the Danube but there Peter and Asen concluded an alliance with the Turkic Cumans. They returned in force the following year and routed the Byzantines, forcing them to abandon the land between the Danube and the Balkan mountains. Since he and his army now controlled what had been the heart of the old Bulgar khanate, Asan now proclaimed himself ruler of Bulgaria. In 1202 the Byzantines had to bow to the inevitable and make a treaty recognising the independence of Bulgaria.

The loss of Bulgaria was part of a wider phenomenon. All over the empire, local warlords were setting themselves up as rulers in their districts, gathering the taxes and defying central authority. At Strumnitsa in Macedonia, a Vlach mercenary called Dobromir Chrysos, who had fought with the Byzantines against Peter and Asan, occupied the fortress and extended his control over the countryside round about. At Philadelphia in Asia Minor, Theodore Mangaphas was proclaimed emperor and started minting silver coins with his portrait on them. In Greece, Leo Sgouros seized Argos and Corinth. These rebels were nothing new. They were taking advantage of the long-standing resentment of many provincials against the distant metropolis with its insistent tax demands and ineffective defence. The difference was the scale on which these revolts were happening.

Separatism in the provinces was matched by instability at the centre. In 1187, Isaac II's rule was challenged when one of the empire's best generals, Alexios Vranas, marched on Constantinople. Isaac survived on that occasion only to be overthrown in 1195 by his own brother who replaced him as Alexios III Angelos (1195–1203). Alexios in turn had to face frequent plots and revolts. One of the most serious occurred in 1200 when John Komnenos Axouchos, a great-grandson of Emperor John II, forced his way into the Great Palace with a band of supporters and seated himself on the throne before a troop of soldiers arrived and chased him through the corridors, caught him and lopped his head off.

* * *

In the midst of the endless round of plot and counter-plot during the 1180s and 1190s, the emperors of the Angelos family might have been forgiven for believing that there was one source of strength on which they could always rely, the Latins. They had helped to save the empire after the loss of Asia Minor and doubtless would do so again. Like Manuel I, the two Angelos emperors used them as secretaries and as ambassadors especially to western powers, but it was their military skills which were prized above all. In 1187, when the fearsome warlord Alexios Vranas was heading for Constantinople intent on seizing the throne, Isaac II's instinctive reaction had been to take refuge behind the Land Walls and hope that the revolt would peter out. As it happened, Conrad of

Montferrat, scion of an Italian princely house, had recently arrived in Constantinople to marry Isaac's sister, Theodora. Marching into the room while the emperor was dining, Conrad caused Isaac to turn red with embarrassment by announcing loudly that his prospective father-in-law should spend more effort on military preparations and less on eating. On Conrad's advice, Isaac's army marched out to confront Vranas. Conrad himself commanded the centre of the force, where the best Latin troops were positioned, and was conspicuous in a bright red tunic and with no helmet to hide his face. He led a head-on cavalry charge against Vranas's centre, crashing through the opposition and coming face to face with the rebel himself, whom he proceeded to knock from his horse. The dazed Vranas then pleaded for mercy and received from Conrad the assurance that nothing untoward would happen – except that his head would be cut off! It ended up, along with one of the general's feet, on public display in the Augousteion.

Time and again Byzantine emperors were saved in similar circumstances. When the people of Constantinople objected to Isaac II's choice of patriarch, it was the Varangian guard who escorted the new incumbent to Hagia Sophia and defused the situation. In 1200, it was Alexios III's Latin bodyguards who stormed the Great Palace and put an end to the revolt of John Komnenos Axouchos. Yet such dependence on the Latins was now more dangerous than ever. Not only had the ecclesiastical schism not been resolved, so leaving a possible justification for aggression, but Byzantium's image in the west had been badly tarnished during the last decades of the twelfth century. The massacre of Italian merchants in Constantinople during Andronicus's coup in 1182 had led to a perception in the west that the Byzantines were secretly nurturing a deep hatred of all Latins. When Jerusalem was lost to Saladin in 1187, much of the blame was placed, quite wrongly, on the Byzantines, who were accused of having aided and abetted the Muslims. They were coming to be seen, at best, as lukewarm supporters of the effort to liberate the Holy Sepulchre and, at worst, as sinister and duplicitous dissemblers constantly plotting to betray the crusades by underhand means. Consequently, prominent crusaders were coming to believe that the empire should be compelled to use its riches to finance the effort to retake Jerusalem. These perceptions made the use of large Latin forces by the Byzantines very dangerous indeed.

* * *

Just as the Byzantine emperors relied on Latin troops to keep them in power, so did those who sought to overthrow them: when Princess Maria, the daughter of Manuel I, had led an uprising against the regency for young Alexios II in

1181, she had immediately recruited some Italians to support her cause. So, when in 1201 a new plot was formed against Alexios III Angelos, it was only natural that those involved should consider how they were to find some Latin military muscle to back their cause. At the centre of the conspiracy was the deposed Isaac II, who had been blinded in 1195 and sent to live at a port on the Bosporus, north of Constantinople. The confinement was a comfortable and relaxed one. The ex-emperor could receive visitors and many of them were Latins. Through them he was able to smuggle out letters to his daughter, who was married to the German duke of Swabia, and to arrange for his son Alexios to escape from Byzantine territory in October 1201 on a Pisan ship which bore him to Italy. When young Alexios returned, some eighteen months later in 1203, it was with a Venetian fleet and a formidable Latin army.

The army was that of the Fourth Crusade, whose leaders had agreed to postpone their expedition against Egypt only because Prince Alexios had promised them vast amounts of money and supplies for the forthcoming campaign. He had also promised to maintain an army in Jerusalem to defend it once it was recaptured and to bring about an end to the schism between the Churches. The deal made sense. Although some time would be lost in Constantinople restoring Isaac II to his rightful throne, the crusaders would then be in a stronger position to carry out their purpose, with the Byzantines at last playing a role proportionate to their wealth and status in the defence of the Holy Land.

As was usual in these cases, there followed a stand-off between the two imperial claimants as those outside the walls sought to persuade someone on the inside to open a gate. Young Alexios Angelos was rowed up and down before the Sea Walls so that he could appeal to the citizens to abandon their allegiance to his uncle, Alexios III. In July, when they had ignored his appeals, there was some fighting as the Latin army broke the chain across the Golden Horn to allow the Venetian fleet to enter the harbour. An attack on the Sea Walls followed. That was enough for Alexios III, who despaired of holding on to his throne and fled the city under cover of darkness. Isaac II was restored, reigning jointly with his son, who became Alexios IV. Once again, as in 1081, the help of the Latins had brought about the downfall of one emperor and the enthronement of another.

Immediately after the restoration, however, it became only too apparent just how dangerous the Latins could be. Useful as they were, their services had always had to be paid for. With the loss of so much territory after 1180, the emperor's tax receipts were shrinking and with them his ability to provide that seemingly inexhaustible fountain of gold that lured so many great warriors into his service. Back in 1187, when Conrad of Montferrat had saved Isaac II from Alexios Vranas, his Latin troops had been recompensed by being given leave to pillage the villages and farms outside the Land Walls. The Italian prince himself, however, had taken umbrage at the smallness of the reward that Isaac had offered him for his services and had left Constantinople. The same difficulty arose now. Alexios IV discovered that the resources of the Byzantine treasury allowed him to pay the crusaders and Venetians only a fraction of what he had rashly promised them. He handed over what he could, even confiscating Church treasures to do so, but a gaping shortfall remained.

At this point the crusade fleet could have cut its losses and departed. After all, the crusaders really had no business to be at Constantinople and had even been expressly forbidden to go there by the pope. On the other hand, their supplies were running low and it was now winter, when sailing on the open sea would be hazardous. So they waited, hoping against hope that Alexios IV would provide them with the aid that he had promised. All hope evaporated in January 1204 when Alexios IV and Isaac II were overthrown in a palace coup led by a courtier called Alexios Mourtzouphlos. The new emperor, Alexios V, immediately suspended all payments to the Latin fleet and army and made ready to defend Constantinople against an attack.

Perhaps the Byzantines hoped that the attack would not come. After all, the crusaders and Venetians were still bound by their vow to fight the infidel and liberate the Holy Sepulchre. Indeed many in the crusade army felt that to turn their weapons on a Christian city would be to betray that oath. These doubts were, however, smoothed over by priests accompanying the army who assured the rank and file that, because the Byzantines were schismatics who had worked against the cause of the crusade, it would be entirely legitimate to attack them. The Venetian fleet was already in the Golden Horn, allowing the ships to sail across and attack the Sea Walls at their weakest point.

When the attack came in April 1204, the Byzantines still displayed that curious ambivalence that had always marked their attitude to the Latins. While there were plenty of Byzantines who were happy to label them as barbarous schismatics, the resistance that was offered to their attack was desultory. It would appear that many defenders still viewed the assault as nothing more than a tussle between two imperial claimants rather than the defence of the city against a foreign enemy, and so saw no reason to fight to the bitter end. The opposition was therefore half-hearted, the strongest resistance to the crusaders on the Sea Walls coming, as ever, from Latins in Byzantine service: the English and Danish mercenaries. The Byzantine troops tended to melt away as soon as the crusaders gained a foothold. One soldier from Picardy clambered through a postern gate that had been broken down with axes and when he waved his sword at the defenders on the other side they all ran off. As the victorious crusaders moved from the Sea Walls into the streets, they found themselves hailed by some of the people they found there with the words 'The Holy Emperor the Marquis!' It was clearly thought that the leader of the crusade, Boniface, marquis of Montferrat and brother of Conrad, would be the new Byzantine emperor. Many persisted in this belief even once the crusaders were in Constantinople and had begun to loot and plunder to their hearts' content, not sparing even the churches. After all, that was only to be expected. Nikephoros Phokas's troops had done the same in 963, as had Alexios I's Latin mercenaries in 1081. No doubt many hoped that when the dust settled things would return to normal.

They were wrong, but only in the days that followed did the enormity of their error become apparent. The Byzantines had lost their capital city, that all-important asset that had enabled them to survive Persians, Avars and Arabs in the past. They had lost Constantinople because the attack had not come from infidels but from those who, as one of them put it, 'bore the cross of Christ upon their shoulders', people whom they regarded as somehow part of their world, even an essential part. It was the Christian Latins who had struck the blow that, up to now, the Byzantines had always been able to parry.

CHAPTER NINE

The New Constantine

Constantinople, the citadel of the inhabited world, the imperial capital of the
Romans, had, with the permission of God, come under the control of the Latins.
By God's gift it was returned to the Romans, through us.
Michael VIII Palaiologos

On 16 May 1204, a grand coronation was held in the cathedral of Hagia Sophia, followed by a colourful procession across the Augousteion to the Great Palace. Constantinople had seen countless such ceremonies over the centuries but this one was rather different. The new emperor was not called Constantine, Leo or Alexios, but Baldwin. He came not from Asia Minor or the Balkans but from the Low Countries, where he had been count of Flanders and Hainaut before setting out on the Fourth Crusade. He was every inch what the Byzantines had come to expect of a Latin, a man of action whose family had a long and proud tradition of riding east on crusade. There were other differences. Baldwin was crowned not by the patriarch of Constantinople but by the archbishop of Soissons and was not, of course, a porphyrogenitos. He had arrived at this supreme office through election by a council of French counts and Venetians who had chosen him from among the other leaders of the Fourth Crusade. Yet in some respects the ceremony was not so different from the coronations of previous emperors. Baldwin was arrayed in the same robes that his predecessors had worn, and the same purple boots. Around his neck hung the great ruby that Manuel I had been accustomed to sport on special occasions. The event was attended not just by Latins but by plenty of Greek-speaking Constantinopolitans who lustily cheered the new emperor.

For a time, it looked as if the new regime would not only be accepted in the capital but would succeed in extending its authority out into the Byzantine provinces. In the autumn, Baldwin made a formal division of the territories of empire among his followers, in much the same way that William the Conqueror had divided up England after his conquest in 1066. Each received a parcel of land commensurate with their rank and in return they were expected to serve with their followers in the emperor's army when required to do so. Boniface of Montferrat received Thessalonica, Nicaea went to Count Louis of Blois, Philadelphia to Stephen of Perche. The local populations of these places initially acquiesced in, and even welcomed, these changes. That August, when Emperor Baldwin and his army had marched west from Constantinople, the people of Thessalonica had streamed out to meet them and to surrender their city without any resistance. At Lopadion in Asia Minor, the new emperor's representative had been met by a procession carrying crosses and Gospel books, to welcome their fellow Christians. The very forces of provincial separatism that had plagued the Byzantine emperors for so long now played into the hands of the Latin conquerors. Renier of Trit, along with his one hundred and twenty followers, was enthusiastically welcomed into the city of Philippopolis in Thrace which Renier had been granted by the emperor Baldwin. The locals hoped that this Latin lord would provide the kind of effective defence against the Bulgars and Vlachs that Alexios III Angelos and his predecessors had conspicuously failed to deliver. Discontented minorities also welcomed the new masters. When Peter of Bracieux and Payen of Orléans crossed to Asia Minor in late 1204, they found allies there in communities of Armenians who hated the previous rulers of Constantinople. So, by the end of 1204, there appeared to be a real possibility that Byzantium would continue and even flourish in a new guise. All that had happened was that an effete and incompetent regime in Constantinople had been replaced by a dynamic and militarily successful one. The very people who had saved the empire time and again for the past century and a half were now in control of its destiny.

Not everyone, of course, welcomed the Latin takeover. Those who had previously been in power now found themselves ousted, destitute and without friends. The fugitive Alexios III Angelos was captured by Boniface of Montferrat and sent off as a prisoner to Italy. The short-reigned Alexios V Mourtzouphlos, who had tried to rally last-minute resistance in April 1204 before fleeing to Thrace, was apprehended and done to death by being hurled from the column of Theodosius, the highest in Constantinople. Seeing that there was no place for them under the new regime, many of the courtiers and advisers who had sustained the Angelos dynasty began to leave Constantinople in the weeks after the Latin conquest. They received little sympathy as they passed through the countryside. Many of the peasants of Thrace took the opportunity to jeer at the sight of those who had once lorded it over them and crushed them with taxation now themselves reduced to destitution.

In the event, the discomfiture of the old elite proved to be only temporary. Those Byzantines who had welcomed the Latins soon discovered that the new regime was not only as rapacious as the last, but it also lacked Byzantium's ability to integrate outsiders, to reward them and to harness their skills. The people of Thrace and Macedonia were among the first to make this discovery. Once Boniface of Montferrat had control of Thessalonica, his benevolence evaporated. Heavy exactions were levied on the population and the best houses were confiscated and handed over to the marquis's own knights. Even then some of the more prominent Thessalonians hoped to find some kind of place in the new order. A delegation approached Boniface and asked him if they could be enrolled in his army. They were contemptuously dismissed. The same request was directed to the emperor Baldwin. He too turned it down. The Latins had no need of effeminate 'Greeks'.

There was another factor that ensured that a large section of the population of the old empire could not be accommodated in the new: the long-running schism between the Byzantine and Catholic Churches. The gulf had been widened by the behaviour of the Latin army once it had Constantinople at its mercy in April 1204. It was not just that these would-be crusaders had looted churches. They had actually gone into the cathedral of Hagia Sophia itself, breaking into the sacred area behind the iconostasis and seizing the communion plate and chalices. They had pulled the gold and silver coverings from the doors and communion rails and brought donkeys into the sanctuary to carry away the loot. The unequalled collection of relics in the Pharos chapel of the Great Palace had been plundered and most of them taken off to the west. The Crown of Thorns ended up in Paris and the Mandylion of Edessa vanished without trace. This was not merely pillage, it was sacrilege. In the aftermath, the patriarch of Constantinople had fled the city, so the Latins had replaced him with their own candidate, a Venetian called Thomas Morosini, and triumphantly announced that the schism was at an end. Some Byzantine clergymen had clung to the hope that their religious tradition could be accommodated under Latin rule. They even wrote to Pope Innocent III proposing that a general council of the Church be called to resolve the schism, though requesting that in the meantime they be allowed to have their own, Greek-speaking, patriarch. In 1206, a group of them met with Morosini and a papal legate in Constantinople to put their case. They were met with a blunt demand that they obey their lawful patriarch, Morosini. When they objected, Morosini bellowed: 'You should accept me. You are disobedient and we shall treat you for what you are!' He was as good as his word and closed many of Constantinople's churches. There followed an exodus of Byzantine clergy from the city into the provinces.

Even now the Latins might have held the loyalty of their Byzantine subjects if they had maintained their reputation for invincibility in war, but that myth was shattered only a year after their takeover. Early in 1205, some disgruntled Byzantine nobles in Thrace had revolted against Latin rule and Emperor Baldwin was soon on his way to lay siege to their stronghold of Adrianople. In desperation the Byzantines appealed for help to the old enemy, the ruler of newly independent Bulgaria, Kalojan. The tsar marched south with an army of Cuman mounted archers. When battle was joined outside Adrianople, the armoured western knights were rather contemptuous of the Cumans, who were clad in rough sheepskin jackets and armed only with small bows. In spite of express orders to the contrary, the knights charged at them at full pelt. They thus gave the Cumans the chance to execute their favourite tactic of feigning flight and then unexpectedly wheeling around and unloosing a hail of arrows against their pursuers. Unnerved by this unexpected ruse, some men fled but Emperor Baldwin and his knights stood their ground only to be shot from their horses one by one. Louis, count of Blois, and Stephen of Perche, who had so recently been given Nicaea and Philadelphia, were among the dead. Baldwin was captured and dragged off to Kalojan's capital of Trnovo, never to be seen alive again. Gruesome tales of his ultimate fate circulated for years afterwards: it was said that Kalojan had had his arms and legs lopped off and ordered him to be thrown down a rocky ravine. He had lingered in agony for three long days, unable to move while birds pecked at his body.

Baldwin was succeeded by his able brother Henry and the Latin empire managed to survive, but the blow to its prestige was immeasurable. The Byzantines had always admired the Latins for their warlike qualities but now that they were suddenly revealed as weak, resistance started to stiffen. Much of Asia Minor, Greece and the western Balkans had still not been effectively brought under Latin rule and in these areas the westerners no longer found themselves welcomed. Already the town of Prousa had refused to open its gates as Thessalonica had when a Latin army approached. To start with, resistance was led by some of the very same local magnates who had defied the Angelos dynasty, such as Theodore Mangaphas in Philadelphia and Leo Sgouros in Greece, but they had few resources to call upon and their defiance proved unavailing even after the disaster of Adrianople. Mangaphas was crushed by Henry of Flanders at

Adramyttion in 1206 and Sgouros was bottled up by the forces of Boniface of Montferrat in the fortress of Akrocorinth that towers above the town of Corinth. After five years, he committed suicide in despair by riding his horse over the precipice. By then, two other leaders had emerged who proved rather more effective in challenging the Latins. In Epiros, in western Greece, Michael Angelos, a cousin of the emperors Isaac II and Alexios III, set himself up as ruler in the town of Arta, while Theodore Laskaris, a son-in-law of Alexios III, established himself at Nicaea in Asia Minor. There they were joined by those members of the former elite who had left Constantinople. A small shanty town even grew up around Lake Nicaea to house these refugees, who had lost everything in 1204.

Arta and Nicaea became the centres of a challenge to the Latin emperor that was not only military but ideological. The rulers in both towns announced that they were the legitimate Byzantine emperor, commissioned by God to eject the schismatic Latins from Constantinople and to restore the empire to its former glory. Theodore Laskaris had himself crowned emperor at Nicaea in 1208 by the patriarch of Constantinople in exile, the rival to Morosini. The ruler of Epiros waited until 1225 after he had pulled off a great coup by recapturing Thessalonica from the Latins, with the archbishop of Ochrid performing the ceremony. The courts of Arta and Nicaea were modelled on that of Constantinople, replicating every detail of administration, civil service and imperial household. Education based on the Greek classics was resumed and became the test for entry into the administration just as it had been in Constantinople. These provincial towns benefited hugely from their suddenly acquired status of capital cities and were transformed by a rash of new building. An impressive five-domed church became the centrepiece of Arta while in Nicaea, six new churches sprang up during the thirteenth century, as well as palaces for the emperor and patriarch.

The challenge was not restricted to rhetoric and display. These successor states were soon in a position to put formidable armies in the field. Careful management of agriculture and trade enabled them to prosper and to accumulate the resources they needed. Moreover, these Byzantines in exile had not lost their touch in dealing with the constant waves of migratory peoples that washed up against their frontiers. During the first half of the thirteenth century, both the Christian and Muslim worlds were gripped by terror of the Mongols, whose empire was expanding westwards with terrifying speed. By 1241, these fast-moving mounted warriors were on the borders of Hungary, where they crushed a Latin coalition that attempted to bar their way. Two years later they meted out the same treatment to the Seljuk Turks of Asia Minor. The sultan of Ikonion was allowed to remain in place but he had to pay an annual tribute to the Mongol khan. Other nomadic tribes fled before the onslaught. In 1237 a group of Cumans crossed the Danube and the Balkan mountains and took refuge in Macedonia, causing considerable damage in the Bulgar territory that they passed through. The Byzantines of Nicaea, who shared no border with the Mongols, were able to turn the situation to their advantage. The Cumans were invited to resettle in the Maeander valley in Asia Minor and they became an important element in the armies of the empire of Nicaea. It was not only Steppe peoples like the Cumans who served the rulers of Nicaea and Epiros as mercenaries. There were even large contingents of Latins, just as there had been before 1204. The Byzantines were perfectly well aware that a man from Normandy or Lombardy would not identify himself with the Flemish emperors and their Venetian allies who held Constantinople, and would serve loyally if he was well paid. In that expectation, they were not disappointed.

Thanks to this process of retrenchment, by the 1220s the goal of recovering the imperial city looked increasingly within reach. More important still was the death of the able Latin emperor Henry in 1216, for his successors were transitory and ineffective. The Latin territories outside the capital shrank drastically and the regime in Constantinople was only sustained by the Venetians, who could keep the city supplied by sea. But although it had become evident that the Latin empire would undoubtedly collapse sooner or later, no one could tell which of the two rival Byzantine emperors would finish it off. A war of words erupted between Arta and Nicaea. The Nicaeans claimed that the emperor at Arta was a fraud because he had been crowned by a mere archbishop. The courtiers at Arta responded that the coronation of Theodore Laskaris was invalid because it had been carried out by a so-called patriarch who was doubling up as archbishop of Nicaea. The arguments would have gone on indefinitely had not developments rendered them superfluous. In 1230, the emperor of Epiros quarrelled with the Bulgarian ruler, John Asen II. His ill-judged invasion of Bulgaria ended in his defeat and capture at the battle of Klokotnitsa and the loss of most of his territory. In 1241, the ruler of Epiros renounced his imperial title and contented himself instead with that of despot, meaning simply 'lord'. The emperor of Nicaea was left to claim undisputed leadership of the campaign to oust the Latins. Under the rule of John III (1221–1254), who had come to power by marrying a daughter of Theodore Laskaris, Nicaea hugely expanded the territory under its control. Thessalonica was taken in 1246. Once he was in control of most of the land around the lost capital, John III seemed poised to take the ultimate prize, but then this very effective emperor died. His son and successor Theodore II reigned for only four years and left the throne to the seven-year-old John IV. The campaign stalled and the

Latin emperor was left to reign on, impoverished but unmolested, in the Great
Palace of Constantinople.

* * *

While he was campaigning in Thrace during the last year of his life, the emperor
of Nicaea, John III, had received information that one of his young subordinates might be in secret negotiations with the Bulgarian tsar and the ruler of
Epiros. The emperor was all the more disturbed by the report because the
governor was Michael Palaiologos, whom he had brought up in the palace as if
he were his own son. The trouble was that Michael had all the hallmarks of a
potential usurper. His family, which had left Constantinople in the wake of the
Latin takeover, had intermarried with the Komnenoi and the Angeloi so he had
a claim to the throne on grounds of descent. He had the look of an emperor
too, for although only in his twenties, he was a very competent administrator
and leader. John had, in fact, appointed him governor of the recently recovered
towns of Serres and Melnik. He was an able soldier and popular with the troops,
including that element vital in any takeover bid, the Latin mercenaries.
Palaiologos was arrested and brought to trial before the emperor but the
hearsay evidence against him did not stand up and he was acquitted. To show
that there were no hard feelings, John gave Palaiologos his great niece Theodora
in marriage and appointed him to the office of Grand Constable, commander
of the Latin mercenaries.

In spite of his rehabilitation, the clouds of suspicion still hung around
Palaiologos, even after John III died and Theodore II took his place. Given
subsequent events, those suspicions may well have been justified. Palaiologos
lived under constant fear of arrest and was apprehensive that he might be blinded
simply as a precautionary measure. Theodore II had already shown himself to be
completely ruthless when the need arose. He had arranged for the son of the
ruler of Epiros to marry his daughter, but when the young man and his mother
had arrived in Thessalonica for the ceremony, he had had them locked up and
refused to release them until he was ceded the port of Dyrrachion. Palaiologos
decided not to take any chances. In the autumn of 1256, while the emperor was
absent in the Balkans, he fled across the border to the court of the Seljuk sultan
at Ikonion. He agreed to return the following year after Theodore II had sworn
on oath not to molest him and Palaiologos had promised never to attempt to
seize the throne.

There matters might have rested had Theodore II not sickened and died in
August 1258. In his will, Theodore named his most trusted minister, George
Mouzalon, as guardian and regent for the child emperor, John IV. The choice

was not a popular one among the numerous enemies that Theodore II had managed to make during his short reign, and it did not stand for long. Three days after the emperor's funeral, a commemorative service was held in the monastery where he was buried. A large and menacing crowd gathered outside, composed of prominent individuals with a grudge of one sort or another. At a given signal they drew their swords and marched into the church, causing the choir to fall silent and the presiding clergy prudently to slip away. The regent Mouzalon and his brothers, knowing that it was they whom the intruders were seeking, tried to hide. A sharp-eyed Latin mercenary noticed Mouzalon's knees sticking out from under the altar, dragged him from his refuge and literally hacked him to pieces.

Michael Palaiologos was not recorded among the perpetrators but it is difficult to believe that he was not involved in some way, given that he was the immediate beneficiary of the murder. He and his brothers immediately took the young emperor John under their protection and within a few weeks Michael was generally recognised as the regent and guardian of the young emperor. A few months more and he was secure enough to take the next step and have himself crowned emperor as Michael VIII (1259–1282), the arrangement being the traditional one that he would reign alongside the legitimate John IV as senior emperor. He may have intruded himself on the house of Laskaris but Michael resumed exactly where his father-in-law John had left off and the rhetoric of imperial renewal, along with the sacred task of recovering Constantinople, was voiced as stridently as ever. He missed no opportunity to present himself as the rightful heir of the Byzantine emperors of the past. An opportunity arose when he was campaigning in Thrace in 1260. Some of his officers informed him that their patrol had brought them within sight of the Land Walls of Constantinople. The fortifications were well garrisoned by the Latins and there was no hope of gaining entry, so the troops retired to the suburb of Hebdomon. There they came across a derelict monastery that was being used as a cattle barn. Entering its dilapidated church, they were startled to see a human skeleton propped up in one corner. It had lost its arms and legs and some wag had stuck a shepherd's reed pipe in its mouth. Nearby was an empty sarcophagus and the soldiers bent down to read the words: 'vigilant through the whole span of my life guarding the children of New Rome'. It was then they realised that they were standing at the tomb of the Bulgar slayer Basil II himself. When Michael heard this, he had the remains reverently wrapped in silk cloths and placed in an ornate casket. This was then carried to nearby Selymbria where it was reburied with the full imperial honours that it was only right for one Byzantine emperor to accord to another.

Symbolic acts and propaganda were all very well but Michael needed to deliver victory if he was to justify his usurpation. With the emperor of Nicaea now in control of all the land surrounding Constantinople, it was likely that he would take the city before too long, and the ruler of Epiros banded together with the king of Sicily and other Latin potentates to stop him. In autumn 1259 Michael's brother, John Palaiologos, did battle with this hostile coalition at Pelagonia in Epiros. Outnumbered though they were, the Byzantines of Nicaea prevailed and every single one of the four hundred knights sent by the king of Sicily was killed. Typically though, the Byzantines did not achieve victory by force of arms alone, for some judiciously spread disinformation played its part too. On the night before the battle, John Palaiologos had sent a message to the ruler of Epiros warning him that his Latin allies planned to betray him. The despot believed the ruse and fled with many of his men, thus helping to even out the odds.

Michael was now in the position of many would-be conquerors of Constantinople. Like Khan Symeon, he had won all the battles but he was still confronted by the impregnable Land Walls. In the spring of 1260 he laid siege to Galata across the Golden Horn from the city but he could not capture that either. His only hope was that, as in 1081, someone on the inside would let his army in, and that was what happened in the end. In July 1261 one of his generals, Alexios Strategopoulos, was in the area with his army when he received information that the city was virtually undefended. Much of the Latin garrison had gone off to attack the Nicaean-held island of Daphnousia. News also came that one of the small postern gates in the walls had been left open by a sympathiser. The chance was seized and a group of fifteen men crept through the gate on the night of 25 July. The reports were correct: there was almost no one manning the walls. The one sentry whom they encountered was grabbed by the legs and pitched headlong over the battlements. The main gates were then hurled open and the army poured in. There was virtually no resistance and by daybreak the city was in Strategopoulos's hands.

Michael VIII was on the Asian side of the Bosporus with his part of the army when the news of the capture of Constantinople arrived. It was still very early in the morning and the emperor was asleep in his tent. The news had to be given to Michael's sister Eulogia, who went into the emperor's tent and tickled his feet with a feather to wake him. At first Michael did not believe it, but then a messenger arrived bringing the crown and sceptre of the Latin emperor Baldwin II, which he had left behind in his rush to escape from the Great Palace. Michael himself arrived in Constantinople three weeks later on 15 August. The date was carefully chosen because it was the Feast of the

Dormition of the Virgin Mary, the city's protector. The emperor entered through the Golden Gate on foot, walking reverently behind the icon of the Hodegetria, and processed towards Hagia Sophia along streets lined with cheering crowds. The interlude of Latin rule was over.

* * *

Michael had achieved what the rulers of Arta and Nicaea had yearned for in the long decades of exile. He had restored Constantinople to the rule of an emperor and a patriarch who adhered to the true Orthodox faith rather than the erroneous version preached by the Latins. He could therefore claim that he was a new Constantine, refounding the city that his illustrious predecessor had inaugurated. He even used the title in official documents, but he needed to communicate it to a wider audience, so he gave orders for the erection of a column outside the church of the Holy Apostles. On top of the column was a statue of Saint Michael and before him knelt the figure of an emperor, presenting the Archangel with a model of the city. It must have been well known that Saint Michael was the emperor's patron saint because the Archangel was often depicted on the coins that were issued during his reign. Hence the emperor depicted on the column could have been either Constantine or Michael himself.

The same idea of restoring things to the way that they should be ran through Michael's programme of rebuilding and renovation in the newly recovered capital. Some of this was purely practical, such as raising the height of the Sea Walls along the Golden Horn to prevent anyone from repeating the tactics used by the Latins in April 1204. Streets and porticoes were repaired and schools and hospitals founded. Some served to emphasise Michael's piety and concern for the Church as opposed to the Latins who had let many religious buildings fall into ruin. Many received new roofs of tiles or lead and new furnishings to replace those which had been stolen. Hagia Sophia was adorned with a new mosaic of the Deisis: a figure of Christ between the Virgin Mary and St John the Baptist. The Blachernae palace was redecorated with scenes of Michael's victories, alongside those commissioned earlier by Manuel I Komnenos.

Being the new Constantine meant not just restoring the capital but also reviving its role as the centre of Orthodox Christianity. Byzantium's cultural and ecclesiastical influence in those countries which it had converted to Christianity had been severely shaken by the weakness of the late twelfth century and by the Latin takeover of 1204. In the wake of the disaster, Slav rulers had sought to accommodate themselves to the new regime. In November 1204, the Bulgarian tsar Kalojan had received a crown from the hands of a papal legate and promised the pope that the Bulgarian Church would henceforth be subject to the Holy See. In 1217 the ruler of Serbia, Stephen Nemanjić, had also received a coronation and the title of king from Rome. But the cultural and emotional bonds of the past were not so easily broken, especially when the weakness of the Latin empire became as obvious to the Bulgars and Serbs as it was to everyone else. They soon came to regard the patriarch in exile at Nicaea, as opposed to his Latin rival in Constantinople, as the rightful incumbent. In 1219 a delegation from Serbia had arrived in Nicaea to request the consecration of an archbishop for Serbia, which the patriarch was only too happy to do. The Bulgarians had returned to the fold in 1235 when their tsar officially recognised the primacy of the patriarch in Nicaea. The Russians had done so too, sending their archbishops to Nicaea for consecration.

Now with the patriarch and emperor back in Constantinople, Byzantine religious primacy could be asserted more forcefully. In 1272, Michael VIII announced that the Churches of Serbia and Bulgaria would henceforth be under the jurisdiction of the archbishop of Ochrid, a town that was now in Byzantine territory rather than in Bulgaria. He was prepared to use force to reassert Byzantine influence in the Balkans. In 1279, he sent a small expedition across the Balkan mountains, in the footsteps of John Tzimiskes and Basil II, to support the Bulgarian tsar John Asen III in a bid to overthrow the rebel Ivajlo. Unfortunately, although they captured Trnovo, the Byzantine troops were not numerous enough to win the war and John Asan ended up fleeing back to Constantinople.

In spite of such setbacks, Michael VIII was remarkably successful in keeping the empire afloat in a situation where it was hopelessly outnumbered and beleaguered on all sides, a role that the Byzantine emperors had played ever since the disaster at Adrianople in 378. As ever, outright military strength was seldom an option and Michael VIII had little alternative to resorting to the usual array of other means. He was, moreover, playing a much weaker hand than had the emperors who had reigned in Constantinople before 1204. His empire as reconstituted in 1261 was a great deal smaller, consisting primarily of about a third of Asia Minor, some islands in the Aegean and a strip of territory across the Balkans. In Greece, the Peloponnese, which had been recovered from the Slavs in the ninth century, remained largely under Latin rule although Michael had been able to recover some of the south of the peninsula, around the towns of Mistra and Monemvasia. Crete, which Nikephoros Phokas had reconquered so spectacularly in 961, was now a colony of Venice, and Cyprus was ruled by the French Lusignan family. On the Black Sea coast of Asia Minor, Trebizond and the area round about was an independent state with its own line of rulers claiming to be the true Byzantine emperor. Epiros remained a separate entity even if its ruler had given up the imperial title. This shrinkage of territory meant that Michael VIII received only a fraction of the tax receipts that his predecessors had enjoyed and his scope for action was limited in proportion.

Michael VIII was therefore fortunate that many of the empire's traditional enemies were no longer a threat. The military power of the Bulgars had waned considerably after the death of Tsar John Asen II in 1241 and while there was still a rival Byzantine court at Arta, its despot did not have the resources to do more than plot and scheme. Muslim powers presented little danger either. The Seljuk Turks had declined into passivity after their dreadful defeat at the hands of the Mongols in 1243. Egypt and Syria were now ruled by the aggressive Mamluks, who were slowly eradicating the last strongholds of crusader rule in the Holy Land, but they had no quarrel with the Byzantines. On the contrary, the Mamluks had a treaty with Michael VIII which allowed him to insert his nominee as patriarch of Jerusalem, since they now controlled the Holy City. In return the emperor arranged for Cuman mercenaries to be shipped from the Crimea to Egypt to serve in the Mamluk armies. Even the most feared warriors of the day, the Mongols, were not a threat to Byzantium. Their empire had by now split into two, the Golden Horde and the Ilkhanate. The Golden Horde did combine with the Bulgars to invade Byzantine Thrace in 1265 but in general Michael went out of his way to keep on good terms with both groups, marrying two of his daughters to Mongol rulers.

On the other hand, there was a threat even greater than any since the Arabs back in the seventh century. It came from the west and was largely created by the pope in Rome. Back in 1203, when he heard that the Fourth Crusade was planning to divert to Constantinople, the pope of the time, Innocent III, had been furious. He had written to the leaders of the expedition to remind them of their vow to liberate the Holy Land and expressly forbade them from going to the Byzantine capital. They had ignored him and in May 1204 sent a very carefully worded letter to inform him that Constantinople had been captured, prompting Innocent to reverse his previous attitude and to accept the conquest of Constantinople as a gift from God. In the months that followed, Innocent had received further, less tendentious reports that did not leave out unsavoury details such as the atrocities and desecration committed during the sack, but he decided to ignore them. The means by which it had been carried out might have been reprehensible but the end itself was something that the popes had longed for over generations. The conquest had, Innocent believed, healed the long-running schism between the eastern and western Churches and brought the Byzantines back into obedience to the Holy See. For this reason, Innocent recognised the *fait accompli* and gave it his blessing, recognising Baldwin as the legitimate emperor and Morosini as patriarch.

That was why, when the reigning pope, Urban IV, heard that Michael VIII had retaken Constantinople, he was allegedly stupefied. What had seemed to be an act of God to bring unity to the Church had been undone at a stroke. Urban therefore preached a crusade for the recovery of Constantinople, promising those who took part that they would enjoy the same spiritual reward as those who went on crusade to the Holy Land. At first, there was little response, for few people in the west were convinced that the defunct Latin empire was a cause worth fighting for. Then in 1266 Charles, count of Anjou, the brother of the king of France, succeeded in establishing himself as king of Sicily and southern Italy. In doing so, he inherited the old ambitions of Robert Guiscard and Bohemond to seize the opposite shore of the Adriatic. It was now in the interest of this powerful and ambitious ruler to mount an expedition to Constantinople and in May 1267 he met with the exiled Latin emperor Baldwin II at Viterbo to agree details of the campaign.

Michael's response to the threat was an extraordinarily energetic diplomatic campaign. Charles was preparing a fleet in the harbour at Palermo so Michael needed naval support. Since Venice had been the staunch upholder of the Latin empire of Constantinople, Michael turned to the rival Genoese, handing over to them the town of Galata on the opposite side of the Golden Horn from Constantinople and providing them with preferential access to Constantinople's trading channels. But shortly afterwards Michael was also able to defuse the enmity of Venice as well. Although the Venetians had always been the staunchest supporters of the Latin empire, they were equally anxious to ensure that no one power controlled both sides of the Adriatic and thereby be able to cut off Venice's exit to the Mediterranean. Charles of Anjou's overweening ambitions made him look extremely dangerous and in 1268 Venice too ratified a treaty with Michael, trading neutrality for commercial concessions.

In the end, Genoese and Venetian help was not needed against Charles of Anjou because his fleet never sailed. Michael VIII ultimately brought him down by deploying other means. Ambassadors were dispatched to Spain to the court of King Peter III of Aragon. They promised the king the sum of 60,000 gold pieces if he would invade Sicily, the soft underbelly of Charles of Anjou's kingdom. At the very same time, Byzantine agents were circulating in Sicily, exploiting and stirring up the discontent of the local population with their French overlords. Both these initiatives met with success. On 30 March 1282 the people of Sicily rose up in revolt against their French rulers – an event known as the Sicilian Vespers – and King Peter invaded the island a few months later. Charles of Anjou was forced to divert his attention from the attack on Constantinople to defending his own kingdom. The invasion was defeated without it ever having been launched.

* * *

Brilliant though the frustration of Charles of Anjou was, the Byzantine recovery during the reign of Michael VIII was not quite the same as those of the past. It was not just the reduced territorial extent of the empire that made a difference but a shift in mentality too. In the eyes of its rulers, Byzantium had always been based not on its physical extent but rather on an idea: that of continuity with the Roman past that gave the emperor his unique status. During the period of exile, even though the traditional ideology had been voiced more stridently than ever to undermine the legitimacy of the Latin conquest of Constantinople, the outlook and mentality of the empire's people and even its ruler had subtly changed. In the past, Byzantium had tamed and absorbed wave after wave of destructive warriors, often by enrolling them in their own service and turning them on other enemies, but in 1204 that policy had gone horribly wrong. One response among the Byzantine populace was to retreat into a much narrower sense of identity and one symptom of that was the way in which they referred to themselves. Officially they were 'Romans', a word that had no ethnic connotations whatsoever. A Roman was simply someone who was a subject of the Christian Roman emperor. It was around this time, however, that some Byzantines began to describe themselves as 'Hellenes'. The word was not new. That was what the ancient Greeks, whose literature the Byzantines so admired, had called themselves. The earlier Byzantines had avoided the term, which had come to mean 'pagan', but now it started to be resurrected, probably to signify one of the traits that marked the Byzantines out from the Latins: their language. Niketas Choniates, former minister of the Angelos emperors who after 1204 had spent his last years living a wretched existence in the shanty town outside the walls of Nicaea, had put it very succinctly. It was wrong, he said, to serve the Latins, who spoke a different tongue. Thus the Byzantines were now defining themselves in terms of their language and ethnicity rather than in terms of a universal ideal. Ironically, in this they were following the practice of the Latin west where the Byzantines had been referred to as 'Greeks' for centuries. But it is not difficult to see why the change was taking place: defeat and occupation always serve to sharpen ethnic and national consciousness.

The development was going on under the surface. Officially the ruler who recovered Constantinople in 1261 was the successor of Constantine and the universal Roman emperor who ruled over all Christians. Behind the scenes a different outlook emerges now and then. In around 1255, the emperor of Nicaea, Theodore II Laskaris, had written a letter describing his plans for his army. He announced that foreign mercenaries were not to be relied on. Instead he was going to build an army composed of Hellenes, who alone could be depended on. As an expression of policy the letter was pure fantasy, for mercenaries were as prominent in Theodore's reign as they had always been. Its significance lies in its claim that the only real Romans were those who spoke Greek, a complete reversal of the very universalist ideology that was still being preached at the court of Nicaea.

There was another way in which the mentality that developed during the period of exile conflicted with traditional universalism. With the court removed from the grand setting of Constantinople and installed instead in two provincial towns, the imperial office lost something of its remoteness and its mystique. In some respects that was a positive thing. The age-old alienation of the provinces from the distant but demanding government in the capital was removed. There was an intense local loyalty to the ruling Angelos and Laskaris dynasties, which was carefully fostered and encouraged. Theodore II Laskaris declared himself in a public speech to be a 'patriotic lover of Nicaea'. Nevertheless, the emperor was being transformed from a universal monarch to a local king.

Both these developments were to cause problems for Michael VIII once he was reinstalled in Constantinople in 1261. Local patriotism meant that not everyone, even among Greek-speakers, was happy to recognise him as the new Constantine, and Michael began to encounter those same forces of alienation that had so worried Basil II. Part of the problem was Michael's treatment of John IV Laskaris. Up to 1261, he reigned alongside the legitimate emperor even if young John had no say whatever on policy matters. When Constantinople had been recovered, however, Michael felt secure enough in the adulation that this achievement brought him to do away with the fiction of joint rule. Some five months after his triumphant return to the capital, Michael sent secret orders to Nicaea that the eleven-year-old John should be blinded. When the deed was done, the child was hurried away to a castle on the Black Sea where he was to remain for the rest of his life. In spite of the secrecy, news of the atrocity leaked out. The patriarch excommunicated the emperor and in the frontier region near Nicaea a revolt broke out. The farmers of the area rallied around a young blind boy who claimed to be John IV. The uprising was short-lived. The rebels soon found themselves surrounded by an imperial army, so they allowed their would-be emperor to slip over the border to the Seljuk Turks. Michael wisely decided against punishing the rebels as they formed an integral part of his frontier defences.

Open rebellion was replaced with sullen resentment in the old Laskaris heartland. Once again the emperor became a distant figure whose only interest in the provinces was to tax them and who provided little of benefit in return. The resentment was increased because the Byzantine frontier in Asia Minor was coming under attack again during the 1260s and 1270s. The Seljuk sultan in Ikonion was not directly responsible for these attacks. They came from other groups of Turks who had fled to his territories to escape the Mongols. Eager to enlist them as allies in the civil wars that were slowly tearing the sultanate apart, the sultan had granted them lands on his western borders where, as his authority waned, they effectively became independent rulers. It was these autonomous emirs who mounted raids on their Byzantine neighbours. At first these were mere forays to steal sheep and cattle but as time went on they became more serious. Preoccupied with the threat from the west, Michael denuded Asia Minor of troops and resources, leaving the inhabitants of the area to become increasingly anxious about their security. That anxiety became mass hysteria in a peculiar incident that occurred at Nicaea in 1265.

It took place on a normal enough Monday morning. Doubtless life had changed somewhat since the imperial court had departed some four years earlier but the people of the city were going about their everyday tasks. For some inexplicable reason a rumour started to circulate in the streets that the advance guard of a Mongol army had surprised the guards of one of Nicaea's gates and cut them to pieces. They were now advancing into the city, killing everyone who stood in their path. The story grew as it spread. Some people even breathlessly described hideous atrocities that they had seen. The entire population was seized with horror and panic. People rushed for their houses, colliding with each other in their haste. Some hid in their cellars, others clambered into old tombs. There were a few who grabbed weapons and gathered around the city governor who led them to the east gate to investigate. They found the guards in one piece at their post and completely bewildered at what the fuss was about. Fearing the breakthrough must have occurred at another of the four entrances, the motley force marched off to each of them in turn. The story was the same. There were no Mongols and Nicaea was in no danger.

Not all alarms were false. In the absence of resistance, the Turkish raids became bolder. In 1280, an army led by a warlord called Menteshe reached as far as the valley of the river Maeander, a fertile region that had prospered under the Laskaris dynasty. The Turks surrounded the town of Tralles whose inhabitants resisted bravely in spite of suffering from hunger and thirst until the defensive walls were undermined and collapsed. In the subsequent sack, much of the town was reduced to ashes. While this was happening, Michael VIII's son

Andronicus was at Nymphaion to the south, with an army. He had arrived in the area the previous spring and had announced his intention to expand and remodel Tralles on a grand scale. Now he had proved that he could not even defend it. In view of the inability of the government in Constantinople to help them, some of the inhabitants lost faith completely. There were reports of them joining with the Turks on their raid and guiding them through the countryside to the best places to attack. Doubtless Michael VIII hoped that he would be able to retrieve the situation once he had fended off the threat from the west, but he was never to have that chance.

* * *

The alienation of the provinces was something that might have been remedied if Michael had had the time and resources to do so. The changing mentality of his people, however, was something that he had no hope of changing. The period of exile had created a narrower sense of Byzantine identity in opposition to the Latins, in more than just language and local loyalties. The idea of religious orthodoxy, as opposed to Latin heresy, had become inextricably merged with that of identity. The emperors and their courts at Nicaea and Epiros had done much to encourage that idea in their campaign to discredit the Latin empire. Now, with Constantinople regained, Michael was to find it something of a liability when he tried to purchase security in a new way.

Given that after 1261 the greatest threat to Constantinople came from the west, Michael sought to defuse it by removing the pretext that previous Latin adversaries had used to justify attacks on Christian Byzantium. In 1273, the emperor wrote to the pope expressing his eagerness to work for the union of the Churches and the end of the schism. His predecessors had made similar approaches but had kept it vague and had certainly made no promises on the issues of papal authority and the Creed. Michael, with typical single-mindedness, decided to solve the impasse at a stroke. In June 1274, a Byzantine delegation arrived in the French city of Lyons where a council of the western Church was already in session. Without having entering into any debate, the delegation read out a letter from Michael in the cathedral of St John. In it, the emperor agreed to end the schism on papal terms. The letter contained a formal acceptance of the *Filioque* clause, an acknowledgement of the Church of Rome's authority over the whole church, and an acceptance of the western position on minor matters such as the doctrine of purgatory and the use of unleavened bread in communion. A mass was then celebrated in which the priests with the Byzantine delegation openly used the *Filioque* during the Creed, not once but three times just to make sure that they were heard. When the delegation returned to Constantinople, the ceremony was re-enacted in Hagia Sophia in the presence of the emperor. At a stroke Michael had put an end to the long-running stumbling block to Byzantine relations with the west. The pope immediately distanced himself from any plans to retake Constantinople and restore the Latin empire. Such an attack would no longer be licit if the Byzantines were pious Catholics in communion with Rome.

Michael must have known that there would be opposition in Constantinople to this rather arbitrary solution. He must have recalled the stories of the iconophile martyrs and their resistance to the iconoclast emperors. He doubtless hoped that he could weather the storm as he had that over the blinding of John IV. A storm there certainly was, led, among others, by Michael's own sister Eulogia, who defiantly insisted 'Better that my brother's empire should perish, than the purity of the Orthodox faith.' Monks, particularly those of Mount Athos, were the most vociferous, disseminating tracts attacking the Union of Lyons as surrender to heresy. The emperor did not spare the rod in his efforts to ensure that the agreement was accepted. Opponents were flogged and imprisoned. One particularly obstreperous monk had his tongue cut out. Even Eulogia was imprisoned, although she later succeeded in escaping to Bulgaria. All this was not unlike the theological controversies that had divided Byzantium over and over again across the centuries. There was a difference, however. The religious issues had become linked to ethnic identity. Those who supported and implemented imperial policy were vilified not because they had become Catholics per se but because they were seen as having betrayed their own people. One of Michael's prominent courtiers, George Metochites, complained that people shouted at him that he had 'become a Frank'. In vain he protested that he was a patriot and not the supporter of a foreign power. The old universalism was on the wane in matters of religion too.

Typically, in spite of all the opposition, Michael stuck to his guns. When the threat of Charles of Anjou was removed by the Sicilian Vespers in the spring of 1282, he seemed to have been vindicated. The following November he was preparing to march into Thessaly where a son of the despot of Epiros was maintaining an independent principality. He was still in Asia Minor after a short expedition to shore up the frontier against the Turks and he decided to cross to Thrace by ship across the Sea of Marmara to save time. The ship was caught in a sudden and violent storm which very nearly sank it but it finally reached the port of Rhaidestos where Michael and his son Andronicus disembarked and rode to meet up with a contingent of Mongols sent by Michael's ally and son-in-law Nogai of the Golden Horde. By the time that they camped in the evening, however, the emperor was clearly unwell from a bowel complaint that he had been suffering from for some time. He was unable to mount his horse to give the customary speech of welcome to the Mongols, giving rise to anxiety among his retinue that they might start pillaging the villages in the area, unless they saw the emperor, whom they had been sent to assist. So with great effort, Michael was sat up with his courtiers supporting him on either side and he was able to speak a few gracious words to the leaders of the contingent. When the emperor was once more in his bed, the physician privately warned Andronicus that his father had not long to live. Andronicus went back to Michael's bedside and a priest quietly entered without the emperor noticing at first. Then the emperor turned his head and, seeing the priest there, knew that he was dying. After receiving communion, he slipped away on 11 December 1282, the Mongols lamenting as loudly as Michael's own men.

* * *

The succession was seamless. Although Michael's seizure of power had been brutal and illicit, he had succeeded in establishing his family as the ruling dynasty of Byzantium thanks to his recovery of Constantinople. It was to remain so until the final downfall of the empire. Andronicus II Palaiologos (1282–1328) has often been seen as a very inadequate replacement for his brilliant if ruthless father, pious and well-meaning but politically ineffective. In fact, Andronicus was the realist that Michael never was. Rather than proclaiming himself the new Constantine who would restore things to the way they were, he understood what kind of an empire it was that he was ruling and was more attuned to the outlook of his people. He grasped the passion with which they held to their Orthodox religion and the aspiration of the provinces for effective local rule, and he did his best to provide for both.

In normal circumstances the body of an emperor who had died outside Constantinople would be brought back for burial in one of the great churches of the capital. Michael VIII had probably envisaged that he would be laid to rest in the monastery of St Demetrius, which he had restored and refurbished. On Andronicus's orders, however, the corpse was taken to a monastery close to where he had died and was buried there. The following spring it was moved to a monastery in Selymbria, the same one that had received the skeleton of Basil II twenty years earlier. There was no public funeral in Constantinople and the late emperor was not even commemorated in the liturgy on the anniversary of his death as was normally the custom. Within days of his father's death, Andronicus had issued an amnesty to those imprisoned or exiled on account of their opposition to the Union of Lyons and dismissed the patriarch of Constantinople, John XI, whom Michael had brought in to implement the agreement. The following April, all bishops who supported the union were dismissed and replaced. The new emperor had effectively abandoned the unpopular agreement, even at the expense of his father's memory. Now that the threat of attack from the west was much diminished, with Charles of Anjou distracted by the Aragonese invasion of Sicily, the union was no longer needed. Moreover, its abandonment was undoubtedly popular and brought Andronicus the devotion and adulation of his people: the release of the anti-union prisoners brought cheering crowds out on to the streets of the capital to hail the restoration of Orthodoxy.

Andronicus also hoped to counteract the alienation of the provinces and to make himself visible and popular there. He made a point of visiting the castle where the unfortunate John IV Laskaris still lived, now aged around forty, and still regarded by some as the rightful emperor. Andronicus asked John's forgiveness for his father's crime, and for his recognition as emperor. From there Andronicus proceeded to the old Laskaris capital of Nicaea. He was to remain in Asia Minor for three years, strengthening the border defences against the Turks. By April 1299, Andronicus was in Thessalonica and the following year he visited the town of Monemvasia in the isolated enclave of Byzantine territory in the southern Peloponnese. He is credited with founding the church of Hagia Sophia there which stands precariously on a cliff top overlooking the sea. He even chose a wife with a view to curbing the separatist tendencies of the provinces. In 1284 he married his second consort, Irene, an Italian who belonged to the same family as Boniface of Montferrat who had ruled Thessalonica as king from 1204 to 1207. Part of the marriage settlement was that Irene's family would give up their claim to the city forever. Andronicus was doubtless aware that the people of Thessalonica had welcomed the Latins into their city in 1204.

Andronicus also gave thought to how to provide a permanent imperial presence in these areas when he was not there himself. In this, he may well have favoured a policy that his father had considered but had never been able to implement. At the end of his life Michael VIII had planned to put his younger son, Constantine, in charge of Thessalonica and Macedonia while leaving the empire as a whole to Andronicus. The thinking was, presumably, that with their own member of the ruling dynasty in residence, the provincials would feel less alienated and neglected. Andronicus might well have been sympathetic to this idea but when it became a reality during his reign it was largely by accident. The emperor came to have a rather strained relationship with his wife Irene and in 1303 she left Constantinople and went to live in Thessalonica to escape him. There she set up something like her own court, with a country residence at Drama in eastern Macedonia where she could retreat when she chose. Thereafter, Thessalonica usually had some member of the imperial family in residence, often ruling the city with the title of Despot.

Thus, for all his failures during his long reign, Andronicus had at least recognised the problems that the empire faced and tried to resolve them. It was not his fault that in the end his efforts did not work. Byzantium had become a much reduced ethnic state and, like the other Christian states of the Balkans, it would be unable to survive when the next wave of invaders from the east arrived. Throughout its history, Byzantium had experienced catastrophe after catastrophe: Adrianople in 378, the Persian, Avar and Arab invasions, Anchialos in 917, Manzikert in 1071 and the Fourth Crusade's seizure of Constantinople in 1204. It had recovered from them all. Now the stage was set for its descent towards oblivion.

An Old Man Remembers

I have been moved to this composition not because of any hatred or friendship,
from which falsehood is generally brought into the world . . .
John Kantakouzenos

Compared with the many fine monasteries of Constantinople, that known as
Charsianites was small and obscure. It was not a great imperial foundation like
Romanos I's Myrelaion or John II's Pantokrator, but was founded as a pious act
by a wealthy nobleman called John Charsianites in the mid fourteenth century.
In his old age he took religious vows there himself. During the 1360s, it was the
home of a monk called Joseph. On the face of it, Joseph was much the same as
all the other monks of Charsianites, garbed in the same long black robe and
close-fitting cowl. Yet, although he was not the abbot of the community, the
brothers could hardly have failed to accord him an instinctive deference,
standing aside for him in the corridors and falling silent when he spoke.
Frequent messages used to arrive for him from the Great Palace and he was
often summoned away on urgent business. For Joseph was the former emperor,
John VI (1347–1354), who like so many of his predecessors had ended his
career in monastic seclusion.

When he was not off on official business, mainly that of advising his son-in-
law John V Palaiologos (1341–1391), Joseph was hard at work at his desk. The
former emperor was writing his memoirs and the task was an urgent one. From
the Land Walls of Constantinople, the Byzantines now looked out on a countryside that was almost entirely lost to them. Even the city of Adrianople was
no longer in their hands and Thessalonica, although still a Byzantine city, was
cut off from the capital by land controlled by their enemies. The task of writing

was so pressing because it was widely said that Joseph himself was responsible for the dire straits in which the empire now found itself and he was anxious to exonerate himself from the charge.

* * *

From his monastic cell, Joseph looked back to that distant time when, as John Kantakouzenos, he had grown up in one of the richest and oldest-established families in the empire. There had been Kantakouzenoi in the armies of Alexios I Komnenos and John III Vatatzes, and their sprawling estates in Thrace pastured 5,000 head of cattle and 70,000 sheep. They had intermarried with the Palaiologoi in the past and, as close relatives of the ruling dynasty, members of the family were frequently to be found at court in the Great Palace. It was only to be expected that, as a child, Kantakouzenos had as one of his companions the third in line to the throne, Andronicus, the grandson of Emperor Andronicus II. Indeed he claimed in his memoirs that the two boys had begun then a friendship which became so close that 'both souls acted together'. The link was reinforced when they grew up and John Kantakouzenos married Irene, Andronicus's second cousin.

For those like Kantakouzenos who lived in Constantinople in the early decades of the fourteenth century, it would have been possible to think that things were much as they had always been. The city would still have looked flourishing and prosperous. There were new buildings and works of art. At the expense of the chief minister of Andronicus II, Theodore Metochites, the monastery and church of St Saviour in Chora, which lay close to the Land Walls, was refurbished and redecorated between 1316 and 1321 and was provided with a library which became the largest in Constantinople. Visitors to the city continued to be impressed by what they saw. When a Russian priest, Stephen of Novgorod, arrived with eight companions they gazed open-mouthed at the tall column with the statue of Justinian on his horse in the Augousteion. At the Brazen Gate their guide told them how the icon there had once been taken down by an impious iconoclast. They witnessed the procession that took place every Tuesday when the icon of the Hodegetria was paraded through the streets. In Hagia Sophia, Stephen and his companions walked around with tears of rejoicing and they were particularly happy when the patriarch of Constantinople allowed them to kiss his hand 'because he is very fond of the Rus'. Intriguingly, in one monastery Stephen and his group were shown a sealed lead casket in which they were assured were the relics of the Passion: the Byzantines appear to have acquired a second set to replace those that had been taken away during the period of Latin rule. Like all Russian pilgrims, Stephen accepted everything that he was told by his Byzantine guide, but a western visitor, Sir John Mandeville, was less accepting because he knew that many of the Passion relics, including the Crown of Thorns, were now in western cities. Nevertheless he described Hagia Sophia as the best and most beautiful church in the world and the Great Palace as very fair and well built. An Arab visitor, Ibn Battuta, who arrived in 1332, was astonished at the size of the city and recalled that when the bells of the churches all sounded together, the very skies shook.

It was all illusory. Constantinople was not the same as it had always been but was enjoying its Indian summer. Moreover, whatever might have been the impression given by the capital, out on the eastern frontier all was not well. Andronicus II had now been on the throne for nearly forty years and the latter part of his reign had been a complete disaster. The Turkish raids into Asia Minor that Michael VIII had belatedly tried to stem had turned into a land grab as the Turks no longer withdrew after their raids but settled, especially in the fertile Maeander valley. In 1302 a military expedition was launched to retrieve the situation but it ended in a fiasco. One part of the army was mauled by an emir called Osman at Bapheus while the other withdrew humiliatingly from Magnesia without achieving anything. By 1320, most of the countryside of western Asia Minor was in the hands of various groups of Turks, with Byzantine rule confined to the cities. The inhabitants of Constantinople could not continue serenely as if nothing had happened. The city became packed with refugees from the east who, with nowhere to go, had to live a wretched existence on the city's rubbish dumps. The patriarch organised soup kitchens to relieve the distress but the contrast between the destitute refugees and wealthy aristocrats such as Kantakouzenos must have been glaring. One day in 1317, a strong gust of wind blew the colossal orb out of the hand of Justinian's statue, sending it crashing down on to the flagstones of the Augousteion. It was eventually restored to its rightful place but many later looked back on the incident and saw it as an omen that the emperor was about to lose the lordship that he had exercised for so long.

* * *

The chain of events that was to send Byzantium spiralling into powerlessness began in the autumn of 1320. Whatever the crisis on the borders, the emperor's grandson Andronicus and his cronies enjoyed a riotous life that caused much anxiety to the older and wiser heads at court. Young Andronicus had become enamoured of a noble Constantinopolitan lady but he discovered that he had a rival for her affections. He hired a gang of thugs to administer physical retribution to this unknown lothario and they lay in wait for him one night near the woman's house. They pounced on their victim and beat him severely only to discover that they had got the wrong man. It turned out to be Andronicus's own younger brother, Manuel, and since the hirelings had done their work only too efficiently, the young man was dead. The emperor Andronicus was horrified. He declared his grandson unfit to rule and disinherited him, adopting as his heir another of his grandsons, even though he was illegitimate. Perhaps unsurprisingly, Kantakouzenos makes no mention of the murder in his memoirs, putting the emperor's action down to the temptation of a demon: one of many instances where he carefully altered the record to his own advantage and that of his friends.

At once a conspiracy began to form to promote the rights of the disinherited grandson and Kantakouzenos was at the heart of it. To be fair, this was not mere dynastic feuding. The conspirators were dismayed at the loss of territory in Asia Minor and strongly believed that the empire needed a younger man to retrieve the situation before the eastern provinces were altogether lost. So in April 1321, young Andronicus left Constantinople secretly by night and joined up with a party of supporters, including John Kantakouzenos, who were waiting for him on the road to Adrianople. The rebels found plenty of support in Thrace, which had recently been subjected to ruinous taxation by Andronicus II, and the tsar of Bulgaria offered to help their cause with a force of three hundred cavalry. So by the end of the year they were strong enough to march on Constantinople and to engage in the usual stand-off before the Land Walls. Andronicus II stood firm and since most of the younger Andronicus's supporters had fled the city, there was little danger of anyone opening the gates to the rebels from the inside. On the other hand, the emperor had no way of loosening the grip of the rebels on the countryside. After six months, the stalemate was brought to an end when the elderly emperor agreed to back down. The two sides met at the Thracian coastal town of Epivatai. Andronicus II formally proclaimed his grandson once more to be his heir and made him an allowance from the imperial treasury to maintain him in appropriate style. Some months later there was a coronation ceremony in Hagia Sophia in which young Andronicus was crowned co-emperor by the patriarch. Kantakouzenos too had his reward in the form of promotion to Great Domestic, commander in chief of the Byzantine army.

The agreement ended the civil war but it did not remedy the disastrous turn of events in Asia Minor where the situation continued to deteriorate. In the south the Turks had started to blockade the city of Philadelphia in 1322 while in the north Prousa was forced to surrender four years later. The young Andronicus begged to be allowed to take a contingent of troops to the aid of

Prousa, but the emperor refused to give his permission. With no sign that Andronicus II was likely to die or abdicate in the near future, there were signs of restiveness at the heir apparent's residence in the town of Didymoteichon in Thrace during the summer of 1327. In the autumn, he appeared once more before the walls of Constantinople with an army. Once again, the rebel had plenty of support outside Constantinople. The citizens of Thessalonica sent him a message surrendering their city to him. Finally, in May 1328, some of the garrison of the Land Walls were persuaded to admit the rebel troops. Riding to the Great Palace, Andronicus found his tearful grandfather clinging to an icon of the Virgin. Touched by the sight, the victor left the emperor unharmed. Andronicus II was sent away to monastic seclusion where he died a few years later, while the new regime installed itself.

* * *

The transfer of power had been protracted but Andronicus III (1328–1341) was now in full control of the empire, with Kantakouzenos as his chief minister and adviser. Irresponsible though he may have been as a youth, Andronicus took his assumption of office very seriously and made immediate preparations to reverse the decades of decline. In June 1329, just over a year after his coup, he and Kantakouzenos landed in Asia Minor with an army and marched inland to the relief of Nikomedeia, which was under siege by the Turks. A long and sporadic engagement took place around the village of Pelekanon and as night fell it became even more confused. The emperor was hit in the foot by an arrow and rumours spread that he had been killed. The Byzantines started to fall back to the coast but they were mercilessly harassed by the Turks the whole way. They finally took refuge behind the walls of a small settlement called Philokrene, the crippled emperor having to be carried for the last stage of the march. The next day, they force-marched to the boats and crossed back to Constantinople.

It was a dismal and dispiriting beginning to the reign and was followed two years later by the loss of Nicaea. Both Andronicus III and Kantakouzenos, however, deserve credit for cool and imaginative thinking in such a disadvantageous situation. Asia Minor, they reasoned, was lost for the time being, even if some towns such as Nikomedeia and Philadelphia still held out. The situation was therefore much the same as it had been when Alexios I Komnenos had taken power back in 1081. He had not immediately attempted to dislodge the Turks but had made treaties with them, buying time to deal first with his western enemies. Turkish mercenaries had proved then very useful in bringing about the defeat of Robert Guiscard and the Normans. Andronicus III and Kantakouzenos decided on the same approach now and it was possible because the disparate Turkish raiders of Michael VIII's day had now coalesced into discrete groups with discernible leaders who could make and observe treaties. The Turks who had worsted Andronicus and Kantakouzenos at Pelekanon, and who had taken Nicaea, were the Ottomans whose emir was now Orhan. In August 1333, Andronicus III crossed in person to Asia Minor and met with Orhan somewhere in the vicinity of Nikomedeia. The emperor agreed to make an annual payment to the emir, who in return agreed not to attack the remaining Byzantine footholds on that side of the Sea of Marmara.

Two years later, while engaged on a naval campaign in the Aegean, the emperor and his chief minister made contact with another emir, Umur, the leader of the Aydin Turks, who had established themselves in and around the port of Smyrna. This time the agreement was rather different. Umur had not defeated the Byzantines in battle and did not need to be bought off. Instead, the treaty seems to have concerned the supply of mercenary soldiers for the imperial army. The wheels of diplomacy were oiled by the remarkable personal rapport which developed between Kantakouzenos and the emir, to the extent that the Turk considered himself to be the blood brother of the Byzantine ever afterwards.

Inevitably in later years, when the Turks were in the process of conquering much of the Balkans, Kantakouzenos's involvement in these pacts was remembered and held against him. At the time, however, the policy was a reasonable one. Although the Turks had ousted the Byzantines from Asia Minor they did not appear to be a threat to the empire's existence. They were, as has been said, divided up into small groups: the Ottoman and Aydin Turks were only two of a patchwork of emirates into which, with the demise of the old Seljuk sultanate at Ikonion, Asia Minor was now divided. These Turks were all Muslim by religion but they were not fanatical warriors thirsting for perpetual battle with the infidel. The motive for their original raids across the Byzantine frontier in Michael VIII's day had been sheep and cattle rustling which had developed into seizure of land when it became clear that the opposition was minimal. The idea that they were ghazis, or warriors of the faith, was largely made up later when the Ottomans were pre-eminent and wanted to justify their absorption of the other Turkish emirates, just like the phoney genealogy that was concocted to give the Ottoman sultans a direct line of descent from the prophet. In the 1330s, things were very different and it made sense to conclude peace with one set of enemies and enlist their help against the others: the reconquest of Asia Minor could be attended to later. It was all in good Byzantine tradition.

The tactic proved to be successful. If Andronicus III and Kantakouzenos had failed to rescue Asia Minor, elsewhere they restored Byzantine rule in territories that had seemed lost forever. In 1329, when the inhabitants of Chios rebelled against their Genoese rulers, Andronicus sailed down with a fleet and occupied the island. Seven years later the Genoese were ousted from another Aegean island, Lesvos. In 1333, Thessaly, the area of northern Greece around Larissa which Michael VIII had failed to recover, was incorporated back into the empire. Finally in 1338, accompanied by a contingent of 2,000 Turks sent by Umur of Aydin, Andronicus III and Kantakouzenos marched west to put down a revolt in Albania. The rebellion was soon crushed, the Albanians fleeing in terror from the strange-looking eastern soldiers in the Byzantine army. While he was in the area, the emperor took advantage of the recent death of the despot of Epiros to send an ultimatum to the court at Arta. The new despot was only in his teens and a council of regency was ruling the country. Its members decided not to put up a fight and surrendered to the emperor. Inevitably there was some resistance to the takeover but by the end of 1340, the old successor state of Epiros had been reunited with the empire. There the momentum halted. In the summer of 1341, when Andronicus III returned from Thessalonica to Constantinople, he was clearly exhausted and unwell. He died in June at the age of forty-five.

* * *

The death of Andronicus III left Byzantium in a situation in which it had been many times before. His heir was his nine-year-old son, John V, and the usual council of regency was formed, headed by the boy's mother, the Latin Anna of Savoy, and the patriarch. But everyone knew that in these circumstances the likelihood was that the empire's most prominent soldier would take over the reins of government, with or without the approval of the regency. Inevitably, many people saw John Kantakouzenos in this role. In September 1341, there was a noisy demonstration in the courtyard of the Great Palace by his supporters, who demanded that he be given a more prominent rank in imperial ceremonial. Kantakouzenos himself, in his memoirs, claims that he was painfully embarrassed by the incident and that he had no designs on the throne whatsoever. Whether that was true or not, suspicion was bound to attach itself to him anyway. When he left Constantinople the same month to resume command of the army at Didymoteichon, the regency council seized his property and imprisoned his family. A message was sent to Kantakouzenos ordering him to resign his command and return at once to Constantinople. Unsurprisingly, he did not do so and was proclaimed emperor by his troops at Didymoteichon on 26 October.

In the usual run of things, the issue should have been settled within a matter of months. Either someone would admit the rebel army through the Land

Walls, or the regency would stand firm and the revolt would peter out. This time it did not work out like that and the stand-off lasted for six years. The duration and intensity of the conflict were at least partly the result of the issue of succession becoming intertwined with a social conflict. As the empire had shrunk, many of its inhabitants had been cruelly impoverished. Some had been violently dispossessed of their homes and properties in Asia Minor by the Turks but most of those who had remained under imperial rule had fared little better. With a smaller population to tax, the authorities were squeezing ever harder to extract what they needed to field the army and maintain the capital city. But not everyone was suffering. The landowners of Thrace and Macedonia, such as the Kantakouzenos family, dominated huge tracts of land and in proportion to their wealth made only a tiny contribution to the fisc. The resentment that had been smouldering for decades now found an outlet in civil war and ensured that it was like no other before it. This time the mass of the population did not sit by and wait for the outcome but were actively involved in the hostilities.

The nature of the conflict became apparent the day after Kantakouzenos's assumption of the imperial purple. When the news was announced in the main square of Adrianople, the wealthier citizens were delighted. Not so their less affluent neighbours, who that evening spilled out on to the streets and began rioting. They targeted the houses of known supporters of Kantakouzenos, ransacking their contents and forcing their owners to flee to Didymoteichon for their lives. The pattern was repeated all over Thrace and Macedonia. In Thessalonica a group of workers and farmers calling themselves the Zealots seized control and announced their loyalty to the regency in Constantinople. When Kantakouzenos arrived with the army, he found the city gates locked and barred against him.

At this point, the would-be emperor could have admitted defeat and abandoned his rebellion. Indeed some of his supporters were already starting to melt away. It certainly would have been for the good of the empire if he had done so. But that would mean either exile or, more likely, capture, blinding and even death. So he persevered and looked for help from outside the empire's borders. In July 1342 he signed a pact with a neighbouring Orthodox ruler, the king of Serbia, Stephen Dushan, who provided a contingent of troops. He also turned to his old friend Umur of Aydin who landed in Thrace with a large force late in 1342. These alliances must have raised Kantakouzenos's hopes but they did not win him the war. The Serbian contingent was small and although Umur's was much larger events later took a turn that forced him to return home to protect his own emirate. The Venetians had become seriously alarmed by piratical attacks on their shipping launched from Umur's base at Smyrna. They persuaded the pope to call a crusade against him and in 1344 a Christian fleet attacked and captured the port. After Umur had withdrawn from Thrace, he was killed in battle with the crusaders in 1348. There would be no further help from that quarter.

In Thrace, the war went on. The opposing armies manoeuvred and circled, towns and villages were captured and lost. By 1345, it was clear that Kantakouzenos was gaining the upper hand. Adrianople was taken, giving him a forward base for the march on Constantinople. Yet he still lacked the strength to deliver the knockout blow. He was therefore extremely interested when some envoys arrived in Adrianople from Prousa, the seat of the Ottoman emir, Orhan. They brought a proposal that their emir should marry Kantakouzenos's daughter Theodora. Kantakouzenos was delighted, for, while some Ottoman troops had already been aiding his campaign, this closer association would pave the way for many more. The marriage took place by proxy at Selymbria in the summer of 1346. Some eight months later, the civil war was finally brought to a conclusion when some of Kantakouzenos's closet supporters managed to open up a hole in the Land Walls from the inside and allow his troops to stage a swift takeover in Constantinople.

* * *

'It remains now', wrote the monk Joseph, referring to himself in the third person, 'to narrate what was accomplished by Kantakouzenos as emperor.' He did not try to hide the fact that, although he was now recognised as John VI, he had come into a difficult inheritance. The long years of civil war had, as he himself put it, reduced 'the great empire of the Romans to a feeble shadow of its former self'. It was effectively bankrupt. When Kantakouzenos was crowned in May 1347, the diadem that was placed on his head was adorned with imitation jewels made of glass. The real crown and regalia had been given by the regency to the Venetians during the civil war, as collateral for a loan. At the banquet afterwards, the guests were served from pewter and earthenware, for the gold and silver dinner service had gone the way of the jewels. The treasury was empty and the possibilities for refilling it were limited. The customs revenues which had once brought in such handsome sums were now only a fraction of what they had once been, partly because many of the merchant ships that entered the Golden Horn now dropped anchor at Genoese Galata rather than on the Byzantine side, and paid their customs duties there. The loss of Asia Minor meant that the only way to increase revenue was to tax the inhabitants of the remaining territories in Thrace, Macedonia and the Peloponnese even more heavily. Kantakouzenos tried to spread the burden by taxing luxuries like wine and he solved the problem of the Venetian loan by simply defaulting so that the crown jewels were never redeemed, but neither of these measures could retrieve the dire financial situation.

If that were not bad enough, within months of Kantakouzenos's victory, Constantinople was struck by a new calamity, the Black Death. The plague had originated in Central Asia and was brought to Constantinople in Genoese ships from the Crimea in the summer of 1347. It cut a swathe through the population and put all commercial and political activity on hold as people avoided each other for fear of contagion. The epidemic raged for a year and among the thousands of victims was Kantakouzenos's youngest son, Andronicus, who was only thirteen. 'Every day we bring out our friends for burial,' wrote one survivor. 'Every day the great city becomes emptier and the number of graves increases.' Even so, Constantinople, with its wide streets and open spaces within the Land Walls, may have fared slightly better than the crowded cities of western Europe which were to experience the disease the following year.

His sober realisation of how damaging the civil war and its aftermath had been was probably the reason that, after all the bitterness and bloodshed, the peace terms offered by Kantakouzenos were remarkably conciliatory. There was no witch hunt against those who had opposed him and young John V Palaiologos did not suffer the fate of John IV Laskaris. Instead it was agreed that he would marry Kantakouzenos's daughter Helena and would reign as co-emperor with his father-in-law. John VI would be the senior emperor for ten years but thereafter the two emperors would have equal status. John V would be the heir to the throne, succeeding on his father-in-law's death. At first this rather unusual agreement seemed to be working and many people had high hopes that Kantakouzenos's accession would mark a new beginning in which the recovery under Andronicus III would be renewed. Indeed in the middle years of Kantakouzenos's reign it did indeed look for a time as if Byzantium might be on the mend. The borders of the empire might have contracted, but Kantakouzenos did his best to ensure the prosperity of those areas still under Byzantine control. Following the precedent set by Andronicus II, he appointed members of the imperial family as semi-independent governors, or despots. He sent his younger son Manuel to the Peloponnese, and under his administration the province enjoyed relative peace and security. Its main town of Mistra, with its impregnable castle, began to grow and prosper. Thessalonica was entrusted to Kantakouzenos's son-in-law John V and his mother Anna of Savoy. It kept them out of Constantinople and they administered the city well enough.

Kantakouzenos also had the advantage that Byzantium no longer had any large and powerful enemies. He remained on very cordial terms with the foremost Muslim power, the Mamluk sultanate of Egypt. He sent an embassy to Cairo in the summer of 1349 to ask the sultan to treat his Christian subjects in Jerusalem with consideration. He received a reply so gratifying that he transcribed it verbatim into his memoirs. The sultan addressed him as 'the foundation of the faith and teaching of the Christians, the unshakeable pillar of all the baptised' and promised to allow the churches of Jerusalem to be maintained in good order and to allow pilgrims to visit the city unmolested. Nor was there any danger from the two Slav powers that had threatened Byzantium in the past, Bulgaria and Russia. Byzantine prestige still stood high among the peoples who had originally been converted to Christianity from Constantinople and who considered themselves Orthodox as opposed to Catholic. The Russians were the most faithful, sending their newly appointed archbishops to Constantinople for approval and consecration by the patriarch, and entrusting the decoration of their churches to Byzantine artists. 'The empire of the Romans', John Kantakouzenos assured the ruler of Moscow, 'is the source of all piety and the teacher of law and sanctification,' and when that same ruler heard that Hagia Sophia had suffered damage in an earthquake of 1346, he sent money to help with the repairs. There was no likelihood of an attack from that quarter.

Relations with Latin powers had also been improving over recent decades. There were still descendants of Baldwin II who claimed that they had been wrongfully ejected from the Latin empire, but no one took much notice of them anymore. Relations with the papacy had thawed. Although Andronicus II had been excommunicated for his abrogation of the Union of Lyons, towards the end of his reign he had reopened contact with the papal curia and the possibility of ending the schism had been discussed. Under Andronicus III, Byzantine ships had taken part in a crusade with the Latins against the Turks in the Aegean. Almost as soon as Constantinople was his, Kantakouzenos capitalised on this development and sent an embassy to the papal court at Avignon to announce his accession. He received a gracious reply from the pope, praising the new emperor's clemency to his defeated foes and inviting him to join in another crusade against the infidel. Kantakouzenos must have known perfectly well that the infidel in question was his old friend and ally Umur of Aydin but he enthusiastically agreed, no doubt safe in the knowledge that he would never have to honour his pledge.

Kantakouzenos even managed to steer a path through the tricky relations with the Italian maritime republic of Genoa, which had taken advantage of the civil war to reoccupy Chios and now dominated much of Constantinople's trade from its colony at Galata. In the summer of 1348, the Genoese became apprehensive when they noticed that Kantakouzenos was building a fleet in the dockyards opposite Galata. Fearing that it was going to be used against them, the Genoese mounted a pre-emptive strike across the Golden Horn and set fire to many of the half-completed galleys. When Kantakouzenos ordered a counter-attack the following spring it was a fiasco: the crews of the Byzantine ships lost control of them when a sudden gale blew up, and many of them jumped into the sea in panic. The Genoese then sallied forth and took the abandoned vessels in tow. The next day the Genoese ships sailed up and down provocatively within sight of the Great Palace, dragging captured Byzantine standards in the water behind them. Nevertheless, Kantakouzenos emerged from the encounter rather well. When the government in Genoa learned about the attack across the Golden Horn they were quick to rein in their irresponsible fellow citizens in Galata. They awarded the Byzantines an indemnity for the damage done and agreed to continue the fiction that Galata was held by the Genoese only with Byzantine permission. Its administrator, the podestà, was appointed in Genoa but on arrival he was expected to present himself before the emperor and take an oath as if he were a Byzantine official. The arms of the Byzantine emperor were incorporated into those of Genoa in the devices displayed on the walls of Galata and in this way honour was satisfied. Thus it was not the Arabs, the Latins, the Russians or any of the old enemies who sent Byzantium plummeting into the crisis from which it would never recover. It was a small and insignificant state that had once been a staunch ally.

* * *

The seeds of the empire's downfall had been sown during the civil war when Kantakouzenos had recruited foreign rulers to bring troops to his aid. There was nothing new in that, of course, for Byzantine rulers had been doing it for centuries. The difference now was that Kantakouzenos lacked that wonderful facility which his predecessors had enjoyed: that of producing seemingly inexhaustible supplies of gold coins to oil the wheels of diplomacy and to ensure the loyalty of his allies. In the past, the Serbs had been a minor Balkan power and they had obediently attacked the Bulgars when called upon to do so. Perhaps that background lulled Kantakouzenos into a false sense of security when he negotiated with Stephen Dushan in July 1342. The Serbian king suggested that a sizeable part of Byzantine Macedonia would be a suitable recompense for his efforts but Kantakouzenos firmly declined. At this point, in previous centuries, a large quantity of gold would have been offered, but Kantakouzenos seems to have been guarded about that too. It would therefore appear that a contingent of Serbian troops served in Kantakouzenos's army without any concrete reward being offered and inevitably their services would have to be paid for somehow or other. As the civil war went on, Dushan helped himself to what he considered his due, and occupied numerous towns. This might have looked like an action on his ally's behalf until the spring of 1346 when Dushan had himself crowned as 'Tsar of the Serbs and the Greeks' and the extent of his ambition was revealed. Like Symeon of Bulgaria before him, he hoped to take over the territories of Byzantium in a new Orthodox empire centred on Serbia. Kantakouzenos had no tricks up his sleeve to stop the Serbs. Once the war was over, they marched almost unopposed into what remained of Byzantine territory and by November 1349, they had taken over most of Epiros, Macedonia and Thessaly. All the areas retaken in the optimistic years under Andronicus III had now been lost.

It was not the Serbs, however, who were to emerge as Byzantium's nemesis, but another minor power and erstwhile ally – the Ottoman Turks. Their emirate was just one of many which had emerged in Asia Minor after the demise of the Seljuk sultanate of Ikonion and was by no means the most powerful. The Karaman emirate had inherited the old Seljuk capital while Umur of Aydin, who had access to the Aegean at Smyrna, was of much greater concern to the Christian powers of the west. From his capital at Prousa, the Ottoman emir Orhan governed a modest territory that included the former Byzantine towns of Nicaea and Nikomedeia and faced Constantinople over the Bosporus, but he posed no direct threat to the Byzantine capital. It was for this reason that Kantakouzenos had been only too happy to receive Orhan's help in the civil war and to agree to the emir's request to marry his daughter Theodora.

Initially the Ottomans were far more reliable as allies than either Stephen Dushan or Umur of Aydin. Orhan kept up a steady supply of troops throughout the civil war and the association did not come to an end with Kantakouzenos's victory. A few months after the takeover of Constantinople in 1347, Orhan travelled to Chrysopolis across the Bosporus from Constantinople. The emperor sailed over to meet him and several days of feasting and hunting followed. When Kantakouzenos returned to Constantinople, Theodora came with him on a visit, bringing several of Orhan's children with her. The emir clearly enjoyed the prestige that arose from his imperial marriage and it seemed only natural that he should continue to provide troops for Kantakouzenos's army. Commanded by Orhan's son, Süleyman, they proved to be fearsomely effective against the Serbs and Albanians. Kantakouzenos was not blind to the drawbacks of employing Turkish troops. He knew that it had made his own subjects extremely apprehensive when they saw them marching into Constantinople with him once he was emperor. There were complaints that their noisy carousals disturbed the worshippers in Hagia Sophia, and in his coronation speech Kantakouzenos felt compelled to issue an apology for employing them.

The greatest difficulty that they posed, however, was what to do with them once they were no longer needed. Most followed their leader Süleyman back across the Dardanelles to Ottoman territory once the hostilities were at an end but a few bands stayed behind to pillage the countryside of Thrace and generally make a nuisance of themselves. These groups of soldiers were not the advance guard of an Islamic conquest but a common phenomenon in medieval warfare. Lulls in the contemporary Hundred Years War saw similar companies of unemployed English soldiers wandering around France, in search of any moveable wealth that they could steal. As time went by the Turkish bands were reinforced by new arrivals, as in the summer of 1348 when some 2,000 Turks crossed the Dardanelles uninvited. Kantakouzenos intercepted the intruders and after a sharp encounter compelled them to lay down their arms. He would probably have liked to have dispensed with the services of the Turks altogether but no sooner had one conflict been resolved than another arose. As his reign went on, it became clear that the civil war was likely to begin again. In Thessalonica, young John V was growing impatient of his father-in-law's tutelage and was gathering a strong body of support. At the same time Kantakouzenos's own eldest son, Matthew, was demanding that he, and not John V, should be his father's heir. The emperor did his best to defuse all these competing claims but he only staved off the crisis and, by the summer of 1352, John V and Matthew Kantakouzenos were fighting each other in Thrace.

These events were watched very closely at the Ottoman court in Prousa. Emir Orhan was still Kantakouzenos's son-in-law and ally. He was in no way responsible for the unruly bands of Turks in Thrace, who were acting entirely on their own initiative. Even so, he cannot have failed to realise what an easy target for conquest Byzantine Thrace would now be. Both John V and Matthew Kantakouzenos were recruiting Turkish troops and Süleyman was sent over with a contingent to help the latter. It was now that there was a change in the way the Ottomans behaved in Thrace. During the summer of 1352, Süleyman quietly occupied the small harbour and fortress of Tzympe on the European side of the Sea of Marmara and ignored repeated requests by Kantakouzenos that he should evacuate the town. Whether under orders from his father or not, Süleyman was clearly thinking in terms of a bridgehead. For the present, though, there was little that the Ottomans could do to exploit this gain. Since they had no fleet, they had no means of ferrying a large army across to Tzympe to reinforce their garrison.

Then, during the evening of 1 March 1354, the inhabitants of Constantinople were alarmed by a series of very strong earth tremors. One described looking on helplessly as his precious books dropped one by one from the shelf to the floor while he was unable to rise to his feet to go to their rescue. Fortunately, the epicentre of the earthquake had been far to the south. When daylight returned, there was general relief that the city had received only a shaking and that there was little structural damage. The port of Gallipoli on the Dardanelles was not so lucky. Much of it was levelled to the ground, as complete houses disappeared into the holes that had suddenly opened up. The entire length of the defensive wall that ringed the town to the landward side was reduced to rubble. On the other side of the narrow strait, the Ottoman Turks had also felt the tremors and could clearly see the damage that had been done to Gallipoli. Before the day was out a band of Turks had clambered into boats, crossed the strait and occupied the town. Standing on the Dardanelles at their narrowest crossing point, Gallipoli was the bridgehead the Ottomans needed. No fleet was required to ferry an army over the short crossing here, for smaller boats could easily do the job. It all happened so fast that no one seems to have been aware of the danger until it was too late. A Byzantine ship taking the archbishop of Thessalonica to Constantinople was seized as it passed through the strait before its crew had realised what had happened. Their illustrious passenger was taken off to Nicaea to await ransom. Shortly afterwards, Süleyman turned up in person to claim Gallipoli for the Ottoman emir.

The prudent reaction would have been to drive the Turks from Gallipoli before they had the chance to repair the fortifications and entrench themselves. But, in the summer of 1354, John VI Kantakouzenos was fast losing control of his empire as his attempts to reconcile his son and son-in-law proved unavailing. He wrote to Orhan, asking for a meeting to discuss Gallipoli and Tzympe but the emir claimed to be unwell and the meeting never took place. The autumn came and the Turks were still in Gallipoli. Then one November night, Kantakouzenos learned that John V had landed in one of Constantinople's small harbours with a body of armed men. The emperor and his supporters barricaded themselves into the Great Palace while John's followers occupied the Augousteion. For several days, the two sides glared at each other from their positions. Then, weary of the burden of power, Kantakouzenos announced his abdication. He handed the administration over to John V and took monastic vows under his new name of Joseph.

* * *

Afters the strains and stresses of the past few years, the undemanding life of a monk must have looked very attractive to Kantakouzenos. He might have considered making for the monastic enclave of Mount Athos. Sequestered on their rocky peninsula, the monks of Athos had been largely untouched by the wars and upheavals of the mid fourteenth century. Cristoforo Buondelmonti, an Italian visitor, was deeply impressed by the order and tranquillity that he found there. Among the olive groves and fig trees, the monks occupied themselves with their allotted tasks, mending nets, stitching shoes and weaving baskets. 'At stated hours,' Buondelmonti wrote, 'all essay to praise God. And peace reigns among them always and forever.'

Sadly, if Kantakouzenos had been hoping for something along these lines when he relinquished power, he would have been disappointed. His monastery of Charsianites was not on remote Athos but in the centre of things in Constantinople, for even though he had stood down the ex-emperor could not escape altogether. The Turks, the Serbs and his own fractious family kept on intruding on his contemplative retreat. John V's rule was still being challenged by Kantakouzenos's son Matthew and in December 1357 the new monk was summoned from his refuge to negotiate between the rivals. He succeeded in persuading Matthew to drop his claim to the throne and to retire to the Peloponnese, leaving John V to rule unchallenged. Kantakouzenos could then return to his cloistered existence.

While all this was going on, one of the quietest and most understated conquests in history was in progress. From their bridgehead at Gallipoli, the Ottomans did not subdue Byzantine Thrace so much as infiltrate it. There were no battles and no sieges. In 1360, they moved into Kantakouzenos's old headquarters at Didymoteichon and took over the town. At some point after that, they occupied Adrianople but nobody bothered to record the date. By taking the city, the Ottomans cut Constantinople off from Thessalonica by land and left it as an island in a countryside that they now controlled. Sensing that the future of his dynasty was now in Europe, Orhan's successor as emir, Murad I, transferred his court from Prousa to Adrianople and built a palace there, an eloquent statement that he intended to stay.

With Kantakouzenos out of the picture, it fell to John V to find some way of stopping the Ottomans. Having yearned for years to come into his birthright and become sole emperor, now in his twenties he had got exactly what he wished for. But he was not the man to deal with the crisis: incapable, according to one chronicler, of negotiating any issues apart from those involving beautiful and shapely women. In any case, his options were limited. The bankrupt and shrunken empire that he had inherited could not field a large enough army to retrieve the situation. Instead he went back to the old ploy of looking to the Latins for salvation.

That was easier said than done, because there was still a pronounced antipathy towards the Latins in large sections of the Byzantine population, fuelled by memories of 1204 and awareness of the ongoing schism. So deep were such feelings that, as one Dominican friar living in Galata complained, the locals would even break a cup out of which a Latin had drunk as if it were something contaminated. As Byzantium visibly declined and the menace presented by the Ottomans became clear, however, a pro-Latin element began to emerge among the courtiers. One of the brightest of them, Demetrius Kydones, decided that he should learn Latin so that he could deal better with the throng of western ambassadors, merchants and mercenaries who visited the Byzantine court every day. Once he had learned the language, Kydones became an admirer of Latin literature and theology and even converted to Catholicism. He became a passionate advocate of the idea that the Latins should be seen as allies and fellow Christians, not as hostile schismatics. They should be called upon to send help against the common Muslim enemy. These were the views that prevailed on John V.

The closest Catholic power was Hungary, an extensive and wealthy kingdom that was well placed to strike at the Ottomans. In the summer of 1365, John V made the decision not only to appeal to its king but, such was the gravity of the situation, to do so in person. Thus it was that the following autumn the representative of God on earth left Constantinople and travelled north to the Hungarian capital of Buda. If he had hoped that the sight of the once mighty Byzantine emperor begging for help would melt the hearts of his hosts, he was disappointed. The supplicant was not well received when he arrived and did not stay long. On the way back he was stopped at the border by the Bulgars, who refused to let him cross into their territory. He had to spend months waiting in the town of Vidin before he could be ferried out by ship along the Danube. Frustrating though the trip was, it brought home the essential truth that any Latin help was going to be contingent on the schism being resolved. That lesson had already been learned by the inhabitants of the last Byzantine town in Asia Minor, Philadelphia. For years their city had been surrounded and besieged by the Turks and no assistance whatsoever had been received from the Byzantine emperor, so they sent an appeal to the pope. All they received was a letter informing them that they would have to convert to Catholicism before any help could be dispatched.

On the other hand, John V knew perfectly well that any attempt to end the schism on Latin terms would provoke exactly the same outrage and opposition among his own people that the Union of Lyons had in 1274. On the horns of this dilemma, the only thing he could do was show himself at least ready to discuss the matter, and in June 1367 a papal delegation was invited to Constantinople. John Kantakouzenos was fetched from his monastery to play a leading role in the debates that followed over the next few weeks. The outcome was inconclusive. The Byzantines insisted that an ecumenical council of the Church should be convened to resolve the schism, while the Latin side could see no reason why that was necessary. In the end, John V came up with a novel solution to break the deadlock. He set out on his travels once more, accompanied by Demetrius Kydones and other pro-Latin courtiers. This time his destination was Rome and in October 1369 he took part in a public ceremony in St Peter's. After kissing the pope's hands, mouth and feet, the Byzantine emperor humbly knelt before him and declared himself a convert to Catholicism who accepted papal authority and the western version of the Creed. The action was carefully thought out: John's submission was a personal one and he made no promises on behalf of his subjects, as Michael VIII's representatives had at Lyons in 1274. The pope was perfectly well aware of that but he knew too that there was now a real danger that the ailing Christian empire would be replaced by a powerful Muslim one. He therefore issued a declaration that the emperor was now worthy of assistance and encouraged Catholic powers to go to his aid against the Ottomans.

Sadly, the hapless John V seems to have been doomed to disappointment and humiliation throughout his life. When he left Rome, he made for Venice to take ship back to Constantinople. There the authorities arrested him for non-payment of a loan that he had taken out to finance his trip to Rome. Once again the Byzantine emperor found himself marooned in a foreign land with no way of getting home. It was only when his son Manuel arrived with a fleet of ships and some cash to pay off the loan that he was finally able to return to his capital. By then it was quite clear that the pope's appeal for aid had been completely ignored and there would be no cohorts of Latin knights riding east to drive the Ottomans back over the Dardanelles. The whole distasteful exercise had been in vain.

One hope remained. Byzantium might no longer be capable of confronting the Ottomans militarily but its Orthodox neighbours were. The great Stephen Dushan had died in 1355 and many of the territories that he had annexed in the 1340s had since seceded, but Serbia was still a power to be reckoned with. It was the Serbs who in the summer of 1371 launched an offensive to drive the Turks from the Balkans. When the Serbian army was annihilated at the battle of the Marica river that September, there could no longer be any doubt that the

Ottomans were there to stay. One by one the Christian rulers of the area made their submission to Emir Murad, agreeing not only to stay at peace with him and to pay an annual tribute but also to provide troops to serve in his army when called upon to do so. First the Serbs, then the Bulgars and then, with no other option available to him, John V, all became vassals of the Ottoman emir. John's son Manuel was dispatched with a contingent of soldiers to fulfil the demand for military service, fighting alongside the Ottomans in Asia Minor where they were slowly imposing their hegemony over the other Turkish emirates. Ironically, one of the actions in which Manuel took part was against Philadelphia, the last outpost in the lost territories of the east. When it finally fell by storm in 1390, Byzantine troops were among the soldiers who breached the walls.

At the time John V became an Ottoman vassal in 1372, Joseph the monk was no longer in Constantinople, having moved south to Mistra. He died in a monastery there on 15 June 1383. He had by then long finished writing his memoirs and had presented his defence against the indictment that he was responsible for bringing the Turks into Europe. To some extent, of course, he was guilty as charged, but in doing so he had only been imitating his predecessors, who had turned the waves of migrants to the empire's advantage. It was his misfortune that he had not commanded the resources enjoyed by his predecesors, and without those he could not stem the flood which swept away his entire world.

* * *

By the time of Kantakouzenos's passing, the empire was effectively at an end. The emperor's writ scarcely ran beyond the Land Walls of his capital while his overlord, the Ottoman emir in Adrianople, ruled a large part of Asia Minor and the Balkans with Constantinople sitting awkwardly in the middle of his domains. The emperor's authority was still recognised in part of the Peloponnese and a few Aegean islands but Thessalonica opened its gates to the Ottomans in 1387. Even so Byzantium maintained a shadowy existence for another sixty years. The Palaiologos emperors continued to style themselves 'emperors of the Romans', and their capital still retained its reputation as a holy city and a centre of the faith among Orthodox Christians, although its influence was dwindling. The Russians stopped sending their archbishops there for consecration after 1448. Life in Constantinople in these last years was very different from the way it had been in the past. The emperor and the court were no longer the centre of everything. Indeed the Great Palace and the palace of Blachernae were slowly crumbling, and the imperial family was confined to a cramped suite of habitable rooms. Some of the emperor's subjects were infinitely richer than he was,

having made their money from trade in co-operation with the Venetians and
Genoese. There was an alternative court at Mistra, where a cadet member of
the Palaiologos dynasty ruled the Byzantine Peloponnese. In contrast to crumbling Constantinople, Mistra was a thriving place, drawing a healthy income
from the agricultural lands round about.

This shadowy existence could not go on forever. The end seemed nigh
when the cautious Murad I was replaced by a new and aggressive Ottoman
ruler, Bayezid I. He styled himself as sultan rather than as emir, to mark the
arrival of the Ottomans as one of the pre-eminent Muslim powers, and he
broke with his father's policy of accepting vassalage rather than absolute
submission from his defeated enemies. In 1393, Bayezid invaded and annexed
Bulgaria, bringing to an end the independence that it had enjoyed since 1187.
He then saw no reason why a shrunken and bankrupt Byzantium should
continue to exist in the midst of his dominions. He laid siege to Constantinople
in 1394 with a view to starving it into surrender. Yet even now the defences
held. Bayezid could not break through the Land Walls and the Genoese and
Venetians continued to bring in supplies by sea. The crisis lasted for seven
years until Bayezid broke off his siege to march into Asia Minor and do battle
with Timur, the lord of Samarkand. When he suffered a catastrophic defeat at
Ankara in 1402, the Ottoman empire temporarily broke up, allowing Byzantium
to survive for several more decades. There was even room for some of the old
tricks as the Byzantines played one claimant to the Ottoman throne off against
another in a series of civil wars.

The respite could not go on indefinitely and by 1450, the Ottoman empire
had recovered. It was the young and ambitious Sultan Mehmed II who finally
put an end to Byzantium. In the spring of 1453 he mounted a siege such as
Constantinople had never known before. An army of something approaching
80,000 men encamped outside the Land Walls, while a fleet of over a hundred
warships took up position in the Bosporus. No previous attacker had been able
to bring such enormous combined naval and military power to bear. Like the
attackers of 1204, Mehmed II succeeded in getting his fleet into the Golden
Horn, albeit by using the stratagem of having the ships carried overland to
bypass the chain. In the end though, it was his cannon that gave him the ultimate victory. No previous attacker had guns the size of those set up by Mehmed's
army outside the Land Walls. While gunpowder weapons were nothing new in
the mid fifteenth century, these monsters, which could hurl a ball weighing
over six hundred kilograms, spread fear and consternation among the
defenders. Although the largest of them were so complicated to load that they
could only be fired seven times a day, after a month of continuous

bombardment they had opened up significant gaps in the once-impregnable Land Walls. A mass attack on the night of 28–29 May overwhelmed the heavily outnumbered defenders and delivered the city into Ottoman hands at last.

Among the victims of the carnage that followed was the emperor, Constantine XI, who died fighting on the walls in the early hours of 29 May along with about 3,000 of the defenders. He was the great-great-great-grandson of the founder of the Palaiologos dynasty, Michael VIII, and the last in the long line of succession from his namesake who had adopted Christianity and founded Constantinople. He was to be the last Byzantine emperor, for although Mistra and the Peloponnese remained in Byzantine hands, neither of Constantine's surviving brothers claimed the imperial title. So central had Constantinople been to Byzantine ideology and psyche that it was inconceivable that the empire could continue without it. In any case, seven years after his triumph at Constantinople, Mehmed invaded the Peloponnese and incorporated that too into his empire. This time there was no coming back.

Epilogue

Nothing could have been more fortunate for mankind, than the destruction
of the degraded Greek empire by the Turks . . .
David Stuart Erskine, Earl of Buchan (1742–1829)

Thus it was that when Pierre Gilles arrived in Constantinople a hundred years after Mehmed II's victory, Byzantium had not only disappeared as a political institution but even physical traces of it were difficult to find. In the years after 1453, the buildings and objects that had defined the empire were eradicated one by one. First to go was the Hodegetria icon, the symbol both of the protection of the Virgin Mary and of that visual spirituality that was so central to Byzantine identity. It had been housed in the Chora monastery during the 1453 siege so that it could protect the defenders on the Land Walls, and soon after the breakthrough it was hacked to pieces by marauding Ottoman troops who wanted the gold and jewels on the frame. Many prominent landmarks followed, for Mehmed II decided to abandon Adrianople and to make Constantinople his capital. That meant remodelling the city to make it a suitable residence for the sultan and many of the old buildings had to go, for in the empire's last impoverished years most of the great churches, monasteries and palaces had fallen into a sad state of disrepair. The church of the Holy Apostles was demolished and was replaced by the Mosque of the Conqueror between 1462 and 1470. The column and equestrian statue of Justinian were taken down in the 1540s so that the metal could be used in casting cannon: only broken fragments remained for Gilles to see shortly before they were carried off to the foundry. What remained of the Great Palace was buried under the Blue Mosque in 1609, while the palace of Blachernae simply disappeared. The Hippodrome became an open square. But not everything was lost. The Ottomans were happy to reuse those buildings that were serviceable. Hagia Sophia had been kept in good repair right up to the end and so could be easily converted into a mosque by the insertion of a *mihrab* to indicate the direction of Mecca and the addition of four minarets. The Pantokrator and other lesser churches also survived by being reused, but in the process most of them lost their characteristic Byzantine feature: the rich figurative decoration that would have covered all the interior space.

Another survival was Byzantium's literary heritage, for Constantinople had been full of richly stocked libraries. On the morning of 29 May 1453, many of these books ended up on bonfires, but plenty survived and were later sought out and purchased by collectors like Pierre Gilles or taken to the west by refugees. Among them were not only the works of Byzantine authors such as Zosimus, Procopius, Michael Psellos and John Kantakouzenos, but also precious copies of the ancient Greek classics that had been used as study texts in higher education right up to the end. They included some of the earliest surviving complete texts of the great thinkers, orators and playwrights of the ancient world such as Plato, Aristotle, Aristophanes, Demosthenes and Lucian, works that had not been available in the Christian west for centuries. In Italy, they were eagerly read, copied and translated by Renaissance intellectuals and provided the texts for the first printed editions of the Greek classics in the early 1500s. It is only thanks to the Byzantines that this literary inheritance survived the upheavals of the centuries and is still available today.

The Byzantine Church was another piece of salvage from the wreck. This was partly because Mehmed II knew that it was in his interests to maintain the schism between Orthodox and Catholic and thus discourage any hope among the Byzantines that their co-religionists in the west might come to their rescue. The office of patriarch was vacant at the time that the sultan conquered Constantinople and he personally ensured that it was filled within a few months of his victory, carefully choosing an incumbent renowned for his opposition to any compromise with the Latins. By doing so, Mehmed also made it easier for his Christian subjects to accept the new order: while Ottomans might be infidels, at least they did not tamper with the ancestral faith as the Latins did. And so, although the emperors were gone, the patriarch of Constantinople continued to preside over the Orthodox Church, his authority respected in Serbia, Bulgaria and Russia, the lands that had originally accepted Christianity from Constantinople. That is still the case today and the establishment of Orthodox communities in western Europe, North America and indeed all over the world has ensured that its religion is Byzantium's most visible legacy. An Orthodox church in Brooklyn, Sydney or London will often reflect Byzantine styles of architecture and interior decoration. Its iconostasis, the screen that divides the sanctuary from the main body of the church, will be covered in icons of Christ, the Virgin Mary and the saints. The services will be conducted in an archaic Greek which would have been comprehensible in Byzantium, or in Old Church Slavonic, the literary language that Cyril and Methodios helped to develop in the ninth century. The most direct survival of all is the monastic enclave of Mount Athos where the Great Lavra, founded in the reign of Nikephoros II Phokas, still functions as a monastery alongside other, later foundations. These monasteries are a direct link to the lost world of Byzantium.

These survivals aside, so much of the Byzantine empire has disappeared so completely that it is depressingly often perceived as some kind of failure. It is compared unfavourably to its predecessor, the classical Roman empire, which has left such a tangible legacy to language, law and architecture, not to mention a series of Hollywood epics. The words of the eighteenth-century Scottish antiquary David Erskine, quoted above, typify this negative perception of Byzantium. The comparison with Rome, however, is unfair. The Roman empire grew because it was able to use its abundant manpower to overwhelm its neighbours one by one. It flourished and prospered because once it was established its borders were seldom attacked. Byzantium, on the other hand, was the product of a violent and uncertain world where for over a thousand years there was almost continuous pressure on its borders, and constant invasion, siege and war. During that time the empire survived and retained its culture and identity while all around it the world was in a state of flux. It did so not by becoming a narrow, militaristic state that battened down the hatches and adopted a siege mentality. On the contrary, it strove to turn the constant tide of humanity that washed up against its borders to its advantage, playing one off against another, bringing some inside its borders to boost its own manpower and integrating them into its own religious system and culture. Thus if Byzantium has one outstanding legacy it is not perhaps Orthodox Christianity or its preservation of classical Greek literature. Rather it is the lesson that the strength of a society lies in its ability to adapt and incorporate outsiders in even the most adverse circumstances.

Chronology

Major dates

303	Persecution of the Christian Church begins, under Diocletian
306	Constantine proclaimed emperor at York
312	Battle of the Milvian Bridge: Constantine's vision
324	Constantine becomes sole emperor
325	First Ecumenical Council at Nicaea
330	Inauguration of Constantinople
337	Death of Constantine
378	Battle of Adrianople
381	Second Ecumenical Council at Constantinople
391	Destruction of the Serapeum in Alexandria
415	Murder of Hypatia in Alexandria
451	Fourth Ecumenical Council at Chalcedon
480	Assassination of Julius Nepos, last western imperial claimant
527	Accession of Justinian I
533	Eternal Peace between Byzantium and Persia
540	Byzantine capture of Ravenna; Persian sack of Antioch
562	Completion of Byzantine conquest of Italy
565	Death of Justinian I
568	Lombards invade Italy
580	Avars become dominant power in the Danube basin
582	Maurice becomes emperor by marrying the daughter of Tiberius II
602	Overthrow and murder of Maurice
610	Accession of Heraclius
614	Persian capture of Jerusalem
626	Persian and Avar siege of Constantinople
632	Death of the Prophet Muhammad
641	Death of Heraclius
642	Arab capture of Alexandria

655	Arabs destroy Byzantine fleet at Phoinix
674	First Arab siege of Constantinople begins
681	Sixth Ecumenical Council condemns Monotheletism
697	Arab capture of Carthage
718	End of second Arab siege of Constantinople
726	Probable initiation of policy of iconoclasm
740	Arabs defeated at Akroinon in Asia Minor
741	Accession of Constantine V, known as 'Kopronymos'
751	Lombard capture of Ravenna
754	Council of Hieria
775	Death of Constantine V
787	Seventh Ecumenical Council restores icon veneration
811	Emperor Nikephoros I defeated and killed by Bulgar Khan Krum
815	Iconoclasm revived
843	Final restoration of icon veneration
858	Photios becomes patriarch of Constantinople
860	First Russian attack on Constantinople
863	Arabs defeated at battle of Poson
865	Conversion of Bulgar Khan Boris to Christianity
867	Accession of Basil I, first emperor of the Macedonian dynasty
917	Bulgar Khan Symeon's victory at Anchialos
919	Romanos Lekapenos seizes power in Constantinople
934	John Kourkouas captures Melitene
945	Overthrow of the Lekapenos family by Constantine VII
959	Death of Constantine VII
961	Nikephoros Phokas recaptures Crete
963	Accession of Nikephoros II Phokas
969	Accession of John I Tzimiskes
975	Campaign of John I in Syria and Palestine
988	Baptism of Prince Vladimir of Kiev
989	Defeat of revolt of Bardas Phokas
1018	Completion of conquest of Bulgaria
1025	Death of Basil II
1043	Revolt of George Maniakes
1056	Death of Theodora, end of the Macedonian dynasty
1071	Battle of Manzikert
1081	Accession of Alexios I Komnenos
1099	First Crusade takes Jerusalem
1143	Accession of Manuel I Komnenos
1171	Arrest of Venetian merchants throughout Byzantium
1176	Seljuk Turks defeat Byzantines at battle of Myriokephalon
1180	Death of Manuel I Komnenos
1182	Usurpation of Andronicus I
1185	Overthrow of Andronicus I, Isaac II Angelos emperor
1187	Revolt of Vlachs and Bulgars

1195	Overthrow of Isaac II, Alexios III emperor
1203	Fourth Crusade restores Isaac II
1204	Fourth Crusade captures Constantinople; establishment of Latin empire
1205	Battle of Adrianople
1208	Theodore I Laskaris crowned emperor at Nicaea
1246	John III Vatatzes captures Thessalonica
1259	Michael VIII Palaiologos crowned emperor at Nicaea
1261	Recapture of Constantinople by Michael VIII
1274	Union of the Churches proclaimed at Lyons
1282	Death of Michael VIII; accession of Andronicus II
1328	Andronicus III seizes power from his grandfather
1331	Fall of Nicaea to the Ottoman Turks
1341	Death of Andronicus III; beginning of civil war
1347	John VI Kantakouzenos captures Constantinople
1352	Ottoman Turks seize a foothold in Europe at Tzympe
1354	Abdication of John VI Kantakouzenos
1369	Visit of John V to Rome
1371	Battle of the Marica: Serbs defeated by Turks
1383	Death of John VI Kantakouzenos
1391	Death of John V Palaiologos
1394	Ottoman ruler Bayezid I lays siege to Constantinople
1402	Battle of Ankara: Ottoman empire in disarray
1453	Fall of Constantinople to the Ottoman Turks under Mehmed II
1460	Ottoman conquest of the Byzantine Peloponnese
1544	Pierre Gilles in Constantinople

Byzantine emperors

Emperors in square brackets ruled in the western half of the empire only.

306–337	Constantine I
337–361	Constantius II
361–363	Julian
363–364	Jovian
364–378	Valens [364–375 Valentian I; 375–383 Gratian]
379–395	Theodosius I [383–392 Valentinian II; 392–394 Eugenius]
395–408	Arcadius [395–423 Honorius]
408–450	Theodosius II
450–457	Marcian
457–474	Leo I
474	Leo II
474–491	Zeno [474–475 Julius Nepos; 475–476 Romulus Augustulus; 476–480 Julius Nepos (in Dalmatia)]
491–518	Anastasius I
518–527	Justin I

527–565	Justinian I
565–578	Justin II
578–582	Tiberius II
582–602	Maurice
602–610	Phokas
610–641	Heraclius
641	Constantine III
641–642	Heraclonas
642–668	Constans II
668–685	Constantine IV
685–695	Justinian II
695–698	Leontios
698–705	Tiberius III
705–711	Justinian II (again)
711–713	Philippikos
713–715	Anastasius II
715–717	Theodosius III
717–741	Leo III
741–775	Constantine V
775–780	Leo IV
780–797	Constantine VI
797–802	Irene
802–811	Nikephoros I
811–813	Michael I Rangabe
813–820	Leo V
820–829	Michael II
829–842	Theophilos
842–867	Michael III
867–886	Basil I
886–912	Leo VI
912–913	Alexander
913–959	Constantine VII
920–944	Romanos I Lekapenos
959–963	Romanos II
963–969	Nikephoros II Phokas
969–976	John I Tzimiskes
976–1025	Basil II
1025–1028	Constantine VIII
1028–1034	Romanos III Argyros
1034–1041	Michael IV
1041–1042	Michael V
1042–1055	Constantine IX Monomachos
1055–1056	Theodora
1056–1057	Michael VI
1057–1059	Isaac I Komnenos

1059–1067 Constantine X Doukas
1068–1071 Romanos IV Diogenes
1071–1078 Michael VII Doukas
1078–1081 Nikephoros III Botaneiates
1081–1118 Alexios I Komnenos
1118–1143 John II Komnenos
1143–1180 Manuel I Komnenos
1180–1183 Alexios II Komnenos
1183–1185 Andronicus I Komnenos
1185–1195 Isaac II Angelos
1195–1203 Alexios III Angelos
1203–1204 Isaac II (again) and Alexios IV Angelos
1204   Alexios V Mourtzouphlos
1208–1221 Theodore I Laskaris (in Nicaea)
1221–1254 John III Vatatzes (in Nicaea)
1254–1258 Theodore II Laskaris (in Nicaea)
1258–1261 John IV Laskaris (in Nicaea)
1259–1282 Michael VIII Palaiologos
1282–1328 Andronicus II Palaiologos
1328–1341 Andronicus III Palaiologos
1341–1391 John V Palaiologos
1347–1354 John VI Kantakouzenos
1391–1425 Manuel II Palaiologos
1425–1448 John VIII Palaiologos
1449–1453 Constantine XI Palaiologos

Glossary

Arian A follower of the teaching of Arius, who claimed that Jesus Christ had been created and was therefore secondary to God.

Asia Minor The Asiatic land mass that is now Turkey.

ascetic One who seeks to become closer to God through extreme self-denial and self-imposed hardship.

Augousteion The main square of Constantinople, between the cathedral of Hagia Sophia and the Great Palace.

basileus A Greek word meaning 'king', used by the Byzantines to denote their emperor.

Chalcedonian One who subscribed to the definitions of the Christian faith made at the ecumenical councils of Nicaea and Chalcedon.

Domestic of the Schools (*Scholai*) Commander of the Byzantine army from the tenth century.

exarch Provincial governor, with wide-ranging civil and military powers.

foederati Term used in early Byzantium to describe tribes allied to the empire.

iconoclast An opponent of the veneration of icons.

iconophile A supporter of the veneration of icons.

Monophysitism The belief that Jesus Christ was predominantly divine and that his human aspect was minimal.

Monotheletism A compromise doctrine that while Jesus Christ had both human and divine natures, he had a single will.

nomisma (plural: **nomismata**) The Byzantine gold coin up to 1092.

porphyrogenitos Literally 'born in the purple', a member of the Byzantine ruling dynasty born in the Great Palace in Constantinople.

porphyry A marble of deep purple colour, flecked with white crystals, from a remote location in Egypt.

strategos (plural: *strategoi*) The governor of a theme, and commander of its provincial army.

tagmata Elite units of the Byzantine army, under the personal command of the emperor, introduced by Constantine V.

theme Provincial administrative region from *c.* 650.

Varangian guard The emperor's personal guard, composed mainly of Russian and Scandinavian mercenaries.

Further Reading

Prologue

The quotation from Ogier Ghiselin de Busbeq is in his *Turkish Letters*, trans. Edward Seymour Forster (Oxford, 1927), pp. 36–7. For Gilles's and Gibbon's views on the downfall of Byzantium, see Pierre Gilles, *The Antiquities of Constantinople*, trans. John Ball (Ithaca NY, 1988, 2nd edn), p. xliv; Edward Gibbon, *The History of the Decline and Fall of the Roman Empire*, ed. David Womersley, 3 vols (London, 1994), vol. 3, p. 791. For general surveys of Byzantine political history 306–1453, see Warren Treadgold, *A History of the Byzantine State and Society* (Stanford CA, 1997), the same author's less detailed *A Concise History of Byzantium* (Basingstoke and New York, 2001), Timothy E. Gregory, *A History of Byzantium* (Oxford and Malden MA, 2010, 2nd edn) and Dionysios Stathakopoulos, *A Short History of the Byzantine Empire* (London, 2014). Among more thematic introductions are Averil M. Cameron, *The Byzantines* (Oxford and Malden MA, 2006) and her *Byzantine Matters* (Princeton NJ, 2014), Jonathan Harris (ed.), *Byzantine History* (Palgrave Advances series, Basingstoke and New York, 2005), Cyril Mango (ed.), *The Oxford History of Byzantium* (Oxford and New York, 2002), Judith Herrin, *Byzantium: The Surprising Life of a Medieval Empire* (Harmondsworth, 2007) and Jonathan Shepard (ed.), *The Cambridge History of the Byzantine Empire c. 500–1492* (Cambridge, 2008).

Chapter 1: Twilight of the Gods

The quotation is from Edward Gibbon, *The History of the Decline and Fall of the Roman Empire*, ed. David Womersley, 3 vols (London, 1994), vol. 3, p. 1068. The rival pagan and Christian views of Constantine can be read in: Zosimus, *New History*, trans. R.T. Riley (Canberra, 1982), and Eusebius, *Life of Constantine*, trans. Averil Cameron and Stuart G. Hall (Oxford, 1999), with analysis in Warren Treadgold, *The Early Byzantine Historians* (Basingstoke and New York, 2007), pp. 23–46, 107–14. For modern accounts of Constantine's reign, see Timothy D. Barnes, *Constantine* (Oxford, 2014) and Paul Stephenson, *Constantine: Unconquered Emperor, Christian Victor* (London, 2009). On attitudes towards homosexuals and Jews: John Boswell, *Christianity, Social Tolerance and Homosexuality: Gay People in Western Europe from the Beginning of the Christian Era to the Fourteenth Century* (Chicago, 1980) and Robert L. Wilken, *John Chrysostom and the Jews: Rhetoric and Reality in the Late Fourth Century* (Berkeley CA and Los Angeles CA, 1983). On the theological disputes of the period: J. Pelikan, *Credo: A Historical and Theological Guide to Creeds and Confessions of Faith in the Christian Tradition* (New Haven CT and London, 2003). On Byzantine theocracy and political thought: Donald M. Nicol, 'Byzantine political thought', in *The Cambridge History of Medieval Political Thought c. 350–c. 1450*, ed. J.H. Burns (Cambridge, 1988), pp. 51–79. On the growth of the cult of the holy man: Peter Brown, *Society and the Holy in Late Antiquity* (London, 1982). On the charitable work of the Christian Church: Demetrios J. Constantelos, *Byzantine Philanthropy and Social Welfare* (New Rochelle NY, 1991, 2nd edn); and on its art and architecture: Irmgard Hutter, *The Herbert History of Art and Architecture: Early Christian and Byzantine* (London, 1988) and John Lowden, *Early Christian and Byzantine Art* (London, 1997). On the role of eunuchs: Shaun Tougher, *The Eunuch in Byzantine History and Society* (London and New York, 2008). On policies towards 'barbarians': Peter Heather, *Goths and Romans, 332–489* (Oxford, 1991). In general on the period 284–500: Averil Cameron, *The Later Roman Empire* (London, 1993), Stephen Mitchell, *A History of the Later Roman Empire, AD 284–641* (Oxford, 2007), Peter Heather, *The Fall of the Roman Empire: A New History* (London, 2005) and his *Empires and Barbarians: Migration, Development and the Birth of Europe* (London, 2010).

Chapter 2: Outpost of Empire

The quotation at the beginning is from Procopius, *History of the Wars*, trans. H.B. Dewing, 5 vols (Cambridge MA and London, 1914–28), vol. 1, p. 267. Procopius's laudatory work is *The Buildings*, trans. H.B. Dewing (Cambridge MA and London, 1935) and his vitriolic attack on Justinian is his *Secret History*, trans. H.B. Dewing (Cambridge MA and London, 1940). The value of Procopius's testimony is assessed, and very different conclusions reached, by Averil M. Cameron, *Procopius and the Sixth Century* (London, 1985) and Anthony Kaldellis, *Procopius of Caesarea: Tyranny, History and Philosophy at the End of Antiquity* (Philadelphia PA, 2004). The story of St Savas's visit to Constantinople can be found in Cyril of Scythopolis, *The Lives of the Monks of Palestine*, trans. R.M. Price (Kalamazoo MI, 1991), pp. 182–7. Recent assessments of Justinian and his reign can be found in John Moorhead, *Justinian* (Harlow, 1994), J.A.S. Evans, *The Age of Justinian: The Circumstances of Imperial Power* (London, 1996), Michael Maas (ed.), *The Cambridge Companion to the Age of Justinian* (Cambridge, 2005) and Peter Sarris, *Economy and Society in the Age of Justinian* (Cambridge, 2006). On the theological disputes of the period: John Meyendorff, *Imperial Unity and Christian Divisions: The Church 450–680* (Crestwood NY, 1989). For the military aspects, see John Haldon, *The Byzantine Wars* (Stroud, 2001). On Justinian's buildings and the cathedral of Hagia Sophia: Robin Cormack, *Byzantine Art* (Oxford, 2000), pp. 37–75, and John Freely and Ahmet S. Çakmak, *The Byzantine Monuments of Istanbul* (Cambridge, 2004), pp. 80–153.

Chapter 3: The Deluge

The quotation at the beginning is from *The Chronicle of Theophanes Confessor: Byzantine and Near Eastern History AD 284–813*, trans. Cyril Mango and Roger Scott (Oxford, 1997), p. 439. The story of the three blind men of Alexandria can be found in John Moschos, *The Spiritual Meadow*, trans. John Wortley (Kalamazoo MI, 1992), pp. 59–60. For an account of the reign of Maurice: L.M. Whitby, *The Emperor Maurice and his Historian* (Oxford, 1988); and of that of Heraclius in Walter E. Kaegi, *Heraclius: Emperor of Byzantium* (Cambridge, 2003). On the Arab invasions: Walter E. Kaegi, *Byzantium and the Early Islamic Conquests* (Cambridge, 1992). On the calamitous seventh century in general: John F. Haldon, *Byzantium in the Seventh Century: The Transformation of a Culture* (Cambridge, 1997, 2nd edn) and James Howard-Johnston, *Witnesses to a World Crisis: Historians and Histories of the Middle East in the Seventh Century* (Oxford, 2010).

Chapter 4: A World Transformed

The quotation at the beginning is from Pausanias, *Guide to Greece*, trans. Peter Levi, 2 vols (Harmondsworth, 1971), vol. 1 p. 28. For a balanced and critical assessment of the theme system, see John F. Haldon, *Warfare, State and Society in the Byzantine World, 565–1204* (London, 1999), pp. 71–85; and on the policy of transferring populations: Hélène Ahrweiler and Angeliki E. Laiou (eds), *Studies on the Internal Diaspora of the Byzantine Empire* (Washington DC, 1998). The defences and sieges of Constantinople are described in Jonathan Harris, *Constantinople: Capital of Byzantium* (London, 2007), pp. 40–58. The whole period is surveyed in Leslie Brubaker and John F. Haldon, *Byzantium in the Iconoclast Era (c. 680–850): A History* (Cambridge, 2011); and the later years in Warren Treadgold, *The Byzantine Revival, 780–842* (Stanford CA, 1988). The possibility that Constantine V was deliberately targeting holy men is explored by Peter Brown, 'A Dark-Age Crisis: aspects of the Iconoclastic controversy', in his *Society and the Holy in Late Antiquity* (London, 1982), pp. 251–301, while Leslie Brubaker, *Inventing Byzantine Iconoclasm* (London, 2012) strongly plays down the significance of iconoclasm and the persecution of monks. On Empresses Irene and Theodora: Judith Herrin, *Women in Purple: Rulers of Medieval Byzantium* (London, 2001). On the impact of iconoclasm on Byzantine art: Robin Cormack, *Byzantine Art* (Oxford, 2000), pp. 86–129.

Chapter 5: The Conquest of the North

The quotation at the beginning is from *Ibn Fadlan and the Land of Darkness: Arab Travellers in the Far North*, trans. Paul Lunde and Caroline Stone (London, 2012), p. 46. For the Russian attack of 860 and Photios's account, see *The Homilies of Photius, Patriarch of Constantinople*, trans. Cyril Mango (Cambridge MA, 1958), pp. 74–110. The classic work on Byzantium and the Slavs is Dimitri Obolensky, *The Byzantine Commonwealth: Eastern Europe, 500–1453* (London, 1971), though this should now be supplemented with Florin Curtin, *Southeastern Europe in the Middle Ages, 500–1250* (Cambridge, 2006) and Paul Stephenson, *Byzantium's Balkan Frontier: A Political Study of the Northern Balkans, 900–1204* (Cambridge, 2000). On Photios and his career: Nigel Wilson, *Scholars of Byzantium* (London, 1983), pp. 89–119, and Francis Dvornik, *The Photian Schism: History and Legends* (London, 1970). On the conversion of the Slavs: Francis Dvornik, *Byzantine Missions among the Slavs* (New Brunswick NJ, 1970) and S.A. Ivanov, 'Religious missions', in *The Cambridge History of the Byzantine Empire c. 500–1492*, ed. Jonathan Shepard (Cambridge, 2008), pp. 305–32. On the Russian visitors Anthony of Novgorod and Philip: W.R. Lethaby and Harold Swainson, *The Church of Sancta Sophia, Constantinople: A Study of a Byzantine Building* (London and New York, 1894) and Cyril Mango, 'A Russian graffito in St Sophia', in Cyril Mango, *Studies on Constantinople* (Aldershot and Brookfield VT, 1993), no. XIX.

Chapter 6: Paths of Glory

The quotation at the beginning is taken from *Digenis Akritas: The Grottaferrata and Escorial Versions*, ed. and trans. Elizabeth Jeffreys (Cambridge, 1998), p. 19. The quotation from the disgruntled clergyman is from *The Correspondence of Leo, Metropolitan of Synada*, ed. and trans. M.P. Vinson (Washington DC, 1985), pp. 198–9; that of the mistrustful nobleman (Kekavmenos) from Deno J. Geanakoplos, *Byzantium: Church, Society and Civilization seen through Contemporary Eyes* (Chicago, 1984), p. 237; and the words of the officials to the bishop Liudprand of Cremona from Liudprand, *The Complete Works*, trans. Paolo Squadriti (Washington DC, 2007), p. 273. For the handbooks compiled under Leo VI and Constantine VII, see *The Taktika of Leo VI*, trans. G.T. Dennis (Washington DC, 2010), pp. 555, 589; Constantine VII Porphyrogenitos, *De Administrando Imperio*, ed. G. Moravcsik, trans. R.J.H. Jenkins (Washington DC, 1967) and *The Book of Ceremonies*, trans. A. Moffatt and M. Tell (Canberra, 2012). On the attempts to limit the land held by the Asia Minor warlords: Eric McGeer, *The Land Legislation of the Macedonian Emperors* (Toronto, 2000). On the military developments of the period: Eric McGeer, *Sowing the Dragon's Teeth: Byzantine Warfare in the Tenth Century* (Washington DC, 1995) and Warren Treadgold, *Byzantium and its Army, 284–1081* (Stanford CA, 1995). On John Tzimiskes' 971 Bulgarian campaign:

Paul Stephenson, *Byzantium's Balkan Frontier: A Political Study of the Northern Balkans, 900–1204* (Cambridge, 2000), pp. 51–8.

Chapter 7: The Long Shadow

The quotation at the beginning is taken from Eric McGeer, *The Land Legislation of the Macedonian Emperors* (Toronto, 2000), p. 117. An account of the 980 Arab embassy to Constantinople can be found in H. Amedroz, 'An embassy from Baghdad to the emperor Basil II', *Journal of the Royal Asiatic Society*, vol. 46 (1914), pp. 915–42. The description of Zoe and advice of Bardas Skleros to Basil II are in the memoirs of Michael Psellos, *Fourteen Byzantine Rulers*, trans E.R.A. Sewter (Harmondsworth, 1966), pp. 43, 158. The quotation from the resentful aristocrat is in Deno J. Geanakoplos, *Byzantium: Church, Society and Civilization seen through Contemporary Eyes* (Chicago, 1984), p. 105. On the reign of Basil II, see Catherine Holmes, *Basil II and the Governance of Empire (976–1025)* (Oxford, 2005) and Paul Stephenson, *The Legend of Basil the Bulgar Slayer* (Cambridge, 2003). On the period after Basil's death: Michael Angold, *The Byzantine Empire, 1025–1204: A Political History* (Harlow, 1997, 2nd edn). On Zoe: Barbara Hill, *Imperial Women in Byzantium, 1025–1204* (Harlow, 1999). On the battle of Manzikert: John Haldon, *The Byzantine Wars* (Stroud, 2001).

Chapter 8: The Enemy Within

The quotation at the beginning is from William of Tyre, *A History of Deeds Done Beyond the Sea*, trans. E.A. Babcock and A.C. Krey, 2 vols (New York, 1943), vol. 2, p. 461. On the flourishing economy of the empire in the twelfth century: Alan Harvey, *Economic Expansion in the Byzantine Empire, 900–1200* (Cambridge, 1989); and in general on the Komnenian period: Michael Angold, *The Byzantine Empire, 1025–1204: A Political History* (Harlow, 1997, 2nd edn). On Alexios I, his relations with the Latins and the First Crusade: Jonathan Harris, *Byzantium and the Crusades* (London, 2014, 2nd edn) and Peter Frankopan, *The First Crusade: The Call from the East* (London, 2012). On the Venetians: Donald M. Nicol, *Byzantium and Venice: A Study in Diplomatic and Cultural Relations* (Cambridge, 1988). On ecclesiastical relations and the schism: Henry Chadwick, *East and West: The Making of a Rift in the Church* (Oxford, 2003); Francis Dvornik, *Byzantium and the Roman Primacy* (New York, 1979, 2nd edn); Steven Runciman, *The Eastern Schism* (Oxford, 1955). On Manuel I: Paul Magdalino, *The Empire of Manuel I Komnenos, 1143–1180* (Cambridge, 1993). On the Fourth Crusade: Jonathan Phillips, *The Fourth Crusade and the Sack of Constantinople* (London, 2004).

Chapter 9: The New Constantine

The quotation at the beginning is from Michael VIII's short autobiography in J.P. Thomas and A.C. Hero, *Byzantine Monastic Foundation Documents: A Complete Translation of the Surviving Founders' Typika and Testaments*, 5 vols (Washington DC, 2000), vol. 3, p. 1245. On the partition of the Byzantine empire in 1204: Peter Lock, *The Franks in the Aegean, 1204–1500* (Harlow, 1995). On the courts in exile at Nicaea and Arta: Michael Angold, *A Byzantine Government in Exile: Government and Society under the Laskarids of Nicaea, 1204–1261* (Oxford, 1975) and Donald M. Nicol, *The Despotate of Epiros I, 1204–1267* (Oxford, 1957). On the Latin empire: Filip van Tricht, *The Latin Renovatio of Byzantium: The Empire of Constantinople (1204–1228)* (Leiden and Boston MA, 2011). On political and ecclesiastical relations with the west: Joseph Gill, *Byzantium and the Papacy, 1198–1400* (New Brunswick NJ, 1979), Deno J. Geanakoplos, *Emperor Michael Palaeologus and the West, 1258–1282: A Study in Byzantine–Latin Relations* (Cambridge MA, 1959) and Nikolaos G. Chryssis, *Crusading in Frankish Greece: A Study of Byzantine–Western Relations and Attitudes, 1204–1282* (Turnhout, 2013). On the reigns of Michael VIII and Andronicus II:

Donald M. Nicol, *The Last Centuries of Byzantium, 1261–1453* (Cambridge, 1993, 2nd edn).

Chapter 10: An Old Man Remembers

Kantakouzenos's words are translated by Robert H. Trone, 'The History of John Kantakouzenos (Book I): Text, Translation and Commentary' (PhD thesis, Catholic University of America, 1979), p. 108. On Kantakouzenos's life and reign: Donald M. Nicol, *The Reluctant Emperor: A Biography of John Cantacuzene, Byzantine Emperor and Monk, c. 1295–1383* (Cambridge, 1996). On early fourteenth-century travellers to Constantinople: George P. Majeska, *Russian Travelers to Constantinople in the Fourteenth and Fifteenth Centuries* (Washington DC, 1984); *The Travels of Sir John Mandeville*, trans. C.W.R.D. Mosely (Harmondsworth, 1983); *The Travels of Ibn Battuta*, trans. H.A.R. Gibb, 3 vols (Cambridge, 1958–71). On the rise of the Ottoman Turks: Cemal Kafadar, *Between Two Worlds: The Construction of the Ottoman State* (Berkeley CA, 1995) and Colin Imber, *The Ottoman Empire, 1300–1650: The Structure of Power* (Basingstoke and New York, 2002). On the influence of late Byzantine art in Russia and Italy: Thomas Mathews, *Byzantium from Antiquity to the Renaissance* (London, 1998), pp. 151–63, and John Meyendorff, *Byzantium and the Rise of Russia* (Cambridge, 1981). On the Ottoman conquest of the Balkans: John V.A. Fine, *The Late Medieval Balkans: A Critical Survey from the Late Twelfth Century to the Ottoman Conquest* (Ann Arbor MI, 1994). On Mistra and Thessalonica: Steven Runciman, *Mistra: Byzantine Capital of the Peloponnese* (London, 1980) and Eugenia Russell, *St Demetrius of Thessalonica: Cult and Devotion in the Middle Ages* (Oxford and Bern, 2010). The last decades before the fall of Constantinople are examined in: Jonathan Harris, *The End of Byzantium* (New Haven CT and London, 2010) and Nevra Necipoğlu, *Byzantium between the Ottomans and the Latins: Politics and Society in the Late Empire* (Cambridge, 2009). On the siege and fall of Constantinople: Steven Runciman, *The Fall of Constantinople, 1453* (Cambridge, 1965); Roger Crowley, *Constantinople: The Last Great Siege, 1453* (London, 2005); Marios Philippides and Walter K. Hanak, *The Siege and Fall of Constantinople in 1453: Historiography, Topography and Military Studies* (Farnham and Burlington VT, 2011).

Epilogue

The quotation at the beginning is from David Stuart Erskine, Earl of Buchan, *Essays on the Lives and Writings of Fletcher of Salton and the Poet Thomson: Biographical, Critical and Political* (London, 1792), p. xvii. Byzantium's literary legacy to the Renaissance: L.D. Reynolds and N.G. Wilson, *Scribes and Scholars: A Guide to the Transmission of Greek and Latin Literature* (Oxford, 2013, 4th edn) and N.G. Wilson, *From Byzantium to Italy: Greek Studies in the Italian Renaissance* (London, 1992). On the survival of the Orthodox Church: Steven Runciman, *The Great Church in Captivity* (Cambridge, 1968) and Timothy Ware, *The Orthodox Church* (Harmondsworth, 1993, 2nd edn). On Mount Athos and other Byzantine monastic survivals: William Dalrymple, *From the Holy Mountain: A Journey in the Shadow of Byzantium* (London, 1998).

Index

Sicily, Sicilian, 82, 166
  reconquered by Byzantines (536), 49, 57
  conquered by Arabs, 108
  Vespers (1282), 210–11, 215
Simplicius of Cilicia, 38
Sinai, 61
Singidunum, 44
Sirmium, 62
Siroy, king of Persia (628), 74
Skleros, Bardas, 146, 151, 153–7, 172
Slavs, Slavonic, 92, 106
  invade Byzantine Balkans, 42–3, 62–4,
    66–8, 71–3, 87
  language and alphabet, 87, 107, 114–16,
    118, 120, 126, 134
  remain in Byzantine cultural orbit, 208,
    241–2
Smyrna, 177, 183, 224, 227, 231
Socrates, 38
Solomon, Byzantine commander, 55
Sophronios, 60–1
Spain, 8
  partly occupied by the Byzantines
    (552–624), 57, 61, 67
Sri Lanka, 43
Staurakios, son of Nikephoros I, 109
Stephen Dushan, tsar of Serbia (1331–
    1355), 226, 230–1, 236
Stephen Nemanjić, king of Serbia (1217–
    1228), 208
Stephen of Novgorod, 220–1
Stephen of Perche, 199, 200
Stephen the Younger, monk, 97
Strategopoulos, Alexios, Byzantine
    commander, 206
Strumitza, 193
Suevi, 33
Süleyman ibn Kutulmush, Seljuk sultan of
    Nicaea (1081–1086), 175
Süleyman, son of Orhan, 231–3
Süleyman the Magnificent, Ottoman sultan
    (1520–1566), 1
Süleymaniye mosque, 1
Sura, 51
Svyatoslav, prince of Kiev (945–972),
    123–4, 146–8, 153, 155
Symeon, tsar of Bulgaria (893–927), 120–3,
    129–30, 131, 146
Symeon Stylites, 25–7
Synada, 134
Syracuse, 49, 73, 166
Syria, 8, 19, 40
  invaded by Persians (613), 67, 70
  lost to Arabs (634–639), 78, 82, 85

Byzantine raids into, 129, 148–9, 157,
    173, 185, 187

tagmata, 93, 97, 100, 104, 130, 164
Tarasios, patriarch of Constantinople
    (784–806), 100
Tarsus, 87, 127, 141
Taurus mountains, 82, 85, 87, 93, 130–1
Teias, king of the Ostrogoths (552–553), 57
Tervingi Goths, 31
tetartaron, 143
Thebes, 177
themes, 85–6, 93
  Anatolikon, 91, 93, 136–7
  Armeniakon, 146, 161, 175
  Cappadocian, 137
  Cilician, 137
  Iberia, 157, 164
  Opsikion, 87, 93, 96
  Teleuch, 166
  Thrakesion, 86, 166
  decline in importance, 130, 136–7, 164
Theodahad, king of the Ostrogoths
    (534–536), 48–50
Theodora, daughter of John VI, 227, 231
Theodora, empress (1055–1056), 162, 169
Theodora, empress, wife of John I
    Tzimiskes, 145
Theodora, empress, wife of Justinian I,
    39–41, 44, 46, 58–9
Theodora, empress, wife of Michael VIII,
    204
Theodora, empress, wife of Theophilos,
    101, 112, 118
Theodora, sister of Isaac II, 194
Theodore I Angelos, despot then emperor
    of Epiros (1215–1230), 202–3
Theodore I Laskaris, emperor of Nicaea
    (1208–1221), 202–3
Theodore II Laskaris, emperor of Nicaea
    (1254–1258), 203–5, 212
Theodore, brother of Heraclius, 77
Theodoret, bishop of Cyrus, 25
Theodoric, king of the Ostrogoths
    (493–526), 36, 48, 50, 58–9
Theodosius I, emperor (379–395), 15–16,
    18–19, 23, 43–4, 47
  column of, 199
Theodosius II, emperor (408–450), 17
Theodosius III, emperor (715–717), 91
Theoktistos, eunuch, 112, 113, 118
Theophano, empress, 140–2, 144–5
Theophilos, Byzantine nobleman, 118
Theophilos, emperor (829–842), 101